Two Days of Infamy

ALSO BY STANLEY J. MARKS

The Bear That Walks Like a Man. A Diplomatic and Military Analysis of Soviet Russia

Murder Most Foul! The Conspiracy That Murdered President Kennedy

Coup d'État! Three Murders That Changed the Course of History. President Kennedy, Reverend King, Senator R. F. Kennedy

Yes, Americans, A Conspiracy Murdered JFK!

Two Days of Infamy:

November 22, 1963;
September 28, 1964

A nonfiction manual for the American of common sense,
the agents of the FBI, CIA, Secret Service, the
ABC, CBS, and NBC commentators, and newspaper
columnists, interested in learning the
deceit, deception, and duplicity
practiced by the upholders of
'basic principles of justice,'
the 'Warren Commission.'
(With comments on the trials of C. Shaw in New Orleans, Sirhan
Sirhan in Los Angeles, and Earl Ray in Memphis.)

'Since the dead cannot speak, should not the living?'

Stanley J. Marks

Edited with an Introduction
by Rob Couteau

DOMINANTSTAR

Dominantstar LLC, New York.

Two Days of Infamy: November 22, 1963; September 28, 1964 Copyright © 1969 by Stanley J. Marks.

"The Stanley Marks Revival: The Prophecies of *Murder Most Foul!* and *Two Days of Infamy*," Copyright © 2020 by Rob Couteau.

All Rights Reserved. No part of this book may be reproduced or utilized in any form without written permission from the author.

ISBN: 978-1-7360049-0-6

1 2 3 4 5 6 7 8 9 10 02

(Library Of Congress Catalog Card Number for the original, 1969 edition: 75-76841.)

Special thanks to James DiEugenio, Jim Lampos, Bobbie Marks, Al Rossi, and Yongzhen Zhang for their help and encouragement.

Cover photo: Crowds gathered in front of the White House after the assassination of President John F. Kennedy. Abbie Rowe, White House photographs. Courtesy of the John F. Kennedy Library and Museum, Boston.

robcouteau.com

dominantstarpublications.com

Contents

Introduction: The Stanley Marks Revival: The Prophecies of *Murder Most Foul!* and *Two Days of Infamy*, by Rob Couteau   ix

Introduction–Prologue–Epilogue, by Stanley J. Marks   xxxvii

1. The Failure to Understand   1

2. From the 6th-floor Window, 3 Bullets   19

3. The Evidence That Never Was   55

4. The Invisible Package   73

5. Charades, Prints and Identifications   85

6. Animate and Inanimate Witnesses–The Tippit Affaire   109

7. Odds and Ends   133

8. The Methodology of the Warren Commission   141

9. The Conspiracy That Murdered President Kennedy   161

10. A Short Reprise of the Evidence   199

Photographs, Maps and Surveys   213

Notes   227

Postscript   237

Index   243

'Justice is achieved only when those who are not injured are as indignant as those who are.'–Anon.

The author inscribed a copy of the first edition of *Two Days of Infamy* to his only child, Roberta Marks:

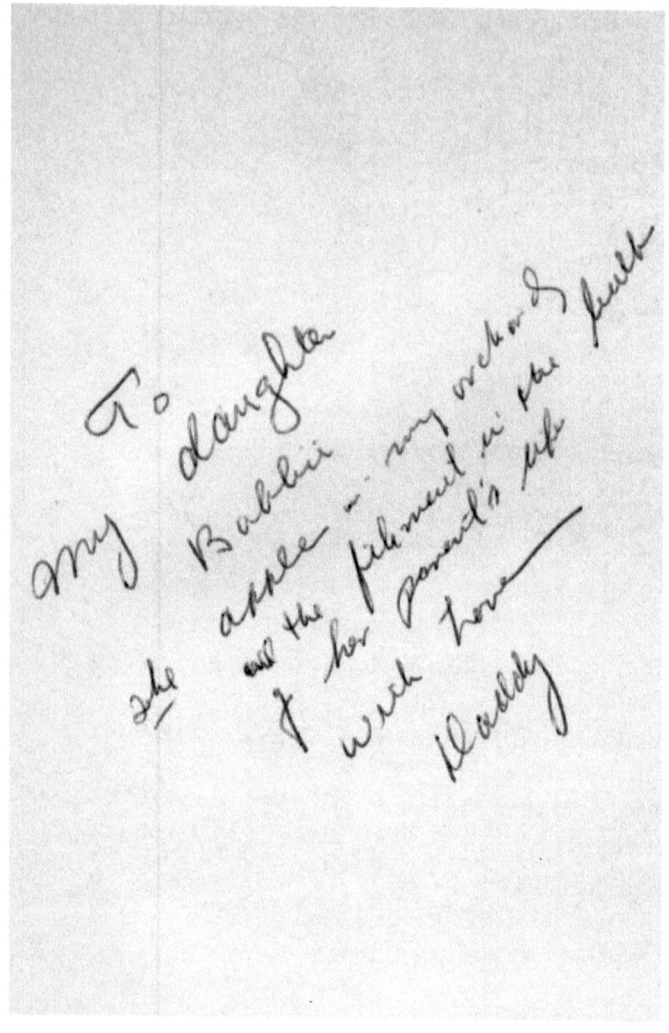

"To my daughter Bobbie, *the* apple in my orchard and the filament in the bulb of her parent's life. With Love Daddy"

The present edition was prepared from this same copy.

THE STANLEY MARKS REVIVAL: THE PROPHECIES OF *MURDER MOST FOUL!* AND *TWO DAYS OF INFAMY,*

BY ROB COUTEAU

Thanks to the help and encouragement of Stanley Mark's daughter, Roberta, *Murder Most Foul!* and *Two Days of Infamy* are now available for the first time since the late 1960s. The timing seems apt. Throughout his oeuvre, Stanley Marks warned time and again of the growing threat of fascism in America, pointing repeatedly to figures such as Allen Dulles, J. Edgar Hoover, and Ronald Reagan, all handmaidens in the march toward the right wing that continued in the decades after the assassination.[1] And now, in the incarnation of the forty-fifth president of the United States, we have a figure who doesn't even bother to disguise his naked grab for power, and the phrase "coup d'état" is being spoken openly, even in the mainstream media.

So much of where we are today is foreshadowed in the writing of Stan Marks: in particular, the fueling of racism and xenophobia, the attempted erosion of civil rights, and the empowerment of the oligarchy and its principal tool of control, the police state. Speaking directly to the readers of a future generation, in *Two Days*, he adds:

> The balance of this small volume now attempts to enter the "dark world" that is slowly, oh, so slowly, being lit, although full light may take until the year 2038–if the "basic principles of American justice" have the strength to remain as principles guiding this long-suffering nation.

---

[1] In *Two Days of Infamy*, Stanley writes of Governor Ronald Reagan: "If it be morally correct for the Czech students to defy Stalinism, should not it be morally correct to defy Reaganism?"

This still remains a big "if"–as the nation continues to suffer while awaiting a firmer grounding in those "basic principles."

When I first shared the work of Stanley Marks with JFK scholar James DiEugenio, shortly after reading *Murder Most Foul!* Jim wrote that Marks' early "condemnation" of the Warren Report in 1967 "is a far cry from, say, Josiah Thompson, who at the end of his book [*Six Seconds in Dallas*; also published in 1967] said he was not really sure that the evidence he adduced justified a conspiracy."

It wasn't until many months later that either of us realized just how astute a remark that really was. For, in Stanley's second JFK-assassination book, *Two Days of Infamy: November 22, 1963; September 28, 1964* (which neither of us had read yet, due to its rarity), Stanley writes:

> As will be shown, the Warren Commission proved the innocence of Lee Harvey Oswald, but his innocence can only be found if the person reading the "Report" will read the testimony in the "Hearings" or the evidence in the National Archives.
>
> Thus, a defense lawyer on Oswald's behalf, because of the prestige associated with the seven commissioners, would be reduced to assume the burden that his client, Oswald, was innocent "beyond a reasonable doubt." The author of "Six Seconds In Dallas" fell into this trap, for he wrote that although he believed there was more than one assassin, Oswald had to be guilty because he could not prove he was innocent! Hence, the burden of proof, as they say in law, shifted from the prosecution–the Commission–to the shoulders of Oswald. This, of course, is contrary to every principle of Anglo-American jurisprudence upon which this nation is founded.

Now, more than fifty years after the publication of *Murder Most Foul!* (September 1967) and *Two Days of Infamy* (March 1969), one is left to wonder to what extent Marks was aware of his own gift of prescience. And we should add that in this 1969 text he was already using the term "conspirators" when referring to the assassins of the Kennedys and King, and he states unequivocally: "All three were murdered as the end result of three interrelated conspiracies," adding: "History has shown that an invisible coup d'état occurred when President Kennedy was murdered." In 1972, after the author Joachim Joesten learned of Stanley's work, he credited him with being one of the first who dared to use the word "coup" in this context: "To my knowledge, nobody but Jim Garrison and an obscure West Coast writer named Stanley J. Marks has ever endorsed before my unswerving contention that the murder of John F. Kennedy was nothing short of a camouflaged coup d'état."

Stanley's work was accomplished in the early days, well before the release of millions of pages of documents that were pried from government archives as a result of the President John F. Kennedy Assassination Records Collection Act (effective October 26, 1992), which led to the creation of the Assassination Records Review Board (ARRB). The ARRB made it possible for an author such as Gerald McKnight to create a classic tome on the Warren Commission deception, *Breach of Trust* (2005), with its in-depth look behind the scenes of the WC drama. But in reading through Stanley's work that was published decades earlier, although it lacks many of the details that would only later emerge, one is struck by how much in parallel his conclusions are with those of contemporary scholars such as McKnight, James Douglass (*JFK and the Unspeakable*; 2008), Jim DiEugenio (*Destiny Betrayed, Second Edition*; 2012),[2] and Lisa Pease, whose book *A Lie Too Big to Fail* (2018) deals with the RFK case.

Marks followed *Two Days of Infamy* with *Coup d'État! Three Murders That Changed the Course of History. President Kennedy, Reverend King, Senator R. F. Kennedy* (February 1970). And then, perhaps inspired by the release of Oliver Stone's film on

---

[2] One could also argue that since *Destiny Betrayed* was first published in 1992 and then completely rewritten a decade later, it serves as a symbolic bridge between the Old World of JFK research and the New.

JFK, in his seventy-eighth year Marks published his last assassination-related title, *Yes, Americans, A Conspiracy Murdered JFK!*. This appeared in June 1992: just a few months before the Assassination Records Collection Act became effective. Thus, the year 1992 marks a milestone not only in JFK research, thanks to the ARRB, but also in the passing of an intellectual torch from the old guard to the new. One also cannot help but wonder what conclusions Stanley might have drawn if he had access to such voluminous records earlier in his life. He died seven years later, in 1999.

While *Murder Most Foul!* remains the author's most seminal work as well the most avant-garde in terms of stylistic approach, its format of over nine-hundred rapidly changing "questions and answers" can be a bit jarring.

Although all of his books on the assassination contain fascinating, insightful observations, I consider *Two Days of Infamy* to be his most well-written work on the subject, due largely to its smooth narrative flow and literary presentation. As we shall see, the text expands upon many of the points first raised a year and a half earlier in *Murder Most Foul!*, as well as introducing fresh ideas and perspectives to the case.

Regarding the literary flair that Marks exhibits in *Two Days*, consider the following passage. Picking up on a theme first introduced in *MMF* (that is, the collective cynicism born as a result of the lies published in the Warren Commission Report, which would eventually accumulate like a growing poison in the national psyche), he writes:

> Perhaps it was the cynicism, inherent in citizens of all nations, that convinced the American citizenry that the "Report" issued by the Warren Commission was supported by rotten timbers incapable of supporting the truth. The suspicion increased in the same ratio and in the same speed as smog increased with the density of automobiles on a Los Angeles freeway. The American people were becoming deeply convinced that the Commission had perpetrated a gigantic, gruesome hoax the like of which concealed a conspiracy that reached into

the very gut of American government and society. Today, that hoax, that whitewash feared by the people has been exposed to the light of day, for the citizenry were, and are, absolutely right in their assessment of the Warren Commission. There now exists overwhelming evidence, provable in a court of law, that the Warren Commission, either willfully or negligently, concealed the conspiracy that murdered President John F. Kennedy. This deed was committed by the Commission in "the interests of national security."

Later on, Marks returns to the subject of perfidy committed in the name of "national security." And he adds that, even if Oswald was "part and parcel of the conspiracy," he represents no more than a "piece of string [tied] around the conspiracy package." He concludes:

The dilemma faced by the Commission resulted in a solution based not on fact or on law, but on a phrase: "in the interests of national security." The Commission published a series of deliberate lies, not to protect the "national interests" of the American people, but to protect those interests that had interests contrary to the interests of the president of the United States, who had the interests of all the American people whom he represented.

That being the dilemma, it would have been far better for the Commission to have proclaimed the conspiracy even though it be directly connected to the right-wing fascist elements in the United States than have this nation live a lie.

Thus, it was "'in the interests of national security' that the Commission was under an obligation to destroy any testimony regarding the possibility of shots not coming from the Book Depository."

This is just one example of a far-reaching, "bigger picture" perspective that Marks should be remembered for. And now, decades after these remarks first appeared in *Two Days of Infa-*

my, we have the latest personification of fascism in America in the figure of President Trump, whose election in 2016 was merely the endpoint of a line first drawn on November 22, 1963.

It's also tempting to reinterpret Marks' phrase "not to protect the 'national interests' of the American people, but to protect those interests that had interests contrary to the interests of the president of the United States" to mean that JFK's interests included the fate of those nations that were struggling to reject the yoke of neocolonialist domination, much to the chagrin of multinational corporate, oligarchic interests that had billions of dollars to lose if Kennedy was allowed to live. As far as this reactionary group was concerned, it would be completely of out character to make an exception for John Kennedy when far less threatening figures were being gunned down during the global war on the left that transpired, often in a clandestine manner, from 1945 to 1990 and that still continues, with far less fanfare, today.

Marks adds to cynicism another deadly poison: loss of faith in the media, because of its betrayal. Back in 1967, Marks was already noting that there was no way of knowing "how many agents of the CIA now work for various organizations in the mass communication media" (*MMF*). In *Two Days of Infamy*, he again picks up this theme, adding: "The investigators of the 'Report have presented the result of their investigations to the public; but the silence of the press lords to further an investigation of the Commission's allegations has led to a further decline of the general public's faith in all forms of mass communication."

Again, keep in mind that this statement was published in March 1969. Since then, we have seen a snowballing–and then an avalanche–of mistrust in what we now refer to as the MSN; and this has occurred on both sides of the aisle, left and right. But Marks goes on to blame not only the MSN and the Warren Commission but the critics themselves for what followed. He refers to the first generation of researchers when he says:

> The critics' primary failure was their repeated implication that the murder of President Kennedy could not be

solved unless, at the same time, they proved a conspiracy. The critics have constantly proclaimed that unless the Zapruder film, the X-Rays, and other photographic evidence was released from the National Archives no solution could be obtained. Their demands obscure the main issue: "Was Lee Harvey Oswald the 'sole and exclusive assassin of President Kennedy' as charged by the Warren Commission?"

The film, X-rays, and other photographic evidence is not the prime evidence in securing an affirmative or negative answer. That evidence is secondary.

The prosecution, in this case the Warren Commission, must affirmatively prove three elements: (1) Lee Harvey Oswald was at the 6th floor S.E. corner window at the time the shots were fired; (2) those bullets which caused the death of President Kennedy came from a weapon he used at that time and (3) the rifle allegedly used was a functional operating lethal weapon from which those bullets were discharged.

As we witness time and again in his assassination-related publications, no matter how far afield Marks goes to explore "bigger picture" implications, as a trained attorney he always circles round and returns to the case at hand. Thus, two of his principal concerns are to show why Oswald could not have been convicted of being a "sole assassin" in any law court that followed the basic principles of American justice; and to prove this with specific facts, on a nuts-and-bolts legal level:

> In a court of law those three elements must be proved beyond a reasonable doubt by the evidence in the possession of the Warren Commission. Each of the three must be proved; not just one, or two, but all three.
>
> Thus, if Oswald was not at the S.E. corner window at the exact time those three bullets were fired, he could not be found "guilty" even though the remaining two elements be proved in the affirmative. If element (2) be proved in the affirmative but element (1) in the negative,

then a trial judge would rule Oswald "not guilty." If element (3) was proved affirmatively, the trial judge would still rule Oswald "not guilty" if (1) or (2) not be proven by the evidence given in court. Further, if (2) be proven but (3) proves that the rifle could not discharge those bullets because it was defective and incapable of firing bullets through its barrel, then Oswald would be found "not guilty." A consensus does not operate in a criminal courtroom.

Peppered throughout the text are examples of straightforward forensic evidence that any lawyer worth his salt would present to demonstrate his case against the WC conclusions: "Any attorney defending Oswald on the charge of being the 'sole and exclusive assassin' of President Kennedy would have an easy task to obtain a 'not guilty' verdict with the testimony of the physicians and federal agents that proved beyond a reasonable doubt that President Kennedy was struck in the back by a bullet striking him from an angle of fire between 45 and 60 degrees. This proved that such an angle of fire could only come from a window of the Dal-Tex Building or the County Building but not from the 6th floor of the Book Depository. Oswald was innocent." And it is the presentation of such clear evidence that allows Marks to then expound upon the risible nature of the Commission's groundless theories:

> In spite of the testimony of the physicians and the federal agencies, the Commission decided to confuse the people by outdoing Baron Munchhausen–a paragon among liars. The Commission therefore proceeded to "produce" a "Tale of Bullet No. 399." This "bullet," sayeth the Commission Barons, first entered the president's back, hesitated a moment, reversed itself, flew up his back, made a 90 degree turn, turned downward into the back of his neck, went through his neck, made another angle turn, entered the governor's body, "tumbled" through the wrist, entered his rib cage, and came to rest when the "tumbling" lacked inertia, in his thigh! The leading Bar-

on aide was a man by the name of Specter.

Even after decades of rehashing the magic bullet fiasco in the voluminous assassination literature, Marks's version leaves one with the impression of a fresh and lively spin. He later concludes:

> It can only be said that the 7 commissioners put the Baron Munchhausen stories out of print. As they say in Las Vegas: The Commission gave it to the Baron in spades!

* * *

Just as he does in *Murder Most Foul!*, by the end of the book Marks turns much of his ire on commissioner and former CIA Director Allen Dulles. And for good reason. Here, like a prosecuting attorney delivering a summation through the use of rhetorical device, Marks' refrain, echoed repeatedly in an imaginary courtroom, is the incredulous: "No conspiracy, Mr. Dulles?" To offer just a few piquant examples:

> The chief of the United States Secret Service not only informed the Commission of a conspiracy but also proved it was a conspiracy. What happened to the men who identified themselves as "Secret Service" agents to the various witnesses and collected evidence from those witnesses, and then those "agents" disappeared with the evidence? The chief of the Secret Service admitted that every Secret Service agent went either to Parkland Hospital or went on to guard Vice President Johnson immediately after the bullets ceased to fire. Then, Mr. Dulles, who were those "agents" seen near and behind the "grassy knolls" when policemen and deputy sheriffs approached them and those "agents" flashed "credentials"? Who were those men discussed in Com. Exh. 2003, No. 79-83? Secret Service agents or conspirators? Uncle Remus and his friends? Or members of the conspiracy? (280-

81.) No conspiracy, Mr. Dulles?

A few pages later:

> And you, Mr. Dulles, now have the gall to say no conspiracy existed!
> To assist your recollection, Mr. Dulles, your Commission's method of operation concerning evidence proving a conspiracy was to bury the proof in either the "Hearings" or the National Archives.

Finally, with a slight change in modulation, he adds:

> The same Dallas police also testified that although Tippit's clipboard was attached to his dashboard they never looked at it or read it! Do you believe that, Mr. Dulles?

Such passages also exemplify Marks' lively, provocative, arch, yet charming humor, which appears as a hallmark of the author's writing and that serves as a counterpoint to the sometimes strident, rage-fueled cadences that mark his discourse with an undertone of righteous indignation.

We should also note that Marks' disdain for Dulles may be traced back to an article that appeared in *Look* magazine in July 1966, in which Dulles remarks: "If they found another assassin, let them name names and produce their evidence." Stanley first quotes this in *MMF*, where he follows it with the remark: "This contemptuous statement directed at the American citizenry revealed the attitude of the Commission." In *Two Days of Infamy*, he further qualifies it as "The most contemptuous statement ever issued by a member of any governmental commission investigating the murder of the head of his government." But Marks cites this quote not merely to inform us of its existence but to take up Dulles' challenge. Indeed, the deeper one reads into Marks' work, the more easily one can imagine that the impetus to produce such tomes grew directly from the outrage spawned by this outrageous declaration. After citing one example after another in which the Commission is caught with its pants down–

or, perhaps more fittingly, called out for being an emperor without any clothing–Marks rests his case by stating:

> The author has produced the evidence; it was the duty of Mr. Dulles and his commissioners to name the names of the assassins and the conspirators.
> That failure is theirs, not the responsibility of the American citizen.

But Marks finds no solace in reaching this conclusion; rather, he reminds us of a terrible truth:

> History has proven that once assassination has become the weapon to change the government, that style and form of government preceding the assassination falls beneath the hard-nailed boots of the assassins. Both right and left favor no democratic spirit in the people. The cold of Siberia and the gas ovens of the concentration camps have proved it.
> The tragedy of the Warren Commission is that they helped set those boots on the road to the destruction of American democracy.

And how could so many have fallen prey to such a deceit? In part, this turning of a blind eye to the possibility of a conspiracy occurred because the citizens of the United States are "living in a dream world concocted by the mass communication systems."

One should also note that not all the ire falls upon Dulles. That other intractable head of so-called intelligence, J. Edgar Hoover, is the subject of so much justifiable vitriol that Marks was certain to have had a file opened on him by the FBI as a result. He lambasts Hoover for declaring just five months after the assassination of Bobby Kennedy that "Justice is incidental to law and order," and adds:

> Mr. Hoover's belief in "law and order" is on the exact same level as Hitler's "law and order"; Stalin's "law and order"; Mussolini's "law and order"; Tojo's "law and or-

der"; "Batista's "law and order"; the Greek Colonel's "law and order, 1968 version"; and so forth. Mr. Hoover's basic philosophy is identical with the philosophy of any other "police state" objective.

But Marks also views Hoover as something of a foxy figure. Since the Bureau's memoranda and reports on the assassination were often as truthful as they were deceitful, and since the official FBI assassination report often contradicts the Warren Commission Report, Marks speculates that Hoover was attempting to have it both ways: protecting himself and the Bureau no matter what the final outcome. Indeed, Hoover's performance was rather sly and of the type that only an attorney could truly appreciate. For example, speaking of the Mannlicher-Carcano rifle supposedly owned and used by Oswald for the assassination, Marks highlights Hoover's brilliant use of legalese:

> In the official FBI Reports, Vol. 1 to 5, there is no statement by the Bureau that that rifle given to them was ever "used" by any rifleman. The FBI constantly referred to this rifle as being "owned" by Lee Oswald; never did they state that he "used" it for any purpose. How can a rifle discharge three bullets when the rifle has never been used?

Note that fine line between truth and deceit: whether or not this rifle was really "owned" by Oswald, the Bureau nonetheless betrays the Commission by refusing to take that extra step of stating that it was "used" by him. Then there's the matter of the WC attempting to prove that it must be Oswald's rifle because Oswald's firearm had the same serial number: "C2766." But Hoover puts an end to such speculation, Marks reminds us, via Commission Exhibit No. 2562, which contains a letter from Hoover that

> informed the "honorable" gentlemen that between 1931 and 1941 every rifle manufactured by Italian rifle manufacturers carried the identical number: "C2766." [...]

Thus, in a court of law, the serial number "C2766" was worthless as the legal identification of any rifle.

Marks attempts to summarize this paradox of the Bureau's seemingly shifting, alternating allegiances in the following manner:

> The federal agency that is the paradox, the Chinese puzzle, in the entire investigation is the Federal Bureau of Investigation. As has been stated in previous chapters, that Bureau overwhelmed the Commission with evidence that proved Oswald innocent in both murders. What is the puzzle is the fact although the Bureau time and time again warned the Commission that its "conclusions" would not stand the scrutiny of the light of day, that agency then turned right around and conducted itself in a manner implying they had something to hide–to conceal their possible involvement in the assassination. The Bureau was involved in suppressing the same evidence they had originally uncovered and exposed to the world! [...]
>
> The Bureau's conduct can only lead to a conclusion that the Bureau was operating on both sides of the fence in the slim hope that any investigation of the "Report" would not be undertaken by a serious investigator of that "Report." "Heads or tails," the FBI could prove that they had given evidence, or uncovered evidence, disproving the Commission's accusation that Oswald was the "sole and exclusive killer of President Kennedy." What is perplexing is Mr. Hoover's defense of the Commission in the face of that evidence, and his various statements, which were obtuse or contradictory, that did nothing to add to the honor of the FBI.

* * *

Stanley Marks was only twenty-seven years old when President Roosevelt called December 7, 1941 "a date that shall live in infamy." Marks was a lifelong FDR Democrat; and, while working for the Democratic National Committee in the late Thirties and early Forties, he wrote publicity for FDR's presidential campaigns. On March 8, 1945, during the end of World War II, he was inducted as a private into the Army. By the summer of that year, he would be stationed in the Pacific under the Command of General MacArthur. Therefore, it's in this context that we must view the borrowing of the phrase, a date of "infamy," for the title of this book. That is, the author's reaction to the first date of infamy in 1941 was visceral and real, not simply an abstraction or a sentence memorized decades later, in a classroom. Marks also devotes many pages to discussing this event in his first book, a well-received study about Soviet Russia (see below).

In the present volume, "two days of infamy" refers to the date of JFK's murder and, ten months later, to the publication date of the Warren Commission Report. By grafting FDR's "infamy" term onto these more recent dates of iniquity, the author is reminding us of the rage and indignation that rise up within many who lived through both the attack on Pearl Harbor and the coup d'état of November 22, 1963. This outrage extends beyond the personal figure of JFK and the experience of his loss; for, as Marks warns in the first chapter of his text: "A nation can be destroyed if its leaders can be murdered with impunity." As a result of the Warren Commission hoax perpetrated by those ignoble seven commissioners, "The truth was never ascertained; the evidence never evaluated; and the truth uncovered was covered. Never was so much done by so many that produced so little." Later on, with typical Marksian aplomb and incisiveness, he adds:

> The historical verdict of the Warren Commission is that the Commission proclaimed a precedent whereby it is now permissible for the president of the United States to be murdered by men who believe that the vice president, who becomes the president upon the death of the president, would be more amenable to the philosophies of the murderers.

* * *

In this book and in his next two assassination-related titles, the author makes several remarks that indicate he was in some sort of communication with Senator Robert Kennedy. Unfortunately, there exists no documentary record of these communiques other than what Marks mentions in his work, so the best we can do is to speculate on how such a contact may have happened and to place what Marks says into the broader context of contemporaneous events.

Although nothing is known about how such a contact may have come about, there is one possibility that presents itself as the most logical and likely one. We know from feature articles about Marks that appeared in the press after the appearance of his first book (a bestseller titled *The Bear That Walks Like a Man. A Diplomatic and Military Analysis of Soviet Russia*) that he worked for the Democratic National Committee from 1936 to 1944 in the role of writing publicity. He also received help from an influential Democrat: Cordell Hull, the longest serving secretary of state and the "father" of the United Nations, who gave Marks access to State Department files while he was conducting his research. And in 1943, the *Bear* was reviewed in the *Chicago Tribune* by FDR's former ambassador to Poland and Belgium, John Cudahy. Decades later, Marks' biography in *Who Was Who in America* notes that he continued in his DNC role in 1948, 1952, and 1960.

Thus, the most likely scenario for a contact with RFK may have been via the DNC. Perhaps they met in the early days of JFK's or RFK's political career or during JFK's 1960 presidential campaign. Or perhaps Marks, an inveterate letter writer,[3] corresponded briefly with Senator Robert Kennedy, mentioned his work for the DNC, and received a reply.

Certainly, the RFK quote that appears on the first page of *Two Days of Infamy*, which Marks says he received from the senator

---

[3] Marks also mentions that he wrote to Dallas Police Chief Curry but that his "letters remain unanswered."

in March 1968 ("Life is but a way station on the track to eternity"), is something that Robert Kennedy could conceivably have penned in a reply to Marks; i.e., it resembles a written remark more than a spoken communication. So, too, regarding the quote with which Marks ends his preface: he says that RFK "expressed to the author" that "No person or nation receives freedom as a gift. Those who possess it must always remember that others will to take it away. The struggle for man's freedom is an eternal one, and those who refuse to struggle remain 'free' only as slaves." JFK assassination researcher Penn Jones later cited Marks' *Two Days of Infamy* and reproduced the last phrase from this quote ("those who refuse to struggle remain 'free' only as slaves") in his *Forgive My Grief* series.[4]

In chapter eight of *Two Days of Infamy*, Marks records an even more surprising exchange. While discussing President Johnson's executive order that established the Warren Commission, he writes:

> The president's Executive Order No. 11130 also committed an act that was never analyzed by the critics of the Commission. That order effectively removed the attorney general of the United States, Robert F. Kennedy, from any supervision of the activities of the FBI headed by the arch foe of the Kennedy family, Mr. Hoover. The person who pointed that fact out to me was Senator Kennedy, and it was placed in my book, "Murder Most Foul." At the time the "Report" was issued, Mr. Kennedy was no longer the attorney general. Thus, at a stroke of the pen, President Johnson removed the one man who would have gone through hell and high water to capture the conspirators who murdered his brother, the President of the United States, John F. Kennedy.

If this actually occurred as described, it would mean that Marks

---

[4] A brave journalist, after Jones received the Elijah Parish Lovejoy Award for Courage in Journalism, President Kennedy sent him a message of congratulations.

crossed paths with Bobby Kennedy at some point prior to September 1967, when *Murder Most Foul!* first appeared.

In his subsequent work on the JFK assassination, Marks attributes several comments to RFK that would never have been committed to paper by the senator and could only have been delivered as the result of a direct spoken communication. For example, in *Coup d'État* (February 1970), he writes:

> The senator, three weeks before his death, informed me that it was not the election he feared but whether or not when he won the national election he would be able to live until he was sworn in as the president of the United States. The senator was a fatalist, and I have no doubt that when the bullets struck him he was not surprised. Prior to the day those bullets struck him in the head, the senator had informed several persons–including Jim Garrison, the New Orleans District Attorney–that when he became president he would establish a new commission to investigate the murder of President Kennedy. But, more dangerously, he was dedicated to the philosophy espoused by his brother; he would be threatening the identical forces that commissioned the assassination of President Kennedy.

Again, since RFK would never have committed such comments to paper, this leads one to conclude that such an exchange could only have come as the result of an off-the-record conversation. We don't know where or how this may have occurred, but, tantalizingly, Marks says that it happened three weeks before the senator's assassination, which would place it on May 15-16, 1968.

A quick look at Robert Kennedy's schedule[5] reveals that he was briefly campaigning in Los Angeles at this time, where Marks had been living since 1964. After a noonday rally in Detroit, Kennedy was scheduled to arrive at Los Angeles Interna-

---

[5] RFK schedule accessed online via the JFK Library.

tional Airport on May 15 at 4:00 p.m., followed by appearances at LA's Century City, Van Nuys, and Los Angeles Valley College, where he gave a speech to an overflowing crowd of university students. Then, at 9:00 p.m., he would return to the Ambassador Hotel to stay overnight, leaving the following day, May 16, for Long Beach, located in LA's metropolitan area. After making several other local stops, including a midday visit to Redondo Beach, Kennedy departed LA Airport that afternoon for Sacramento, followed by a trip that evening to Portland. (Indeed, RFK's final weeks of campaigning were remembered for their hectic, high-pitched, frenetic pace.)

If Marks' contact with Robert Kennedy occurred during one of these appearances in LA, one can only imagine what else was said–and whether Marks attempted to pass along a copy of his book to the senator.

All this calls to mind another strange event that occurred just a few years later. Robert Kennedy's trusted colleague, Dave Powers, who served as JFK's personal assistant and whom RFK later placed in charge of assembling materials for the official JFK Library, would probably have been familiar with at least the title of Marks' *Murder Most Foul!* because the JFK Library wrote Marks a letter on March 12, 1973, requesting information on how to purchase a copy for their collection.

How to explain such an interest in this little-known work?

Thanks to Vincent Palamara's *Survivor's Guilt: The Secret Service and the Failure to Protect President Kennedy*, I recently learned that Powers had long maintained a skeptic's view of the Warren Commission Report. In discussing the possibility of Secret Service involvement in the conspiracy, in *Survivor's Guilt* Vince writes that, in 1996, ARRB Director Tom Samoluk informed him that Dave Powers "agreed with your take on the Secret Service." If Powers held this belief, it might explain why this unusual purchase of *Murder Most Foul!* was authorized for the JFK Library.

A photo of this letter addressed to Marks, composed on U.S. General Services Administration stationery, is reproduced here.

UNITED STATES OF AMERICA
GENERAL SERVICES ADMINISTRATION

National Archives and Records Service
John F. Kennedy Library
380 Trapelo Road
Waltham, Massachusetts 02154

Telephone: 617 223-7250

March 12, 1973

Bureau of International Affairs
6769 W. Lexington Avenue
Los Angeles, CA 90038

Gentlemen:

The Kennedy Library is interested in acquiring the book listed below from your company. Please consider this letter our order and bill us accordingly.

    Marks, Stanley J.
        MURDER MOST FOUL. 1967

Our purchase order number is: JB-NLK-147. If you would be kind enough to send the book and invoice to my attention, it would be much appreciated.

Thank you in advance for your cooperation in this matter.

Sincerely,

JOAN BARONIAN
Purchasing Agent

Keep Freedom in Your Future With U.S. Savings Bonds

In this edition of *Two Days of Infamy*, minor changes in grammar and punctuation have been made, and the spelling of proper nouns has been corrected. Textual changes involving anything more complex, such as inserting missing words or phrases, are indicated by brackets. A bibliography of works cited in the text has been added, along with annotated footnotes and a general index. Otherwise, the original *Two Days of Infamy* is reproduced here without any substantial changes.

Unlike *MMF*, the original text of *Two Days of Infamy* features the author's endnotes. There, Marks cites two key assassination titles published between September 1967 (when *Murder Most Foul!* first appeared), and March 1969 (the publication date of *Two Days of Infamy*): Sylvia Meagher's *Accessories After the Fact* (November 1967), and Paris Flammonde's *The Kennedy Conspiracy* (early 1969). Also mentioned is Jim Garrison's *Playboy* interview of October 1967, as well as various newspaper reports and magazine articles.

But we can surmise from these notes that Marks mainly continued to delight in exposing the many contradictions that exist between the official WC Report and the twenty-six volumes of WC "Hearings and Testimony." ("As the investigator digs into the 'Hearings,'" writes Marks, "he becomes amazed at the duplicity practiced by the Commission.") He never ceased to aggressively rifle through this data as he applied the principal mediums of the attorney's art–common sense coupled with in-depth knowledge of the law–and ripped the WC Report to shreds. Indeed, it's for this reason that the opening phrase in the subtitle of the present book reads "A nonfiction manual for the American of common sense." Later on, Marks again refers to this rare virtue that we call "common" when he writes: "Be not so contemptuous of your fellow-citizens, Mr. Dulles, for although many of them may not be blessed with your intelligence, you should not forget that Abraham Lincoln placed common sense above intelligence." Finally, in one of the many digs that he loved to make against his own profession, he says: "Of course, the commissioners were not men of common sense; they were 'lawyers'!"

In the main body of text, the author's endnotes are referenced by numerals in parentheses. When citing the WC Report or the WC Hearings and Exhibits, Marks uses the abbreviation "R" for the Report and "H" for the Hearings and Exhibits. (Thus, "R81, 235" refers to the WC Report, pp. 81, 235; while "3H294-95" refers to the third volume of the Hearings and Exhibits, pp. 294-95.) "C.E." is an abbreviation for "Commission Exhibit." "C.D." refers to the FBI's Commission Document. (E.g., "C.D. 1" is Commission Document 1, the Bureau's thirty-nine-page assassination report.) Some of the witness statements quoted by Marks are not verbatim transcripts but rather a condensation of their remarks.

Rob Couteau
November 22, 2020

$4.95

TWO DAYS OF INFAMY

November 22, 1963

September 28, 1964

Stanley J. Marks

A Bureau of International Affairs Publication

The first edition of *Two Days of Infamy*, which features teal blue lettering on a white background. An ad for the book appeared in the July 11, 1969 *Los Angeles Free Press* and included the caption: "Now available at bookstores with courage."

Marks circa 1934. When he was only four years old, Stanley lost his parents to the 1918 influenza pandemic, which infected a third of the world's population. Roberta Marks recalls her father saying that "he never had enough food. When you see pictures of him as a youth, he was bone-thin and skinny. That is, until he married my mother, whose cooking he adored." Stanley's privations and experience with hunger on Chicago's hardscrabble streets may have helped to open his eyes to a certain political awareness and helped to mold him into a lifelong FDR New Dealer.

Private Stan Marks at an army base library, circa 1945. By his late twenties Marks had accumulated a private collection of over 5,000 books.

Stanley with Roberta Marks at Union Pier, Michigan, circa 1950.

January 25, 1962: President Kennedy at an award ceremony of the National Newspaper Publishers Association (formerly the National Negro Publishers Association), founded by John H. Sengstacke, publisher of the *Chicago Defender*, a widely celebrated African American newspaper. Sengstacke stands beside the president, the fourth figure from the left. Just hours after the assassination, Sengstacke declared: "I regard the death of President Kennedy as the greatest tragedy that has befallen America since the assassination of Civil War President Abraham Lincoln. Kennedy's tragic ending is the greatest blow that the Negro people has sustained since the demise of the great Emancipator."

In the spring of 1943 Stanley Marks published a dozen essays in the *Chicago Defender*. During WWII the *Defender* promoted the "Double V Campaign": "Dual Victory" over foreign *and* domestic "enemies" who remained opposed to racial equality, thus incurring the wrath of J. Edgar Hoover, who tried to convince FDR to prosecute its editors for treason. Stanley's publications eventually led to his blacklisting by the House Un-American Activities Committee.

XXXV

INTRODUCTION–PROLOGUE–EPILOGUE

November 22, 1963–March, 1969

"Life is but a way station on the track to eternity."
—Robert Kennedy to author; March, 1968

As 1968 passed into history, several major historical events have occurred since the first victim of the conspiracy–President Kennedy–was claimed. The first event was the announcement early in 1967 that a C. Shaw had been indicted by a New Orleans grand jury for being a member of a conspiracy whose objective was the murder of President Kennedy. The second event was the murder of Dr. Martin L. King in Memphis, Tenn. And within ninety days after that event Senator Robert Kennedy was fatally struck down by another assassin. All three were murdered as the end result of three interrelated conspiracies.

The citizen's failure to understand law, in theory and practice, has permitted the mass communication media to thoroughly confuse the citizen's knowledge regarding the application of the law to those three murders.

To understand what Mr. James Garrison, the district attorney of New Orleans was attempting to achieve in the trial of C. Shaw necessitates the definition of the word "conspiracy." A Webster's Dictionary definition is "an agreement, especially in secret, to do some unlawful deed; to plot together. To concur or to work to one end." Thus, in the State of Louisiana v. Shaw trial, the grand jury did not accuse him of being a member of a conspiracy that did murder President Kennedy, only that Mr. Shaw conspired to commit the murder.

For example: Group I meets to discuss methods to murder K. Unbeknownst to the members of Group I, members of Group II not only meet secretly and plot to murder K but actually do commit the murder. Members of Group I can only be indicted for planning or conspiring to commit an unlawful act; namely, murder. However, all the members of Group II, either singly or in combination, can be indicted and found guilty of murder. A conspiracy must be composed of not less than two persons, for no one can conspire with himself. Furthermore, mere talk to commit an unlawful act is not in itself illegal. From talk, action, which is in furtherance of the illegal act, must take place. What constitutes action to precipitate a conviction of conspiracy to commit murder is determined by the jury based upon all the evidence presented to them.

The New Orleans grand jury simply indicted Mr. Shaw as being an alleged member of a group of persons who conspired to murder President Kennedy. They did not say he was guilty. An indictment simply means that the district attorney had submitted sufficient facts which impelled the grand jury to issue an indictment. Nor did that grand jury's indictment state Mr. Shaw's alleged conspiracy committed the murder.

In an effort to have this indictment declared null and void, Mr. Shaw appealed to the New Orleans criminal court panel of three judges to have this panel declare the "Report" of the Warren Commission be legally binding upon the court. Thus, if the panel had upheld Mr. Shaw's request the effect would have been to legally state that Lee Harvey Oswald was the "sole and exclusive assassin of President Kennedy." Hence, no conspiracy existed, and since no conspiracy existed Mr. Shaw should not have been indicted. The New Orleans court panel refused this request with the statement that the Warren "Report" was "hearsay piled upon hearsay"! Mr. Shaw then appealed through the state court system and all the way up to the United States Supreme Court. That court refused to consider the appeal and Mr. Shaw had to defend himself. Thus, at the commencement of the Shaw trial, in January, 1969, every court that had heard Mr. Shaw's legal argument upheld the indictment. In other words, the Warren "Report" is not a legal document in any sense of the word, for no legal document can be based upon "Hearsay piled upon hearsay."

The reader of this book may become somewhat confused by the various legal statements regarding the conspiracy that murdered President Kennedy, Dr. King and Senator Robert Kennedy. The first problem is to distinguish between a federal or state crime. Generally, all unlawful acts are punished in the state where the crime was committed unless such acts are made unlawful by Congress and not in violation of our Constitution. When Congress enacts a law which states a specific act is illegal, then the violator of that act can be indicted and tried in the federal district court in the state where the act was committed. Contrary to newspaper opinion, there are many cases of murder where the perpetrator can be punished by a federal jury. For example, the murderer of an FBI agent killed in the line of duty is tried in the federal district court in the state where the murder took place.

The citizen must remember that District Attorney Garrison's case against Mr. Shaw was hampered by this vital distinction between state and federal laws. For example, the district attorney had no power to compel the attendance of any doctor who attended the president at either the Parkland or Bethesda Hospitals. He had no power to compel any FBI, Secret Service, or Dallas police agent to testify either before the New Orleans grand jury or at the Shaw trial. He could not compel the FBI, the Secret Service or the members of the Miami, Fla., Police Department to testify to the remarks of the statement by a right-wing follower prior to the president's murder. Mr. Garrison had no power to compel Police Chief Curry, Sheriff Decker, Capt. Fritz, or Lt. Day to testify before either jury concerning their activities prior, during, and after the murder of both the president and Officer Tippit.

Nor could Mr. Garrison, under state law, introduce the amazing affidavit signed by W. S. Walters, an FBI security clerk in the FBI Dallas Office relating to a TWX[6] message expressly stating that an attempt would be made to assassinate President Kennedy in Dallas on November 22, 1963! This TWX message was sent November 17, 1963. To this day the FBI has never denied the existence of that message. (Garrison's "Playboy" interview; also see "The Kennedy Conspiracy" by P. Flammonde, 1969.)

A verdict of "not guilty" in the Shaw trial proved only one

---

[6] A switched teleprinter network first developed in 1932 by AT&T. FBI memo, later unearthed by Mark Lane, concerning the TWX message discussed by Marks.

thing: that Mr. Shaw was not a member of a conspiracy to murder President Kennedy. The verdict of "not guilty" does not mean that the Warren Commission's conclusion that a conspiracy did not exist was correct. A "not guilty" verdict does not imply that a conspiracy by another group did not exist. It must also be remembered that a "guilty" verdict did not imply, in any manner, that Mr. Shaw was implicated in the actual murder of the president. He was not a member of a group that conspired to commit the murder. This is a vital distinction. Much of the testimony and evidence in the Shaw trial can be read in the author's first book: "Murder Most Foul! The Conspiracy That Murdered President Kennedy." (Bureau of International Affairs, 1967.)

The startling testimony of Lt. Col. Finck in the Shaw trial that no complete autopsy was made upon the president's body, and his statements that the autopsy physicians were under pressure from "high ranking military officers," must compel the acceptance that the conspiracy takes in high figures in our government. From newspaper reports [it appears that] Lt. Col. Finck was an extremely nervous witness called by the Shaw defense. The military physician's statement that this incomplete autopsy report (not to be confused with the autopsy chart which has been labeled authentic by both the Warren Commission and the Bethesda, Md. Hospital autopsy panel) was also based on press reports is a shattering example of how extensive and impressive the pressure was used upon those physicians. It is imperative to realize that at no time did the Lt. Col. testify that the autopsy chart was incorrect or that the location of the bullet hole in the president's suit jacket was incorrect. Thus, a conspiracy did murder President Kennedy.

In March, 1969, as this book was going to press, there quietly appeared an unpublicized book titled: "The Kennedy Conspiracy" by Paris Flammonde. The book has appeared in no book review sections of any of the major newspapers in the United States. It is receiving the same treatment that was given to "Rush to Judgment" by Lane; 'Whitewash" by Weisberg; "Accessories After the Fact" by Meagher, "The Affair" by Sauvage; 'Oswald: Assassin or Fall Guy" by Joesten. Mr. Flammonde's book is the first book to deal with Mr. Garrison's investigation of Mr. Shaw, and the evidence uncovered by Mr. Flammonde relating to Mr. Shaw's "liberal" background gives lie to Shaw's facade created by the press. This book is essential for anyone who desires to understand the Garrison investigation. However, due to the distinction between state and federal laws, Mr. Garrison cannot examine the evidence enumerated in Mr. Flammonde's book.

The murder of Dr. King in April, 1968, was part and parcel of the same group of conspirators that murdered President Kennedy. The identical "modus operandi" was used to commit both assassinations. For example: (1) [A] high powered telescopic rifle was used. (2) A building was used as the ambush site. (3) The police radio network was used. (4) Both "murderers" were "patsies"! (5) In both murders, the murder itself was incidental to the main objective. In the Kennedy assassination an invisible coup d'état occurred. In the King assassination the objective was to obtain a race war.

The important fact in both murders is that the man captured with a rifle in his hands on the grassy knoll by deputy sheriffs, taken into custody at 12:45 p.m., and then mysteriously disappeared from the Dallas police station is the identical man described by witnesses to the Dr. King murder as the man they saw flee from the King murder site. For proof the reader is referred to the illustrated section of this book, where the official FBI sketch of one of Dr. King's alleged murderer-conspirator's is published for the first time in a book. The man taken into custody in Dallas and the FBI man in the sketch are identical! Although the Warren Commission had full knowledge of this man they refused to have any investigation made as to how he was able to "flee" from the police. The man is not James Earl Ray, the alleged murderer of Dr. King.

Sufficient testimony has been given at the trial of Sirhan B. Sirhan, for the murder of Senator Robert Kennedy on June 6, 1968, in the kitchen hallway of the Ambassador Hotel in Los Angeles, Calif., to prove the existence of a conspiracy. Again, a conspiracy was proved, but who all the conspirators were is not the subject of this book.

The vital fact proving, or disproving, a conspiracy rests solely upon the number of bullets found either in the person of the six victims or in the kitchen wall. Sirhan, as his part of the conspiracy, used a .22 snub-nose Johnson revolver having 8 bullets.[7] Until the trial commenced the public was led to believe that Senator Kennedy was struck only twice. However, at the trial, the official police ballistic expert, Mr. D. Wolfer, testified that Senator Kennedy had three bullet holes and, in addition, a bullet in his head. That is a total of four bullets.

But, five other persons were struck by bullets. A woman and two young men were each struck by a bullet. That is three more bullets. A union official was struck by two bullets and a television producer was, by his own statement made in the hospital, struck by three bullets. In an attempt to make the number of bullets conform to the number of bullets that could be fired from Sirhan's revolver, the authorities released a statement that those two injured men were each struck by one bullet. But, as the mathematics of the murder revealed, that still left the authorities with 4 extra bullets. 12 bullets! Nor did the mass communication media question any police officer as to how four bullet holes appeared at the baseboard of the kitchen wall in that hallway.

Thus, any way the authorities wiggle, the blunt fact remains that Sirhan had an accomplice. The fact remains that the number of bullets proved to have been fired exceeds the number of bullets, 8, in Sirhan's revolver. The fact remains that the tapes of a national television system contain the statement that another man was arrested, in addition to Sirhan, and turned over to a man dressed in a "policeman's" uniform. The fact remains that four bullets were extracted from four bullet holes located at the base-board of the kitchen wall. The fact remains that a minimum of ten bullets were fired at Senator Kennedy. The fact remains that although there were seven exits which could be used by Senator Kennedy when he left the ballroom, Sirhan stationed himself, upon orders from his fellow conspirators, in the kitchen

---

[7] Sirhan was *alleged* to have used an eight-shot Iver-Johnson .22 caliber Cadet 55-A revolver. Evidence has since emerged that he was firing blanks form a starter pistol, thus distracting attention from the actual shooter. See Lisa Pease, *A Lie Too Big to Fail*.

two hours prior to the murder and never left that area.

The fact remains that the Los Angeles authorities deliberately lied when they first said that there was "no woman in a polka-dot dress." Whether or not the girl they produced as that "woman" is true or false cannot be objectively commented upon, since the original witness who saw the woman was never summoned by the authorities to testify at the Sirhan trial. Why? Was it because the original witness saw a "woman in a white polka dot dress" who did not limp, while the authorities' witness said she wore a different color dress and limped?

Thus, in conclusion, the evidence is overwhelming that a conspiracy murdered all three political leaders. The Warren "Report" was an out-and-out whitewash; the Shaw trial was hampered deliberately by the federal agencies although Mr. Garrison legally proved the existence of a conspiracy. The jury, based upon the evidence, correctly found Mr. Shaw "not guilty." The testimony of Lt. Col. Finck conclusively proved the falsity of the conclusions of the Warren Commission when Col. Finck testified that the autopsy was incomplete. In law, an incomplete autopsy presented to the court as a complete one is false from its inception and no verdict can be rendered which is based upon a falsehood. Thus, conclusive proof is evidence of a whitewash. The press coverage of Shaw's trial is another chain in the gradual erosion of the phrase "freedom of the press," since it was the deliberate misrepresentation by the press that has confused the legal issues in the Shaw trial.

The trial of Sirhan Sirhan also proved the existence of a conspiracy that murdered Senator Robert F. Kennedy. An eight-bullet revolver cannot discharge 9, 10, 11, or 12 bullets. Nor did the state or defense explain the existence of four bullet holes at the base of the kitchen wall.

The March 10, 1969 four-hour trial of James Earl Ray was another cover-up. Earl Ray, the confessed "killer" declared, in open court, that he was a member of a conspiracy that murdered the Rev. Martin L. King. After he made that statement, the FBI announced that the Bureau was still seeking evidence of a conspiracy and that the case was not closed. Of course, the FBI merely has to place the tape recording they received from the

Miami, Fla., Police Department thirteen days prior to the murder of President Kennedy and the names of the conspirators would be heard. The picture of the man captured on the "grassy knoll" on November 22, 1963 and the FBI sketch of the man who witnesses said fled the King murder site can be found in the illustrated section of this book. It is the same man and he is not Earl Ray! His name is known to both the FBI and the U.S. Secret Service and, by a coincidence, to the Dallas police who had him in custody!

In view of the fact that the president, the senator, and the reverend were murdered in the exact manner as stated on that tape recording, and in view of the fact that that recording also contains the names of the political, social, and business leaders who are scheduled to be murdered by the same organizations, then this nation can look forward to more days of mourning. At the 1968 Democratic Convention Senator Eugene McCarthy escaped serious injury or death by less than five minutes when his Chicago headquarters were invaded and his staff beaten by "unknown Chicago policemen."

This "election by assassination" is now the new rule of political conduct in our nation and is the direct result of the Warren Commission's "investigation" that "proved" no conspiracy murdered President Kennedy.

Senator Ted Kennedy's statement to a newsman on the plane carrying his brother's body back to New York that "faceless" men were carrying a vendetta against his family is half right and half wrong. The vendetta is against the American Republic and the philosophy upon which it stands.

As Robert Kennedy once expressed to the author: "No person or nation receives freedom as a gift. Those who possess it must always remember that others will to take it away. The struggle for man's freedom is an eternal one and those who refuse to struggle remain 'free' only as slaves."

The murders of President Kennedy, Dr. King, and Senator Kennedy must be viewed as being part of that struggle. It remains upon us, the living, to see that the struggle never ceases.

–Stanley J. Marks; February, 1969

Chapter I

The Failure to Understand

The Warren Commission issued its "Report" with the knowledge that the failure of the general public to understand the law would enable it to perpetuate its theory that "Lee Harvey Oswald was the sole and exclusive assassin of President Kennedy." Citizens of any nation understand the fact that for a nation to exist they must have laws. Whether those laws are good or bad is not the subject of this book. What is involved is the fact that the Warren Commission knew that the citizens have never understood the "whys" and "wherefores" that are necessary for the law to function properly.

One court of law has legally rendered a decision regarding the validity of the Warren "Report." That court, in the Parish of New Orleans, State of Louisiana, in the preliminary hearing between that State vs. Clay Shaw, issued a legal opinion that the "Report" was "hearsay piled upon hearsay." When the citizen read of that decision in his newspaper he simply shrugged and turned to the sports or financial page.

Yet, this court of law, presided over by three judges, rendered a decision that branded the Warren "Report" a tissue of lies. A lawyer and a law student can spot "hearsay" but not the average citizen. So, what is "hearsay"? Hearsay, in the language of the average citizen, is nothing more than "over-the-fence" gossip. One person telling another person what that person told him about another person or fact. Or, A telling B what he heard D say about C. A did not see or hear anything said or done by C but was informed by D of what C had allegedly done or said. A told B that he was informed by D that C had committed rape. Therefore, on the basis that A told B, the police arrested C for the charge of rape. That is hearsay. A rumor is also hearsay.

The Warren Commission also relied upon the fact that the general public could not distinguish between a statement and an affidavit. A statement not made under an oath is absolutely worthless in any court, whether the case be civil or criminal. However, where a person signs a statement to an authorized person and swears an oath that the statement is true, then that statement is considered to be true in a court of law unless testimony is produced in court that the statement is untrue. If that occurs then the person making that statement or affidavit can be tried, convicted, and imprisoned for perjury. A liar is not necessarily a perjurer, but a perjurer is always a liar.

The major reason why the Warren Commission suppressed many affidavits that proved the innocence of Lee Harvey Oswald is the simple fact that the affidavits proved the witness whose "testimony" was used by the Commission to convict him was lying, Affidavits are statements made under oath which are generally given by a notary public licensed by the state and made prior to the commencement of the trial. Thus, the person making the affidavit has committed himself as to the truth of his statements in that affidavit. However, where a witness in a criminal case has simply made a statement to the police authorities or to newsmen that witness can admit he made a mistake in that statement when testifying in open court under oath but he cannot be charged with perjury for making that statement. The opposing attorney, either the prosecutor or the defense attorney, may point out to the jury that that witness said one thing at one time and another thing at the trial but that contradiction only means that his "credibility" is subject to doubt. The lack of credibility does not imply perjury.

The methods used by the Commission permitted many of the FBI agents to submit written statements that perverted the original statements made to the agents by witnesses. Various witnesses, under oath, accused the agents of "putting" words in their (the witness's) mouth that were contrary to what the witness had said. In spite of those accusations against the FBI agents, the Commission never once placed the accused agent on the witness stand to affirm or deny the charge. In addition to those civilian witness accusations, the Secret Service agents also accused the FBI agents of perverting both the statements and the evidence given by them to the FBI. In analyzing the accusations it was found that the Commission accepted the falsified version submitted by various FBI agents which, in its perverted state, supported the "guilt" of Lee Harvey Oswald.

However, when the original statement is converted to paper and signed by that person under oath, he then commits perjury when he goes upon the witness stand, and, under oath, gives facts that contradict the original affidavit or statement. The Warren Commission repeatedly published statements made by witnesses under oath when those same statements were in direct contradiction of what the witness had sworn to in an affidavit. In several instances the Warren Commission completely perverted not only the affidavit but also the sworn testimony of the witness who swore that the facts in the affidavit were true. The witness was not the perjurer; only the Commission.

Several classic examples can be quoted. The Warren Commission used the "testimony" of Mr. Brennan to place Oswald at the southeast (S.E.) 6th-floor window of the Book Depository, from where the Commission alleged Oswald fired three shots from an Italian Mannlicher-Carcano rifle. Yet, in the files of the National Archives, in Washington, D.C., is Mr. Brennan's affidavit, not a statement, but an affidavit that he could not identify the man at the 6th-floor window. When appearing before the Commission, Brennan made several statements which were contradicted by his original affidavit. Furthermore, this same Brennan made an affidavit to the Dallas police that also contradicted his testimony before the Commission. Thus, in law, he was a perjurer; and, under the law, his testimony was not worth a tinker's damn. In spite of his perjury, the Commission accepted his "testimony" to "prove" Lee Harvey Oswald guilty of the murder of President Kennedy.

Another example of the prostitution of the law by the Warren Commission is the manner and method used to convict Oswald of the Tippit murder. In that case the Commission accepted, as true, the "testimony" of Mrs. Markham, who admitted perjury but whose "testimony" was accepted. In her example, the Commission willfully deceived the American people by ignoring two statements made at the scene of the murder by this—according to the Commission—"reliable and truthful" witness. She gave a description of the Tippit murderer which in no way resembled Lee Harvey Oswald to (1) the Dallas police who took her description; (2) her statement to the Columbia Broadcasting System which was also broadcasted to the public; (3) her statements made at the identification parade lineup at the Dallas police station; (4) her testimony before the Commission which denied the Commission's statement that she had identified Oswald as the murderer; (5) her affidavit to the FBI which totally disproved the Commission's 'reliability" of Mrs. Markham, and (6) her statement given to District Attorney Wade.

In the author's opinion, the greatest perversion of the truth relates to the outright perjury committed by the various members of the Dallas Police Department relating to the number of bullets taken from "Tippit's" body. The Dallas police swore that Tippit was struck by three bullets and had only three bullet holes; yet, when that testimony was given to the Commission, they had in their possession four bullets which the same police department testified came from Tippit's body. No Dallas policeman was indicted for perjury.

Some time has been spent upon the differences between statements and affidavits, because the general public has little knowledge of this important matter when used in a court of law. And it was this fact of little knowledge that was used by the Commission to deceive the American people.

In the murder of President Kennedy the citizenry knew that he had been murdered. The Warren Commission was theoretically organized to answer three questions: (1) Why he was murdered; (2) How was he murdered; and (3) Who murdered him? It became essential to the nation that these three questions be answered honestly, for a nation can be destroyed if its Leaders can be murdered with impunity. Therefore, when the Commission announced its "Conclusions" on September 28, 1964, that Lee Harvey Oswald was the "sole and exclusive murderer of President Kennedy," the nation accepted those "Conclusions.' However, prior to the issuance of the "Report," rumblings were heard and published that the "Report" was a whitewash, a hoax. A reading of the "Report" revealed that statements contradicted statements.

The reader quickly realized that nothing in the "Report" answered those three questions of "who," "why" and "how." The reader soon grasped the fact that the Commission had simply organized a series of rumors to convict the Commission's own predetermined killer when they named him to be Lee Harvey Oswald. The Commission's "Report" is nothing more than a conglomeration of unsubstantiated statements or deliberate lies when those statements and lies are compared with the sworn testimony in the 26 volumes of the "Hearings" or with affidavits now in the National Archives.

The Warren Commission was created for the specific purpose which was enunciated in President Johnson's Executive Order No. 11130: "to ascertain the truth and evaluate the evidence so that the truth will be exposed to the world." The Commission failed in all three directives. The truth was never ascertained; the evidence never evaluated; and the truth uncovered was covered. Never was so much done by so many that produced so little.

Neither the Congress of the United States, which approved the seven-man Commission under a Joint Resolution of Congress, nor the President of the United States, Lyndon B. Johnson, ever restricted the use of money or time by the Commission. The Commission was also granted unlimited use of the power of subpoena and the right to grant full immunity if any witness claimed the 5th Amendment.

The seven-man Commission, chaired by Chief Justice Warren of the United States Supreme Court, selected J. Lee Rankin as its general counsel. Those eight men then proceeded to select, as its operating staff, twenty-six lawyers, or aides, to assist the men attaining their objectives under Order No. 11130. The Commission, after due deliberation, decided that no other profession was capable of having the ability to "ascertain the truth and evaluate the evidence." In their opinion, only the members of the legal profession had the integrity, the stability, and the wherewithal to stand before the winds that would hurl both the seed and the chaff from which the legal profession would sift the facts to ascertain the truth.

The Commission, with its arrogance leading the charade, embarked upon a course, not to answer those three questions, but one which, in their "inherent wisdom," protected the "interests of the nation." This "papa knows best" attitude of the Commission overlooked the inherent inquisitiveness of people. Many of them never swallowed the story that the murderer of the president was arrested by the police within 90 minutes after the president was shot. Other persons, from their reading of national and international press, knew that some evidence had been suppressed, and they desired to know why that evidence had been suppressed.

Many persons were hearing or reading of stories of key witnesses being killed in mysterious ways, like the woman who "hung" herself in a Dallas police station 30 minutes after she had been arrested for "disorderly conduct." What the people could not understand was how that key witness could hang herself with her toreador pants when the legs of those pants were too small to make a hangman's knot around her neck and attach them to the prison bars, and then also the fact that the same pant legs did not have the strength to hold her body off the floor. Nor could those same inquisitive people understand how an ex-CIA executive could shoot himself by using the wrong hand to hold the gun which also caused the bullet to enter his head from an impossible angle. And, of course, some people became a little suspicious when a famous newspaper woman, who had the only exclusive interview from Jack Ruby when he was imprisoned, could accidentally die from being a "habitual user" of a drug she never bought or used at any time in her life, nor the fact that the coroner issued a verdict in her death that the leading pathologists of New York could not determine what drug caused her death. The same inquisitive citizens could not understand how a newspaper reporter, who was also a friend of Jack Ruby, could be killed in a police station by a gun dropping from the holster of a cop when that bullet struck the reporter at an impossible angle.[8]

Those citizens also wanted to know whether the Lee Oswald named by the Commission as the president's killer was the same Lee Harvey Oswald linked to the FBI and the CIA by none other than the Dallas Intelligence Department and the Dallas Sheriff's

---

[8] The "toreador" victim was Nancy Mooney, aka Betty MacDonald, who was found dead in her jail cell on February 13, 1964. The ex-CIA executive is most likely a reference to Gary Underhill. The famous female journalist was Dorothy Kilgallen. And the reporter killed "accidentally" in a police station was Bill Hunter.

Department. Of course, it is the nature of man to be inquisitive when, in 1967, it was revealed that the Miami, Florida, Police Department had a confession of a right-wing leader that President Kennedy would be murdered from an ambush in the next Southern city he visited.[9] And, being inquisitive, those same citizens wondered why the Federal Bureau of Investigation and the United States Secret Service calmly stood by and permitted the president of the United States to be driven into the Dallas ambush when the Dallas officials used the now infamous "double detour" route.

Perhaps it was the cynicism, inherent in citizens of all nations, that convinced the American citizenry that the "Report" issued by the Warren Commission was supported by rotten timbers incapable of supporting the truth. The suspicion increased in the same ratio and in the same speed as smog increased with the density of automobiles on a Los Angeles freeway. The American people were becoming deeply convinced that the Commission had perpetrated a gigantic, gruesome hoax the like of which concealed a conspiracy that reached into the very gut of American government and society. Today, that hoax, that whitewash feared by the people has been exposed to the light of day, for the citizenry were, and are, absolutely right in their assessment of the Warren Commission. There now exists overwhelming evidence, provable in a court of law, that the Warren Commission, either willfully or negligently, concealed the conspiracy that murdered President John F. Kennedy. This deed was committed by the Commission in "the interests of national security."

Any citizen able to read, write and understand the English language will, if they take the time, locate, read, compare, and analyze the statements printed in the "Report" with that of the testimony in the "Hearings," the affidavits, photographs, and charts

---

[9] A right-wing extremist named Joseph Milteer was secretly tape-recorded thirteen days before the assassination by a Miami police informant. Milteer was a leader of the National States' Rights Party and a member of the Congress of Freedom and the White Citizen's Council of Atlanta.

in the National Archives, and find that the "Report" is contradicted in every major element laid upon the body of Lee Harvey Oswald. Only the Commission had the gall to say that their statements in their "Report," the testimony in the "Hearings," and [in the] National Archives supported each other.

There is, furthermore, absolutely no testimony or material evidence provable in a court of law that could be used to convict Lee Harvey Oswald for the murder of Police Officer Tippit, the wounding of Governor Connelly, or the attempted murder upon the life of ex-Maj. Gen. Walker.

The Commission assumed that they, and only they, could read and understand the English language. There is no rule of law that says one needs a legal background to read and understand the language of the land. Does one need a legal background [to know] that when a person testified he saw a man in a white jacket it does not mean "black," "blue," "brown," or "grey"? Is a legal background necessary to understand that where a witness saw a 7.65 German Mauser rifle equipped with a "brownish-black sling" with a telescopic sight attached, he did not mean a 6.5 Italian Mannlicher-Carcano rifle with a white sling rope as a camera cord? When that same witness is an experienced deputy sheriff with 8 years' experience as the owner-manager of a sporting goods store that sold both types of rifles, then common sense, not legal background, accepts the deputy sheriff's original affidavit of what he saw as part of the "res gestae"[10] of the murder scene. Common sense dictates the acceptance of the fact that a German Mauser rifle was found by Deputy Weitzman when the Commission conveniently "lost" the two original Dallas police official "memos" which accurately described that rifle.

Since when is it necessary to have a legal background to read the contents of a letter signed by the chief of the Federal Bureau of Investigation to the Commission that a witness who informed two FBI agents that when that witness saw the shooting he was seated and wearing a "red and white striped shirt buttoned up to his neck," then that same witness was lying when he changed his

---

[10] "The facts that form the environment of a litigated issue and are admissible in evidence." (Merriam-Webster's.)

affidavit story on the witness stand? Common sense, not a legal background, informed the reader that the witness had committed perjury. How is a legal background necessary to read the official statement by the physicians attending President Kennedy at the Parkland Hospital that the cause of death was due to a "massive head wound over the left temple"? Common sense, not a legal background, compelled the acceptance of the autopsy physicians' report that the president "had a wound in his back, five inches below his neck," [which] was a back wound as distinguished, medically and legally, from a wound in the back of his neck.

A citizen, using his common sense, and not holding an exultant position in the legal profession, would hesitate to contradict the official photograph of the FBI showing the location of the wound in the president's back to be five inches below the shoulder and say that was a neck wound. Only lawyers, not citizens with common sense, would have the gall to dispute both an official autopsy chart and the testimony of every physician in both the Parkland and Bethesda, Md. Hospitals.

Of course, the legal profession, being what it is today, would not accept common sense, which dictates the fact that a telescopic sight mounted on a rifle for a left-handed rifleman could not be used by a right-handed rifleman. Common sense, not the ability to read law, dictated the acceptance of the fact that perjury was committed by the Dallas Police Department when they said only three bullets were recovered from Officer Tippit's body when that department gave the FBI four bullets from "three" bullet holes. Nor does one need a legal background to know that a .38 automatic shell cannot be discharged from a .38 revolver.

It was the common sense of the average citizen that accepted the fact that a conspiracy murdered President Kennedy when they were informed that not only were curtain rods discovered in the Paine garage (after that same garage had been searched by the various police agencies) by a Commission aide and a U.S. Secret Service agent; but also found in the Irving, Texas, Post Office was the "brown paper bag" used by Oswald to carry those curtain rods into the Texas [School] Book Depository! The common sense of the American people knew it was not the phrase "in the interests of national security" that compelled the

Warren Commission to deliberately conceal those two facts proving Oswald's innocence from the public but that fact proved that a conspiracy murdered President Kennedy.

Common sense, not a legal background, compelled the American people to accept the fact that a conspiracy murdered the president of the United States when the people learned that the Commission suppressed from them two vital affidavits which proved Lee Harvey Oswald was nowhere on the 6th floor between 12 noon and 12:30 p.m., but, in fact and in law, was seen on the first floor and at the front door entrance of the Book Depository. Those two affidavits can be found in File No. CD. 5 in the National Archives and in Com. Doc. No. 354. Why did the Warren Commission deliberately conceal those two affidavits? To protect the nation from whom? How did the Commission protect the "national interests" when those two documents proved beyond a reasonable doubt that Lee Harvey Oswald was innocent? Common sense proved a conspiracy when the Commission suppressed the fact that the Dallas police suppressed the fact that they found three expended cartridges on the 3rd floor of the Depository nearly thirty minutes prior to the finding of three additional cartridges on the 6th floor. Why did the police suppress these three cartridges from public knowledge?

Under the law of the United States murder is a crime in the state where it was committed. Since Oswald was murdered he was unable to secure a trial by jury of his peers. Therefore, the only true indictment was the one issued by the Warren Commission. Hence, the only question involved is: "Does the 'Report' sustain the indictment?" To answer this question, an investigator must rely upon the sworn testimony printed in the 26 volumes of the "Hearings" plus the affidavits and material available in the National Archives.

American criminal law, in theory, is no different from criminal law practiced in other Western states. The procedures may differ, but the philosophy remains the same. Under American criminal law it is the duty of the state to prove the accused guilty beyond a reasonable doubt. A part of that duty places upon the state to prove, by evidence or statements legally presentable to a court, that the weapon used to murder the victim was capable of being used as a lethal weapon. Thus, if the alleged weapon was not the weapon that was the direct cause of the death of the victim, then the accused must be found "not guilty." An ounce of pure spring water is not as deadly as an ounce of cyanide!

The Warren Commission, acting as the prosecutor on behalf of the State of Texas, indicted Lee Harvey Oswald as follows: (1) Lee Harvey Oswald was the sole and exclusive killer of President John F. Kennedy and Police Officer Tippit; (2) wounded Governor Connally; (3) attempted to murder ex-Gen. Walker; (4) attempted to murder another police officer while resisting arrest; and (5) Oswald had the capability of using the rifle used to commit the murders. To substantiate the above accusations the Commission set forth nineteen additional allegations.

Under American criminal law, what did the Commission do? The Commission, having promulgated its "Conclusions" or allegations, then plunged ahead and stated that those 19 additional allegations would be proven beyond a reasonable doubt by legal evidence that those 19 allegations would support the five major conclusions. It must not be forgotten that those allegations, or accusations, were not made by the critics of the Commission. Since the Commission constructed the platform upon which rested those accusations, it was the legal and moral duty of the Commission to prove to the jury, the American people, that the Commission's statements in the "Report" would be supported by the evidence in the "Hearings" and in the National Archives. In other words, "the truth was out," and nothing was hidden from the jury that would prevent that jury from accepting the Commission's charge that Lee Harvey Oswald was the "sole and exclusive killer of President Kennedy."

The Warren Commission, if it had in fact acted as the prosecution for the State of Texas, would not have indicted Oswald in the manner set forth in its "Report." What the Commission attempted to achieve was to create a state of mind in the American public that Oswald was a psychopath. The more murders, the more attempts at murder, the greater the acceptance by the public that Oswald was a machine-mad murderer.

Thus, from a practical legal method of procedure no prosecutor would have indicted Oswald in the manner enunciated by the Commission.

The majority of citizens know that a man may be guilty of one crime but that that guilt does not presuppose he is guilty of other crimes. Yet, the manner in which the Commission indicted Oswald could have led to his release for, ipso facto, if he had not killed Police Officer Tippit; and if he had not attempted to kill another police officer while resisting arrest; and if he had not attempted to murder ex.-General Walker; and if he had not wounded Governor Connally; then he did not murder President Kennedy.

This would be the reverse of the Commission's reasoning. That is not logic; either forwards or backwards. But the Commission employed this type of logic to fashion the cloak of murder and murderous intent around the shoulders of Lee Harvey Oswald.

The unanimous opinion of the Commission convicted Oswald as follows:

"Based on the evidence analyzed:

(A) "The Commission has concluded that the shots which killed President Kennedy and wounded Governor Connally were fired from the 6th-floor window at the S.E. corner of the Texas Book Depository Building. Two bullets probably caused all the wounds suffered by President Kennedy and Governor Connally. Since the preponderance of the evidence indicated 3 shots were fired, the Commission concluded that one shot probably missed the presidential limousine and its occupants, and that the 3 shots were fired in a time period ranging from approximately 4.8 seconds in excess of 7 seconds.

(B) "Having reviewed the evidence that (1) Lee Harvey Oswald purchased the rifle used in the assassination, (2) Oswald's palm print was on the rifle in a position which shows that he handled it while it was disassembled, (3) fibers found on the rifle most probably came from the shirt Oswald was wearing on the day of the assassination, (4) a photograph taken in the yard of Oswald's apartment showed him holding this rifle, and (5) this rifle was kept among Oswald's possession from the time of its purchase until the day of the assassination, the Commission concluded that the rifle used to assassinate President Kennedy and wound Governor Connally was owned and possessed by Lee Harvey Oswald.

(C) "The preponderance of the evidence supports the conclusion that Lee Harvey Oswald (1) told the curtain rod story to Frazier to explain both the return to Irving on a Thursday and the obvious bulk of the package which he intended to bring to work the next day; (2) he took paper and tape from the wrapping bench of the Depository and fashioned a bag large enough to carry the disassembled rifle; (3) he removed the rifle from the blanket in the Paine's garage on Thursday evening; (4) carried the rifle into the Depository Building, concealed in the bag; and (5) left the bag alongside the window from which the shots were fired.

(D) "Fingerprints and palm print evidence establishes that Oswald handled two of the four cartons next to the window and also handled a paper bag which was found near the cartons. Oswald was seen in the vicinity of the S.E. corner on the 6th floor approximately 35 minutes before the assassination and no one could be found who saw Oswald anywhere else in the building until after the shooting. An eyewitness to the shooting immediately provided a description of the man in the window which was similar to Oswald's actual appearance. This witness identified Oswald in a lineup as the man most nearly resembling the man he saw and later identified Oswald as the man he observed. Oswald's known actions in the building immediately after the assassination are consistent with his having been at the S.E. corner window of the sixth floor at 12:30 p.m. On the basis of these findings the Commission has concluded that Oswald, at the time of the assassination, was present at the window from which the shots were fired.

(E) "The (foregoing) evidence established that (1) two eyewitnesses who heard the shots and saw the shooting of Dallas police Patrolman J. D. Tippit and seven eyewitnesses who saw the flight of the gunman with the revolver in hand positively identified Lee Harvey Oswald as the man they saw fire the shots or flee the scene; (2) the cartridge cases found near the scene of the shooting were fired from his revolver in the possession of Oswald at the time of his arrest, to the exclusion of all other weapons; (3) the revolver in Oswald's possession at the time of his arrest was purchased by and belonged to Oswald; and (4) Oswald's jacket was found along the path of flight taken by the gunman as he fled from the scene of the killing. On the basis of this evidence the Commission concluded that Lee Harvey Oswald killed Dallas police Patrolman J. D. Tippit.

(F) "On the basis of the evidence ... the Commission has found that Lee Harvey Oswald (1) owned and possessed the rifle used to kill President Kennedy and wound Governor Connelly; (2) brought this rifle into the Book Depository Building on the morning of the assassination, (3) was present at the time of the assassination, at the window from which the shots were fired, (4) killed Dallas police Officer J. D. Tippit in an apparent attempt to escape; (5) resisted arrest by drawing a fully loaded pistol, and attempting to shoot another police officer; (6) lied to the police after his arrest concerning important substantive matters, (7) attempted, in April, 1963, to kill ex. Maj. General Edwin A. Walker, and (8) possessed the capability with a rifle which would enable him to commit the assassination. On the basis of these findings, the Commission has concluded that Lee Harvey Oswald was the assassin of President Kennedy."

As Clarence Darrow once said: "That's a lot of crime to pin on the little man." An indictment is not a presumption of guilt; it merely notifies the accused that the state "thinks" or "believes" that they have sufficient evidence to prove "beyond a reasonable doubt" that what is said in the indictment is true. The Warren Commission published its "Report" with the implication to the American people that the Commission's eight conclusions had been proven beyond a reasonable doubt and that the evidence they published in the 26 volumes of the "Hearings" would support all their "Conclusions." As will be shown, the Warren Commission proved the innocence of Lee Harvey Oswald, but his innocence can only be found if the person reading the "Report" will read the testimony in the "Hearings or the evidence in the National Archives.

Thus, a defense lawyer on Oswald's behalf, because of the prestige associated with the seven commissioners, would be reduced to assume the burden that his client, Oswald, was innocent "beyond a reasonable doubt." The author of "Six Seconds in Dallas" fell into this trap, for he wrote that although he believed there was more than one assassin, Oswald had to be guilty because he could not prove he was innocent! Hence, the burden of proof, as they say in law, shifted from the prosecution–the

Commission–to the shoulders of Oswald. This, of course, is contrary to every principle of Anglo-American jurisprudence upon which this nation is founded.

If a defense attorney could prove by the evidence in the "Hearings," by affidavits, or by official reports given to the Commission by local, state and federal investigating agencies that the evidence in those categories directly conflicted or contradicted the statements in the "Report," then a reasonable doubt can be cast upon the conclusions issued by the Commission. But, if in addition to casting a reasonable doubt on the evidence used by the Commission to convict Oswald of his "crimes," the defense attorney could prove to the jury–in this case, the American public–that the Commission deliberately lied and upon those lies the Commission issued its verdict, then Oswald must be judged "not guilty" of (1) murdering President Kennedy; (2) murdering Officer Tippit; (3) wounding Governor Connelly; (4) attempting to murder Walker; (5) attempting to murder another police officer while resisting arrest; and "lying" on substantive matters relating to 1, 2, 3, 4, and 5.

The Commission has proclaimed that a bullet fired from the S.E. corner window on the 6th floor went through President Kennedy's neck and also wounded Governor Connelly; then it follows as night the day, that if a defense lawyer can prove, with the Commission's own witnesses, that if Oswald was not on the 6th floor at the time the shots were fired, he was innocent of both charges. In addition, if Oswald's defense attorney could prove, by the Commission's own witnesses and documents, that Oswald was not at the Tippit murder site prior, during, or after the murder, then a trial judge would be compelled to instruct the jury to return a "not guilty" verdict without the jury retiring to the jury room.

The Oswald Affaire is a modern paradox for there is substantial evidence that he was, in some manner, involved in the conspiracy that murdered President Kennedy; yet the Commission emphatically denied the existence of a conspiracy. Under American law a conspirator is as guilty as the man who "pulled the trigger." Hence, an investigator must arrive at the conclusion that Lee Harvey Oswald was not "the sole and exclusive assassin of President Kennedy, nor of Officer Tippit; nor did he wound Governor Connally; nor did he ever attempt to murder ex-Maj. Gen. Walker."

If Lee Harvey Oswald was part and parcel of the conspiracy, even though he be only a piece of string around the conspiracy package, then he would have been guilty as charged concerning the two murders and the nonfatal shooting of the governor, for he would have been as guilty as the four men who actually fired those bullets.

The dilemma faced by the Commission resulted in a solution based not on fact or on law, but on a phrase "in interests of national security." The Commission published a series of deliberate lies, not to protect the "national interests" of the American people, but to protect those interests that had interests contrary to the interests of the president of the United States, who had the interests of all the American people whom he represented.

That being the dilemma, it would have been far better for the Commission to have proclaimed the conspiracy even though it be directly connected to the right-wing fascist elements in the United States than have this nation live a lie.

The seven commissioners, being lawyers, should have known that a good prosecuting attorney prosecuting a person accused of murder will always ask himself five questions: "Did the accused commit the crime; when was it committed; where was it committed; was the alleged weapon used to commit the crime a lethal weapon; and how was the crime committed?" In other words, who, what, when, where and why?

The Warren Commission attempted to answer all those questions except: "Who killed President Kennedy?" "How was he murdered?" "When was he murdered?" "Why was he murdered?" In a murder trial the motive is generally not involved, for an irrational person will kill without any motive–unless hatred of man is considered the reason for the murder. However, where the president of the United States is the victim, a motive is always involved. Lee Harvey Oswald, according to the evidence in the "Hearings," was not an insane or irrational person. And he certainly did not commit the murder because his wife did not agree to a reconciliation on the night prior to the day of the murder. Only an author writing fiction at $10.00 a copy would dream a theory like that one! Thus, from the "Report" those questions remain unanswered until the reader has completed the reading of this small book.

Under our system of government, the theory is that a man is presumed innocent until proven guilty beyond a reasonable doubt. It is unfortunate that the mass communication media has now convinced the public that due to "law and order" a man is guilty as soon as he is arrested by the police. The constant harping by the press has encouraged the belief a person becomes a criminal immediately upon his arrest by the police. No person arrested for a crime becomes a criminal until he is convicted by due process of law; and that includes the review of the conduct of the trial by an appeals court.

Lee Harvey Oswald was never granted the right to exercise his rights granted under the Bill of Rights.

We now proceed to review that which was said; that which was suppressed; that which was perjury; to see if the truth can be ascertained.

CHAPTER II

FROM THE 6TH-FLOOR WINDOW, 3 BULLETS

The Warren Commission, in its indictment of Lee Harvey Oswald as the "sole and exclusive assassin of President Kennedy," devoted four paragraphs which they said conclusively proved their accusation that Oswald was the sole killer. The Commission stated that Oswald fired three bullets toward President Kennedy, two of which hit their target, one missing completely. In fact, although they considered Oswald the world's greatest marksman on that tragic day, the Commission admitted that he not only missed the president, but also Mrs. Kennedy, Mrs. Connelly, two Secret Service agents in the front seat of the automobile, the automobile itself, the street, the entire area of the Dealey Plaza park area, lamp posts, trees, and spectators. Yet, according to the Commission, Oswald held the rifle at such an angle that any bullet leaving the rifle held by a rifleman at the 6th-floor window would have dug itself into the street a few feet behind the president's automobile,

Oswald was such a great marksman he was able to pull the trigger of a dilapidated 22-year-old rifle, and by using a telescopic sight that was mounted on the rifle for the use by a left-handed rifleman, pulled that trigger three times within a timespan ranging from not less than 4.8 seconds to in excess of 7 seconds. He was such a tremendous rifleman that he was able to hand load 4 bullets into this rifle within that time limit and, still calm, cool, and collected, discharge that rifle with deadly accuracy. What is interesting in the Commission's statement is the use of words that permitted the Commission to "leap around the mulberry bush." The Commission qualified the time limit since they used the phrase "probably caused" all the wounds in both victims.

The Commission then proceeded to publish a phrase that means everything to all men: namely, "the preponderance of the evidence." The Commission, including the 26 aides, all lawyers, knew that every one of the states does not permit the conviction of an accused person by the preponderance of the evidence. Criminal law principles are not determined by a "consensus" of the jury. Finally, the Commission's third weasel-wording phrase was their attempt to obtain the time limit of the rifleman in discharging three bullets from his rifle by saying "from approximately 4.8 seconds in excess of 7 seconds." If one understands the English language correctly, the rifleman could have pulled the trigger three times in a period of not less than 4.8 seconds and in excess of 7 seconds, 30 seconds, 1 minute, and so on. A witness whose testimony was used to "convict" Oswald testified that he heard the shots ring out for a period of not less than 30 seconds.

In a criminal case for murder in the first degree an impartial judge would never permit a jury to convict the accused on the basis of words used by the Commission. The prosecutor must prove beyond a reasonable doubt that what they allege in their indictment is true and that what they use as evidence is true. Thus, by using words, not evidence, the Commission hoped to sustain their accusations and convince their citizenry that what they published in the "Report" was true. At the same time the Commission very cleverly shifted the burden of proof from themselves onto the shoulders of the critics of the Commission. The critics thus have the burden of proving the "Report" and the Commission false, not by the preponderance of the evidence, but "beyond a reasonable doubt."

Where was the evidence that the Commission said proved that the bullets were discharged from the barrel of an Italian 6.5 Mannlicher-Carcano rifle, which bullets killed President Kennedy, and that rifle was held by a man firing from the 6th-floor S.E. window of the Book Depository? There was none! The Commission's statement was a figment of the Commission's imagination, for there is overwhelming evidence which proved no bullets were ever fired from any type of rifle, on November 22, 1963, from the S.E. window on the 6th floor.

The Commission officially stated that the rifle found on the 6th floor was a 6.5-mm Italian Mannlicher-Carcano rifle. This was a self-serving statement, since the only evidence given to 3the Commission by eyewitnesses said the found rifle was a

7.65 German Mauser. The finder of the rifle, Deputy-Sheriff Weitzman, immediately identified the rifle as a German Mauser and, after he had thought about it for hours, made an affidavit the next day. (1.) However, several months later, the deputy-sheriff informed a Commission aide that he was mistaken because "in a glance it (the rifle) looked like it (7.65 German Mauser)." (2.) Therefore, Oswald's defense attorney would have to cross-examine the deputy sheriff to determine the meaning of "in a glance."

In his affidavit of November 23, 1963, the deputy, in one glance, not only saw enough to determine that type of rifle–a German Mauser–but also the size of the bore, 7.65 mm. In addition, he saw that the rifle was equipped with a 4/18 telescopic sight; and finally, he saw the type of sling, "a thick leather brownish-black sling on it." The testimony of this witness developed the fact that, prior to his employment as a deputy sheriff, Weitzman managed a chain of sporting goods stores in which he purchased and sold a line of rifles including German Mausers. (3.)

This "brownish-black" sling has been overlooked by far too many investigators of the Warren Commission, for it was to be that sling that proved beyond a reasonable doubt that the rifle originally found by Deputy Weitzman was a 7.65-mm German Mauser and not the 6.5-mm Italian Carcano rifle, which, the Commission said, was published by "Life" [magazine] as the true and authentic rifle used to murder President Kennedy.

In a court of law the value of weight of evidence is determined by the jury. Furthermore, when a witness signs his name and gives his oath to an affidavit, the law assumes that what is stated in that affidavit is the truth. When those facts are, in turn, corroborated or substantiated by other witnesses under oath, then the trial judge will instruct the jury that the statements in the affidavit takes precedence over the testimony of the affidavit-signer at the subsequent trial. There is an excellent reason for this age-old principle of law, for the law presumes that the signer of the affidavit will give his immediate impressions of what he saw and heard at the scene of the murder. His original affidavit will not be subjected to any type of pressure that could be exerted upon him after his signing.

Thus, the testimony or evidence of a witness can be strengthened or destroyed by other witnesses to the same event connected with the crime. In the "Hearings," the record revealed that the Commission examined five other witnesses relating to the discovery and the identity of the rifle found by Deputy Weitzman. Two deputy sheriffs, who were on the 6th floor at the time the rifle was examined by Capt. Fritz, testified that he said to Lt. Day that the rifle was a German Mauser. (4.) At no time did either the captain or lieutenant "promptly" identify the rifle as an Italian Mannlicher-Carcano. (5.) Further substantiation that the rifle was a German Mauser came from District Attorney Wade who made that statement to a national press conference. Mr. Wade, was a former FBI agent qualified in the use and examination of firearms. (6.)

When Deputy-Sheriff Boone was shown the Commission's Italian Carcano rifle, known as Com. Exh. No. 139, he flatly refused to identify it as the rifle he had seen with Deputy Weitzman, who discovered the German Mauser. (7.) During the time Deputy Weitzman was testifying the Commission aide refused to show him the Italian Mannlicher-Carcano rifle for purposes of identification as to the rifle he found at 1:22 p.m. on the 6th floor. That aide's conduct was contrary to all rules of criminal law, for no man accused of murder can be found guilty of that crime where the prosecution refuses to enter into the court record the weapon, in possession of the prosecution, which the state specifically alleged was the weapon used to cause the death of the victim. The failure to produce that weapon under those circumstances would compel the trial judge to issue a verdict of "not guilty." When Deputy Weitzman was on the witness stand, on the prosecution's desk (the Commission) was the alleged weapon, but the aide knew that Weitzman would refuse to commit perjury by stating that the Italian rifle, Com. Exh. No. 139, was the weapon he found on the 6th floor.

One major element that has been consistently overlooked by the critics of the Commission is that at no time from 1:22 p.m., when the German rifle was found, did the Dallas police or the FBI examine the rifle internally to see if the rifle had been discharged on that day. There is no evidence, in the "Record," the "Hearings," or in the National Archives, that such an examination was ever made of either the German Mauser or the Italian Mannlicher-Carcano rifle. There is testimony from the FBI that clearly implied that the rifle sent to them by the Dallas police had never been discharged. In the official FBI Reports, Vol. 1 to 5, there is no statement by the Bureau that that rifle given to them was ever "used" by any rifleman. The FBI constantly referred to this rifle as being "owned" by Lee Oswald; never did they state that he "used" it for any purpose. How can a rifle discharge three bullets when the rifle has never been used? The constant repetition by the FBI of the word "owned" is conclusive proof that the FBI never believed, nor did any FBI agent ever testify, that the Italian Carcano rifle was "used" by Oswald as the murder weapon.

Nor is there any statement by any agent of the FBI or Chief Hoover that the rifle the Bureau received from the Dallas police was the identical rifle found by Deputy Sheriff Weitzman at 1:22 p.m. on November 22, 1963.

An investigator of the work of the Commission must attempt to locate the reason for this use of the word "Owned" instead of "used." After the sifting and analyzing of all the testimony and exhibits, a definite statement can be made that the FBI knew, or had suspicion, that not only was a switch made concerning the rifles but that more than a switch had been involved. Namely, that there were a minimum of two Italian 6.5-mm Mannlicher-Carcano rifles in addition to two 7.65 German Mausers with telescopic sights.

How are the above statements proved beyond a reasonable doubt? The Oswald defense attorney, since the burden of proof has been shifted to his shoulders, would have available to him various witnesses who were vouched for by none other than the unanimous opinion of the Warren Commission. The Commission witnesses who proved Oswald's innocence would be Mrs. Marina Oswald, the wife of Oswald; Mrs. Paine, who kept the FBI informed of Oswald's activities; FBI ballistic expert, Mr. Cunningham; and various photographs labeled authentic by the Commission.

The first witness to be summoned by Oswald's lawyer would be one who received high praise from the Commission as being a truthful witness whose veracity and integrity was accepted "in toto" by them. It was the wife of the accused who was the key witness used by the Commission to "convict" her husband. Waiving aside the rule of criminal law that a wife cannot testify for or against her husband in a criminal case, there is no evidence the Commission could use in a law court to convict her husband.

Mrs. Marina Oswald, who was held "incommunicado" by various federal agencies and threatened with deportation to the USSR, gave a long statement to those various agents. (8.) Her statement is now in the National Archives under Code Number 344. In that statement is her admission that she first saw a rifle handled by her husband, Lee, in February, 1963. She said: "that it (the rifle) was either in a corner, standing up in a corner, or on the shelf." She also testified that at no time did she ever see that rifle have on it a telescopic sight. (9.) Thus, the Commission was placed in an awkward position, for her testimony destroyed the Commission's charge that Oswald purchased a rifle with a telescopic sight from Klein's of Chicago in March, 1963. Here, the Commission's chief witness was testifying that Lee had owned a rifle in February, 1963, one month prior to the so-called purchase of an Italian rifle in March, 1963.

The Commission has admitted that Oswald had only one rifle in his possession, but what the Commission failed to do was to inform the American people that the rifle he had was in his home one month before the purchase allegedly taking place. The Commission cannot have it both ways. The Commission accepted Mrs. Oswald's testimony as being 100% true and accurate. QED Lee Harvey Oswald never purchased a rifle from Klein's in March, 1963.

The Commission could not brand their chief witness a liar and perjurer, for that would destroy her evidence "convicting" her husband on the charge he attempted to kill a retired General and also the charge that it was Lee's revolver that murdered Officer Tippit. Therefore, in an attempt to prove that Oswald had indeed purchased an Italian 6.5-mm Italian Mannlicher-Carcano rifle from Klein's of Chicago in March 1963, they placed on the witness stand Postal Inspector Holmes of Dallas, Texas. His testimony proved absolutely worthless, since he stated that although Oswald leased a post office box the Inspector never saw any package, including one that could have been large enough to contain a rifle, delivered to Oswald's box. (10.) He also testified that the Klein advertisement, allegedly used by Oswald to purchase the Italian rifle, was published in the November, 1962 issue of "Field & Stream." The Commission immediately disagreed with the "learned" Inspector by saying that Klein's received Oswald's money order on March 13, 1963, to which was attached a coupon from the February 1963 issue of "American Rifleman." This advertisement was for a 36" rifle weighing 5-1/2 pounds. How did the "Oswald" Italian rifle lose 2 inches and gain 3 pounds? By organic dieting? The Commission, however, failed to reveal the fact that the "American Rifleman" of that date carried no Klein's of Chicago advertisement or coupon for an Italian 6.5-mm Mannlicher-Carcano rifle! Finally, no such rifle was offered at the price of $12.65. Klein's advertisement did offer a rifle 40.2", weight 8 lbs., but the Commission said the "Oswald" rifle was only 38.4 inches overall. Based on the evidence, Oswald never ordered a rifle from a nonexisting advertisement.

The Commission's attempt to manufacture evidence to convict Oswald can easily be recognized in their method to connect the Italian rifle to the accused assassin. According to the money order, the rifle was purchased by a man named "Hidell." The rifle was to be sent to a p.o. box rented by a Lee Harvey Oswald. (11.) According to past and present P.O. regulations, No. 355, Sec. III (b), para. 4, no person other than the lessee of a p.o. box can receive or obtain mail addressed to that box number. (12.) There is absolutely no legal proof or testimony in the "Report," the "Hearings," or in the files of the National Archives that Klein's Italian rifle was ever received by the Dallas Post Office to be placed in Oswald's post office box. No evidence whatsoever.

Oswald's defense attorney, not being impressed by the "prestige" surrounding those seven "honorable gentlemen," would have dug into the National Archives and placed before the American jury evidence conveniently overlooked or suppressed by those "honorable" gentlemen.

Oswald's attorney would have produced Commission Exhibit No. 2718 and Commission Exh. No. 2562. Very interesting is

No. 2562, for it showed the deceitfulness of the Commission in that its "Report" stated that the Italian rifle used by the Commission to "convict" Oswald had a manufacturer's number "C2766" stamped upon it, The impression in the "Report" was that the FBI traced that rifle by that number "C2766" through five years of World War II, through the hands of various surplus weapon dealers, directly to Klein's of Chicago, and from that company to the hands of "Hidell," who was, in reality, Lee Harvey Oswald. What a scenario! What a pipe dream! Commission Exhibit No. 2562 is a letter from the Chief of the FBI, J. Edgar Hoover, which informed the "honorable" gentlemen that between 1931 and 1941 every rifle manufactured by Italian rifle manufacturers carried the identical number: "C2766." Millions of that type and number were manufactured,[11] and they were being sold in the United States by the thousands. Thus, in a court of law, the serial number "C2766" was worthless as the legal identification of any rifle.

Equally interesting is Commission Exhibit No. 2718, for that suppressed document was a vital piece of evidence substantiating the innocence of Lee Oswald as the "sole and exclusive assassin of President Kennedy." This document revealed the startling fact that Oswald's P.O. Box No. 2915 was under surveillance from the day he leased that box in April, 1962, until the day the lease was completed, in May, 1963. The Federal Bureau of Investigation had full knowledge of every letter and every package placed in that mail box from the beginning to the end of its use by Lee H. Oswald. The person who conducted that surveillance was none other than Inspector Holmes of the U.S. Office! There is no testimony by any officer or agent of the Post Office or the FBI that Oswald ever received a package that was large enough to contain an Italian Mannlicher-Carcano rifle or, for that matter, a rifle of any size. (13.)

Oswald used his Post Office Box No. 2915 as a "message

---

[11] Since Commission Exhibit No. 2562 does not mention exactly how many "C2766" rifles were manufactured, Marks statement that it was in the "millions" must have been sourced elsewhere. (Thanks to Jim DiEugenio for pointing this out.)

drop" for the FBI and CIA.

Oswald's defense that he never purchased a rifle from Klein's under the name of "Hidell" was substantiated not only by his wife but by the evidence given to the Commission by Mrs. Paine and the firearm experts, Agents Frazier and Shaneyfelt. The great majority of the Commission's critics have overlooked this testimony of the two FBI agents. As has been noted the sling that was seen by Deputy Sheriff Weitzman was a "brownish-black" one, in one piece, and made of leather. (14.) FBI Agent Shaneyfelt testified that when he examined the Italian Carcano rifle (Com. Exh. 139), the sling on the rifle was made of rope! (15.) By this testimony the Commission had knowledge that the rifles had been switched, since they only had to compare the agent's testimony with its own statement that two (2) straps comprised the "sling," which, in turn, was from a musical instrument strap or a camera bag strap. This vital discrepancy must be solved by an investigator of the Commission's activities. Who was testifying truthfully, the Commission or the FBI agents? Mrs. Oswald and Mrs. Paine? The testimony published in the "Hearings" supported the witnesses and not the Commission.

Mrs. Oswald, applauded by the Commission as being a truthful witness, stated that the sling she had seen on the "rifle standing in the corner" did not have on it the sling shown to her by the Commission. Mrs. Paine, the friend of the Oswald family and an FBI informant, also upheld Mrs. Oswald. (16.) To corroborate both Mrs. Oswald and Mrs. Paine, the FBI, by the testimony of Agent Shaneyfelt, informed the Commission that the "Life" photograph showing Oswald holding a rifle had on it a "different sling." Since the Commission has labelled the "Life" photograph as an authentic photograph of the rifle used by Oswald to murder President Kennedy, then the only conclusion that can be drawn from the testimony was that the rifles had been switched. (17.) Who switched the rifles?

Devastating testimony was presented to the Commission by another FBI firearms expert, Mr. Frazier, who testified: "that it (the rifle sling) was too short, actually. It is rather awkward to wrap the forward hand into the sling in a normal fashion." (18.) In other words, the Italian 6.5-mm Mannlicher-Carcano rifle which the Commission said was the weapon used to murder President Kennedy was proved to be a weapon that was impossible to be used in the fashion for which it was manufactured. Again, who switched the rifles?

From all the evidence it can be seen that a minimum of six rifles are involved: (1) the 7.65 German Mauser found by Deputy Weitzman; (2) an Italian Carcano with a rope sling; (3) an Italian Carcano rifle known as Comm. Exh. No. 139 with a leather sling composed of a musical instrument strap or camera strap; (4) the rifle with no telescopic sight seen by Mrs. Oswald "standing in the corner"; (5) the Italian rifle published by "Life" and labelled authentic by the Warren Commission; (6) the rifle published by the "Associated Press" and also labelled as authentic by the Warren Commission; and (6) the rifle which first appeared in the news in the "Free Press," 1968, and in the "Midlothian Press" in 1968, concerning a "deputy sheriff having a German Mauser equipped with a telescopic sight posted on the roof of the County Building[12] which overlooked the presidential "double detour" and which, strangely, had a "direct angle of fire" into the president's body. Six different rifles and the Commission never discovered how the Dallas police were able to switch those rifles around!

The overwhelming contempt the Commission had for the intelligence of the American people can be seen in its handling of the "AP" photograph of the rifle labelled by the Commission as authentic. The discrepancies are as follows: (1a.) The front sight of Com. Exh. No. 139 has a tapered sight. (1b.) The "AP" photograph has a round sight. (2a.) The front end of Com. Exh. No. 139 of the telescopic sight is 4/16" behind the barrel. (2b.) In the "AP" photograph the front end is directly in line. (3a.) Com. Exh. No. 139 shows the rifle bolt to be even to the telescopic sight mount. (3b.) The "AP" photograph rifle bolt is behind the mount. (4a.) In Exhibit No. 139 the telescopic mount is slanted. (4b.) In the "AP" photograph the rear of the mount is vertical. Thus, it can be seen that only the legal profession would attempt

---

[12] The Dallas County Records Building, hereafter referred to as the County Building.

to convince their client that white is black for having labelled both their Exh. No. 139 and the "AP" photograph as the authentic rifle. The Commission deliberately concealed the fact from the American jury that not less than two Italian Carcano rifles were involved. When, in addition, the "Life" photograph is also added to those rifles, then the jury knows that a minimum of three Italian rifles are now involved. No court of law would permit any prosecutor to present to the court or jury three rifles as the murder weapon, and then request the jury to make the decision.

According to the principles of Anglo-American law the 6.5-mm Italian Mannlicher-Carcano rifle given to the FBI by the Dallas police was a vital piece of evidence "planted" by the police to "convict" Lee Harvey Oswald. In view of the statements made by the Warren Commission, the evidence proved beyond a reasonable doubt that the Commission had full knowledge that the Italian rifle, Com. Exh. No. 139, was evidence manufactured by the Dallas police. Since the evidence revealed that not less than three Italian rifles were used by both the police and the Commission in an attempt to "convict" Oswald, an impartial law court would direct the American jury to return a verdict of "not guilty" without permitting the prosecution (the Warren Commission) to continue their "case." Based on the Commission's "evidence," Oswald could not be found "guilty" of the murder of President Kennedy or wounding Governor Connelly.

In a murder trial it is the duty of the prosecution to prove that the weapon they allege was used to commit the crime was a weapon capable of committing the crime. No person can be convicted of driving an automobile under the influence of liquor if he is sitting behind the steering wheel of an automobile that has no wheels. In the Oswald "trial" the Commission had the duty to prove beyond a reasonable doubt that the weapon they alleged was used to discharge the two bullets into the body and head of President Kennedy was a weapon capable, at the time of the shooting, of discharging those two bullets.

The evidence published in the "Hearings" and the affidavits in the National Archives conclusively prove beyond a reasonable doubt that the Italian Carcano rifle given to the FBI by the Dallas police and used by the Commission to convict Lee Harvey

Oswald was, as a lethal weapon, absolutely worthless and was not the weapon used at any time during the consummation of the murder. The Federal Bureau of Investigation revealed that the weapon was repaired by Mr. R. Simmons, a firearms expert. Mr. Hoover informed the Commission that the rifle had to be repaired because, prior to that repair, the rifle was inaccurate. (19.) The Bureau admitted that although Oswald was right-handed the telescopic sight was mounted for a left-handed rifleman. (20.) In addition, the FBI informed the Commission that not only was that telescopic sight mounted for a left-handed rifleman but that the telescopic sight had to be entirely rebuilt in their laboratory and the same sight had to be supported by adding three shims under the mount! (21.) As to the internal condition of that Italian rifle given to the FBI by the Dallas police, the FBI's firearms expert, Mr. Frazier, testified that "the lands and grooves were worn, the interior of the surface was roughened from corrosion and wear." At no time did FBI Agent Frazier testify that the Commission's Italian rifle was ever used by any rifleman on November 22, 1963. Nor did the agent testify that that rifle, given to the FBI by the Dallas Police Department, had any bullets discharged through its barrel on November 22, 1963.

All the above evidence was not published in the "Report" but hidden from the American jury. There is no testimony from any state or federal ballistic department that stated that the Italian Carcano rifle was examined immediately after it came into their possession to determine whether or not that rifle had been discharged on November 22, 1963. The person who had possession of the Carcano rifle for examination purposes, Lt. Day, never testified that he examined that rifle for that purpose; only that he examined the rifle for fingerprints.

To support a verdict of "not guilty," Oswald's defense attorney would also place before the court two other vital aspects relating to this planted rifle. One would relate to the ammunition clip and the other to the bullets or cartridge shells found not only on the. 6th floor but also on the 3rd floor. Yes, cartridges found on the 3rd floor, approximately thirty minutes before other cartridge shells were found on the 6th floor! The Commission kept a discreet silence regarding those third-floor cartridges; in fact, it was more than a discreet silence, for those cartridges are classified as "top secret" by the Dallas Police Department. Fifteen minutes after a Dallas police officer found the three cartridges on the 3rd floor, another police officer walked out of the Book Depository with a rifle that had no telescopic sight on it! This rifle was found twenty-two minutes prior to the time Deputy Weitzman found the 7.65-mm German Mauser on the 6th floor.

The Commission, as quickly as possible, skimmed through the failure of the Dallas police to find an ammunition clip near the Carcano rifle "found" on the 6th floor. The Commission simply published their statement that an ammunition clip had been found, for without that clip it was conclusive proof that Oswald, even if he had handled that rifle, was absolutely innocent. The reason for the Commission's fraudulent statement is the ballistic fact that no rifleman in the world, yesterday, today, or tomorrow, can hand load four bullets in any type of a military rifle, aim through a defective telescopic sight, and pull the trigger of that rifle within the 4.8–7 seconds time limit specified by the Commission. It may be done with an ammunition clip attached to the rifle, but according to the tests (fraudulent in themselves) conducted by the Commission only one rifleman, in eighteen tests, succeeded in pulling the trigger within that time limit but without aiming at a target the size of a person's head or the upper torso. (22.)

The Commission had admitted Klein's of Chicago sent no ammunition and no ammunition clip with the Italian rifle to "Hidell" under mysterious circumstances. Thus, unless the Commission could prove that Oswald had somehow been able to purchase an ammunition clip for an Italian rifle last manufactured in 1941, their case against Oswald would be destroyed. A close reading of all the testimony of the deputy sheriffs, the Dallas policemen, FBI and Secret Service agents who were on the 6th floor from 12:40 p.m. until the completion of their search, revealed that none of them ever saw an ammunition clip either attached to the "Carcano" rifle or lying on the floor. That is, until the Commission summoned their "pinch hit" witness, none other than Lt. Day, a man with 40/40 vision who always saw everything never seen by men with 20/20 eyesight.

Lt. Day testified he saw this ammunition clip, handled it, and then forwarded it to the FBI Fingerprint Laboratory where the clip was examined for prints by the Bureau's number one expert, Mr. Latona. The FBI expert testified that although Lt. Day had handled this clip with his bare hands and fingers, Mr. Latona never found either Oswald's or the Lieutenant's fingerprints! When Lt. Day "found" the "brown paper bag" he had enough sense to write a few words on a small tag, but when he "found" this clip his excitement overcame his police training and he wrote nothing. Of course, it is possible that since no one else saw the clip the efficient officer had nothing to write. (23.) There is no "official" report in either the "Report" or "Hearings" regarding this important clip, but Lt. Day did testify on behalf of the Commission that the ammunition clip carried the letters: "SMI, 9x2" on its surface. However, the FBI testified that the clip sent to them by the Dallas Police Department had a different code number: "SMI 952." (24.) Just as [with] the rifles, the Commission now had two different ammunition clips and the Commission knew that no rifle manufacturer stamps two different numbers on a single clip. A trial judge would instruct the jury that the testimony of Lt. Day was of no value. Without that clip, Oswald was an innocent man.

The testimony in the "Hearings" and in the National Archives has revealed that Lt. Day's testimony was not substantiated at any time by any police agent. Nor, at any time, did the same Lt. Day ever inform any officer on the 6th floor that he had "discovered" the ammunition clip. In fact, Deputy Sheriff Craig, who was on the 6th floor engaged in searching for evidence, testified that he never saw any ammunition clip. That the clip was nothing more than "evidence" manufactured by the Dallas Police Department is seen by the fact that a rifle with a clip will automatically eject the clip when the final shell comes into the chamber. Furthermore, conclusive proof is that the official Dallas police "material" list has no statement that Lt. Day found or gave to Officer Hicks, the officer in charge of enumerating the material evidence found on the 6th floor, an ammunition clip. [The] Dallas police "material" list has no statement that Lt. Day found or gave to the officer-in-charge, Hicks, an ammunition clip. In view of all the testimony, the proof is absolute that there was no ammunition clip found on the 6th floor.

Finally, Mr. Hoover's letter called Lt. Day mistaken when the

Bureau informed the Commission that there was "no ammunition clip, for the 3rd shell had been loaded into and extracted" from the rifle chamber. No rifleman, and that includes Oswald–whom the Commission regarded the World's greatest rifleman on November 22nd–would, once the shooting had commenced, load by hand a third shell into that chamber, extract it, and then reload. The Commission expected the American jury to believe every statement made by them, but no rational jury would swallow that concoction! Not even the Dallas police accepted the Commission's imaginary tale, for a Dallas police executive admitted that "we can only speculate [on] his (Oswald's) reason for working the bolt and putting a fourth bullet in the firing chamber." In other words, there was no ammunition clip. Oswald, according to the police, hand loaded that rifle and they admitted no rifleman in the world could hand load four bullets into a rifle chamber, sight the weapon, and pull the trigger three times in 4.8 seconds or even 7 seconds. The Commission conducted no tests to prove or disprove the time element in hand loading. (25.) Nor would an experienced Marine, expertly trained rifleman put four bullets into [a] 6-bullet ammunition clip, fire 2 shots, and then remove the third bullet from the ammunition clip by hand. All expert riflemen know that the clip would automatically be ejected from the rifle. To insult the intelligence of the American people, the Commission then stated that Oswald calmly placed the 3rd bullet back into the clip, removed the 4th bullet already in the chamber, reinserted the clip, and proceeded to pull the trigger!

The Warren Commission, being composed entirely of lawyers, knew that in a criminal trial for murder the weapon allegedly used by the murderer must be capable of discharging those bullets from that rifle into the victim's body causing death. Thus, as part of the crime, the finding of the shells or cartridges is of vast importance. Five years after the murder of the president, light was cast on the manner in which those 3 cartridges were found. The Commission implied that they had been ejected in the normal manner, that is, haphazardly. However, Deputy Craig disclosed the fact that "the shells found on the floor in front of the window, I saw 'em, they were laying, all the shells were facing the same direction–there was not one of them more than 3/4 inch apart. And I've fired many a bolt-action rifle and I have never had two shells land in the same place." (26.) The author of "Six Seconds in Dallas" wrote, after his investigation, that the Commission's photograph, if true, was a physical and scientific impossibility when one bullet shell would land 5 to 6 feet away from the other cartridges. The author,[13] who saw service in the Pacific in World War II, can also state this as an impossibility.

What the Commission did conceal was the deadly testimony suppressed in the National Archives under Com. Exh. No. 705, p. 402, that a Dallas police official, prior to the discovery of the rifle and shells on the 6th floor, contrary to statements made to him by witnesses who said they saw someone on the 6th floor, went to the 3rd floor window and found three cartridges! This information is on the Dallas police radio tapes of the broadcast made by this officer at 12:45 p.m. (27.) What the Dallas police did not report was the discovery of the rifle taken from the Depository at approximately 1 p.m. A photograph of this event is now in the possession of Mr. James Garrison, District Attorney of New Orleans, Louisiana.

Those 3 shells have disappeared from the eyesight of man, but they could have come from a rifle being used by a rifleman at the 3rd-floor window. Or they could have been sent to the FBI by the Dallas police as being the ones found on the 6th floor. That they were vital pieces of evidence can be seen from the fact that this evidence was willfully suppressed by the police and the Commission. Thus, the implication that a conspiracy existed to murder President Kennedy became stronger and stronger as the Commission's concoction slowly but surely sank before the weight of the testimony in the same length of time that the Reagan image,[14] hidden by the California smog, emerged into the full light of the day's sun.

---

[13] Marks is speaking of himself here. He was inducted into the U.S. Army on March 8, 1945 and discharged sometime after December 1945. See my "Introduction to the Life and Work of Stanley J. Marks" in Marks, *Murder Most Foul!* (New York: Dominantstar, 2020).

[14] A reference to Ronald Reagan, who served as governor of California and, later on, as president of the United States.

The Commission, in a law court, would be compelled to solve the question of whether or not those three cartridges given to the FBI by the Dallas police had, in fact, been discharged from the Commission's Italian Carcano rifle. The FBI informed the Commission that the answer was "no." Mr. Hoover wrote to the Commission that (1) the live bullet in the rifle chamber has "marks on it which were not identified with the rifle; (2) three sets of marks were on the cartridge base which could not be found on the other two cases; (3) and the third shell had been loaded into and extracted from the weapon at least twice." (28.) This was definite proof that no ammunition clip was in the rifle chamber, for no rifleman would extract the third shell when the clip was in the chamber. Any rifleman could have informed the Commission that it would be a mechanical impossibility to take out the 3rd shell and then replace it in its identical position without the 4th shell going into the chamber! Not even the "prestige" of the Commission can overthrow physical and scientific laws.

In addition to this formal letter, the FBI's ballistic expert testified that (1) "one of the shells was so deformed it could not fit into the rifle chamber; (2) there were no fingerprints of any person found on any of the 3 cartridges or on the live bullet; (3) no fingerprints were found on the shells, rifle bolt, or stock of that rifle." (29.) This letter was a warning to the Commission from the FBI which proved the existence of a conspiracy. First, the FBI was stating that the rifle given to them by the Dallas police was a "phony," since the live bullet had marks on it not consistent with the rifle markings. Second, and this is a vital statement, Mr. Hoover was pointing out that one of the shells was so deformed it could not fit into the rifle chamber!

Mr. Hoover and the FBI ballistic experts were asking the Commission to answer this question: "How could the president be struck by a bullet from a shell so deformed that it could not be fired through the barrel of the alleged murder weapon?" The Commission never responded to that question, for the reason that the Italian Carcano rifle, Comm. Exh. No. 139, was never used by any rifleman on November 22, 1963. (30.) Both the Dallas police and the FBI testified that [never] in their search of the areas of Dallas, Ft. Worth; Irving, Texas; and New Orleans area did they find an ammunition gun shop that sold Oswald either bullets of any kind or an ammunition clip. (31.) It must be noted that at no time did the FBI ever testify that the shells and live bullet were identical to the ones found on the 6th floor; the Bureau simply testified that they received 3 shells and one live bullet from the Dallas police.

Therefore, there was no substantiation in law that the identical shells and live bullet were given to the FBI. As a matter of fact, on November 25, at 1 a.m. in the morning, the FBI had to retrieve a shell from the possession of Capt. Fritz, which, he so stated, was one of the shells found on the 6th floor. However, the efficient Captain first had to rummage around in his desk drawer which contained other shells to give the agent (Mr. Drain) a shell. There were no markings on this turned-over shell to prove that it was, indeed, one of the three shells found on the 6th floor. (32.) Oh, for the life of a police captain in the city of Dallas! Fee, fie, fum; and a ho ho hum!

It has been previously noted that between 12:30 and 12:40 p.m. a Dallas police inspector found three cartridges on the 3rd floor of the Book Depository. What happened to those 3 shells? Were they the ones given to the FBI by the ever efficient Dallas police? Did they match a 7.65 German Mauser instead of a 6.5 Italian Mannlicher-Carcano rifle? Is it not true, members of the Warren Commission, that the president could have been in the "angle of fire" from the third floor window but was not, as the evidence has proved beyond a reasonable doubt, from the 6th-floor window? Was it not true that both the president and the governor could have been struck from bullets fired from a 3rd-floor window? Why was this evidence suppressed? Because it proved Oswald innocent of being the "sole and exclusive assassin of the president"? (33.)

In a court of law, where the defendant is accused of murder by using a rifle from which came bullets that caused the death of the victim, an impartial judge, based on the above testimony of the FBI, would direct the jury to bring in a verdict of "not guilty."

There is absolutely no legal evidence or proof, not a single, solitary scrap of evidence, given to the Commission by the FBI, the Secret Service, the CIA, the U.S. Marine Corps, the Post Office, the Texas Rangers, the Dallas police, the Dallas Sheriff's

Office, Mrs. Marina Oswald, or Mr. and Mrs. Paine that Lee Harvey Oswald ever possessed or used that Italian rifle, Com. Exh. No. 139, prior to or on November 22, 1963. QED Lee Harvey Oswald was innocent of the charge that he was "the sole and exclusive killer of President John F. Kennedy.

Thus, we leave the rifle, bullets, and ammunition clip to investigate the Commission's allegation: "Were those three shots fired from the S.E. corner window on the 6th floor of the Texas Book Depository?" The Commission, on their "honor," said "'yes"; the evidence said "no." The citizenry is thus left to read the evidence and form their own conclusion, for if the evidence proved beyond a reasonable doubt that those three bullets were not fired from that S.E. 6th-floor window, then Oswald was "not guilty." In a murder trial there is no such thing as he "probably" was the killer any more than there be a woman who is "half a virgin." She is or she ain't!

In the National Archives there is a file, suppressed from the "Report" and the "Hearings," known as File No. 87. In this File can be found the official U.S. Government photographs taken by the United States Secret Service reconstructing the location of the president's automobile when he was struck by two bullets and the governor by still another one. In the identical file is the official survey made by Mr. R. H. West, dated December 5, 1963, which showed the location, in a surveyor's sense, where the president's automobile was located as each of the 3 bullets struck their target. From those two suppressed documents it was a scientific and physical impossibility that any bullet fired from a rifle held by a rifleman at the S.E. corner window from the 6th floor [of the] Book Depository Building could or would hit either the president or the governor. (34.)

Based on those official reports Lee Harvey Oswald was an innocent man. The official U.S. Secret Service Report to the president of the United States, dated November 28, 1963, without equivocation, informed the Chief Executive, Mr. Johnson, that the late President Kennedy was struck first by one bullet, then a second bullet struck Governor Connelly, and the third bullet struck the president, that bullet being the cause of death. This suppressed Secret Service Report bears the title: "Preliminary Special Dallas Report #1. Assassination of the President: Assassination Scene." This Report has never been challenged by any member or aide of the Commission. (35.) It was the Commission, not its critics, that proposed an "angle of fire" which was disproved by every survey conducted by the FBI, the Secret Service, and by the path of the bullet in the president's back and another one in the front of his throat.

A prosecutor conducting a trial for the murder of any person must prove not only the cause of death but also the manner of death. In a formal indictment it is not necessary for the state to include the autopsy report, but such report must be given in open court so that the defense has an opportunity to prove, for example, that the victim did not die from bullet wounds but from knife of the Medici. A defendant accused of killing the victim with his fists is "not guilty" if the evidence proved the victim died of a bullet in his heart. The Commission, not its critics, made the accusation that Oswald fired a bullet which not only penetrated the back of the president's neck but that same bullet proceeded through the neck and continued on into the governor's body. Having made that accusation it was the duty of the Commission to prove it beyond a reasonable doubt.

If the evidence revealed that more than three bullets were fired at the president, then the Commission's case that Oswald was the "sole killer" is destroyed and a conspiracy proved beyond a reasonable doubt. What does the evidence reveal? President Kennedy was struck by two bullets in the head, one bullet in the back, and one bullet entered through the front of his throat. Governor Connelly was struck by not less than two bullets. One bullet struck the curb, and fragments of that curb struck a Mr. Tague in the face, Thus, uncontroverted proof is in the National Archives that a minimum of seven (7) bullets were fired. Since the evidence is overwhelming that seven bullets were fired, then a conspiracy, in fact and in law, existed and Oswald was "not guilty" of being the "sole assassin of President Kennedy."

With that evidence of seven bullets being fired at President Kennedy, the Commission decided to exercise the "inherent wisdom" given to them by themselves. God had nothing to do with it despite reports to the contrary. That "wisdom" informed the Commission to announce only three bullets were fired at President Kennedy and one of the three missed entirely.

The value and importance of the Commission's "wisdom" can readily be seen in the manner in which the Commission interpreted the medical reports and autopsy chart of the Parkland and Bethesda Hospital staffs. The physicians at Parkland Hospital placed the president face up when he was placed on the operating table. They never saw the wound in his back, but what they did see, and what they did do in an attempt to save his life, is of equal value to the medical autopsy performed at Bethesda, Md. Nor does the work conducted by either medical staff conflict with each other's work. Both staffs proved the existence of a conspiracy.

The Parkland Hospital team of physicians did see a bullet wound at the "necktie" knot, and Dr. Perry was to state, legally, that the "bullet ranged downward in the throat and did not exit." His statement was substantiated by Dr. Shaw, who was the Chairman of Thoracic Surgery at Parkland Hospital when he announced, legally, that "the first bullet entered the president's trachea, in front of his neck, coursing downward into his right lung." (36.) Both physicians had their statements corroborated by Dr. Clark when he stated that the president was "hit by a bullet in the throat just below the Adam's apple." To substantiate those three physicians, the remaining two Parkland Hospital physicians testified that the bullet wound in the throat was an "entrance wound." (37.)

As the reader probably knows, great controversy has raged over the wound in the president's throat; was it a bullet from the rear of his neck or one from the front? Everyone became heatedly involved for the reason that the critics say that if it were an "entrance" wound it would prove a conspiracy. As has been shown thus far there is no doubt that a conspiracy in law and in fact existed; hence, in spite of the controversy over the location of the neck wound, the evidence proved a conspiracy. Thus, that wound is, in law, corroboration of the conspiracy!

The importance of the physicians' statements is due to the fact that anyone reading those statements in conjunction with Commander Humes' Autopsy Chart No. 397 can see that there resides in the coffin of President Kennedy portions of a bullet lodged in his right lung. (38.) This chart thus supports Dr. Shaw's statement that the bullet "went downward into his right lung." Dr. Perry, who enlarged the opening in the front of the president's throat, said "the bullet went downward in the throat and did not exit." No physician at any time before the Commission ever testified that the bullet in the throat was the fragment of another bullet.

Thus, there is no reason for the argument that rages over the nondisclosure of the X-Rays. The evidence of the physicians and the autopsy chart proved beyond a reasonable doubt that a conspiracy existed, since no bullet fired from the 6th floor of the S.E. window of the Book Depository could go through the back of the neck when the bullet in the front of the throat "coursed downward into his right lung."

At this point of the trial, if the trial judge had refused to order a not-guilty verdict based on the evidence relating to the rifle being a nonlethal weapon, a trial judge would now order the jury to bring in a "not guilty" verdict. The question of whether or not Oswald was a member of a conspiracy is not involved since the prosecution (the Commission) said there was no conspiracy. As there was no conspiracy involved, then Oswald was not involved with a bullet that entered the front of the president's throat; and not being involved, he could not be guilty of a crime he did not commit.

The Commission impliedly accepted a conspiracy when they said that Bullet 399, in its pristine condition, was the only bullet to hit both the president and the governor. As Bullet 399 did not explode, how did portions of a bullet enter the president's throat and course downward into his right lung? Since no portions of Bullet 399 entered the president's lung or throat, it follows that portions of a bullet in his lung came from the rifle held by a conspirator hidden behind the wooden fence on the grassy knoll.

In a murder case, the law requires the state to inform the accused and the people of the cause of death. The murder of the president was no exception and, accordingly, Dr. R. N. McClelland of Parkland Hospital officially announced that the cause of death was due to "a massive head and brain injury from a gunshot wound of the left temple." The Humes autopsy chart, No. 397, does show two bullet wounds in the head, but the "inherent wisdom" of the Commission overruled the chart and published a lie stating that only one bullet hit him in the head. Not even the authenticated photographic film from the Zapruder camera, nor the statement of Mr. J. Edgar Hoover, swayed the Commission from publishing a lie. Frames 311 to 315 of the Zapruder film showed the president's head being struck by two bullets, one which drove his head forward, the other bullet driving his head backward.

The question of whether or not there was any evidence to support a wound over the left side of the president's head can be answered "yes." Three Parkland Hospital physicians, all members of the operating group, testified that the president was so struck (Drs. Shaw, Giesecke, and Jenkins). (39.) Catholic Father O. L. Huber, who administered the last rites to the president, said "he noticed a 'terrible wound' over his (the president's) eye." (39a.) Furthermore, spectators and police motorcyclists were splattered with blood and tissue. (40.)

The body of President Kennedy was flown from Dallas to the Bethesda, Md. Naval Hospital where those physicians commenced their autopsy at 8 p.m. and concluded their examination shortly before midnight. Unfortunately, none of those physicians had any background in forensic medicine–a highly specialized field of medicine. Regardless of their background, only two basic questions arose involving the autopsy. (1) Did a bullet enter the president's throat from the front or rear; and (2) what happened to the bullet that entered the front of the throat if that did occur? Question No.2 has been answered by the staff of the Parkland Hospital: it entered through the front of the throat and "coursed downward into his right lung."

The answer to Number 1 was answered by none other than an aide to the Commission when he asked a physician to describe the wounds. Since the question was put in a vague manner, the physician asked the aide to which wound he referred. The aide replied "Start with the head wound, or the back wound, either one." (41.) A Commission attorney may not understand the English language, but a person of common sense knows the meaning of the word "or" and the phrase "either one." The physician then proceeded to describe two wounds, one in the back, and one in the head.

Jay Epstein's "Inquest" is credited with the revelation that the Commission had suppressed the entire FBI Report relating to the murder. That Report stated: "The president had been struck by a bullet which entered his back, just below his shoulder to the right of the spinal column at an angle of 40 to 60 degrees downward, there was no point of exit and the bullet was not in the body." The Report was signed by FBI Agents O'Neill Jr., and Sibert, File 89-30, dated 11/26/63. The same report also stated the "bullet which entered his back penetrated less than a finger length. "

To support the signed statement of the two FBI agents was none other than Comdr. Humes, who, at first, denied and then admitted that the facts in the agents' statements were true and authentic. (41A.) The reason is obvious, for the clothes worn by President Kennedy were a silent but eloquent witness to a bullet in the back at the identical locations reported by the two FBI agents. The bullet hole in the president's back was one that "I found on the back of the president's shirt, a hole 5 and 3/4" below the top of the collar, and, as you look at the back of the shirt, 1 and 1/8" to the right of the mid seam." (42.)

When "Inquest" appeared, a mass attack was launched upon the integrity of the FBI and Secret Service agents who signed the report. The main charge was that those two agents were not in the autopsy room all the time during the examination and thus they had manufactured evidence. However, Agent Kellerman of the Secret Service was in the room when Lt. Col. Finck, while examining the bullet wound in the back, said: "There are no lanes for an outlet in this entry and this man's shoulders." (43.) Agent Kellerman's testimony, in turn, was substantiated by Secret Service Agent Greer. (44.) This statement by Lt. Col. Finck was so astonishing that Secret Service Agent Hill was brought into the autopsy room and shown the bullet hole which was in the president's back and had no path of exit. (45.) In the face of this overwhelming evidence the Navy doctor admitted that he did not discern any bullet-hole path through the president's body. (46.)

In view of the testimony of the physicians and from both the agents of the FBI and Secret Service, there is, in law, no need for the X-Rays of which the critics have raised such a storm. Mr. McCloy, a member of the seven-man Commission, has admitted that no member or aide saw the X-Rays at any time. The X-Rays were in the possession of the U.S. Secret Service from November 23, 1963 until April 26, 1965, when they were turned over to the Kennedy family, who then gave them to the National Archives. (47.) The statement by the FBI that Robert Kennedy had refused to permit the Warren Commission to see and use the X-Rays was a deliberate falsehood, for the Commission had only to summon the Secret Service, under the command of the Secretary of Treasury, to turn over those photographs to them. The Kennedy family never had possession of those X-Rays, or any other material relating to the death of President Kennedy until the year 1965, when the Warren Commission had completed their "investigation." According to Mr. McCloy, any aide who said that he, the aide, or any member inspected the X-Rays is a liar.

But what Mr. McCloy never answered was the question: "Why did the Commission refuse to inspect the X-Rays and other photographs of the scene of the murder, prior, during, and after the murder?" Whether Mr. McCloy ever answers that question does not vitiate the statement that those X-Rays are not needed in determining the innocence or guilt of Lee Harvey Oswald. The testimony of every physician and that of the FBI and Secret Service agents in the Bethesda, Md. Hospital clearly secures a "not guilty" verdict. With their evidence freeing Oswald, that identical evidence proved the conspiracy.

Any attorney defending Oswald on the charge of being the "sole and exclusive assassin" of President Kennedy would have an easy task to obtain a "not guilty" verdict. With the testimony of the physicians and federal agents, that proved beyond a reasonable doubt that President Kennedy was struck in the back by a bullet striking him from an angle of fire between 45 and 60 degrees. This proved that such an angle of fire could only come from a window of the Dal-Tex Building or the County Building but not from the 6th floor of the Book Depository. Oswald was innocent.

The intriguing figure of Comdr. Humes will puzzle historians for many years, for he was the only physician who had announced that he issued an autopsy report based on comments in a daily newspaper, the Washington "Post"! No law court would accept his report based not only upon an unsubstantiated newspaper story but also the fact that his report contains many subtractions, alterations and additions to his autopsy report.

An altered document has no value in a law court when those alterations are not supported by other testimony giving the reason for those alterations. Fortunately, there is a Chart 397, which has been authenticated by Comdr. Humes and the other attending autopsy physicians, which clearly shows the wound on the rear portion of the body as a back wound, not a wound in the back of the neck! Substantiating this "wound in the back" is none other than Comdr. Humes' testimony given under oath, which upheld the aide's phrase: "the wound in the president's back." (48.) When describing for the record the location of the bullet hole in the president's jacket, the Comdr. said [it was] "approximately 6 inches below the top of the collar, and 2 inches to the right of the middle seam." (49.)

With his testimony the Comdr. clinched the case for the defense, since no bullet fired from the S.E. corner window of the 6th floor of the Book Depository could, according to the FBI and the official surveys of the United States Secret Service, strike the president from that angle of fire.

A conspiracy, in fact and in law, was now proved beyond a reasonable doubt.

In spite of the testimony of the physicians and the federal agencies, the Commission decided to confuse the people by outdoing Baron Munchhausen–a paragon among liars. The Commission therefore proceeded to "produce" a "Tale of Bullet No. 399." This "bullet," sayeth the Commission Barons, first entered the president's back, hesitated a moment, reversed itself, flew up his back, made a 90 degree turn, turned downward into the back of his neck, went through his neck, made another angle turn, entered the governor's body, "tumbled" through the wrist, entered his rib cage, and came to rest when the "tumbling" lacked inertia, in his thigh! The leading Baron aide was a man by the name of Specter.

The physicians who operated on Governor Connally never supported this Commission theory. According to the FBI Laboratory, Bullet No. 399, after creating all this damage, weighed less than 1/180th of an ounce after it had gone through the rifle barrel. Mr. Dulles, who cross-examined Dr. Shaw and Dr. Shires, received the information from them that the governor's wounds had to be caused by not less than two bullets. (50.) Dr. Shires also informed the commissioner that there still remained within the governor's body fragments which would exceed 1/180th of an ounce. (51.) Every physician testified that Bullet No. 399 could do none of the things attributed to it by the Commission. (52.)

The problem of Bullet No. 399 and its relation to its journey from the Parkland Hospital in Dallas, Texas to the Commission room in Washington, D.C. presented an interesting legal problem of proof. In criminal law it is essential that each item of evidence that is necessary to secure the conviction of the accused be identified by witnesses who handled that item. This is generally called the "path or chain" of evidence, and each witness must be able to prove he received it, or gave it to a person, or delivered it to a specific location. This is done to prevent "planting," "switching," or "manufacturing" of evidence. Thus, the "path of evidence" relating to Bullet No. 399 has revealed that, in all probability, there was not only a "switching" but also a planting of evidence. As has been seen, every physician testifying to the matter of the governor's wounds stated that Bullet No. 399 did not cause the damage in the governor's body. Thus, the only common sense answer that can be attained is that Bullet No. 399 was a "plant."

The evidence in the "Hearings" has revealed that on November 22, 1963, at approximately 1:40 to 1:45 p.m., Mr. Tomlinson, Parkland Hospital employee, found a bullet on the floor of the elevator. (53.) He immediately took it to Mr. Wright, personnel director of the hospital.[15] Mr. Wright, in turn, gave this bullet to Secret Service Agent Johnsen who, in turn, gave it to that Bureau's Chief, Mr. J. J. Rowley. (54.) Mr. Rowley took it with him to Washington, D.C. and, during the night of November 22nd, gave A bullet to FBI Agent Todd in the FBI Washington office. (55.) Agent Todd now gave "A" bullet, which he marked with his initial, to FBI Agent Frazier who, in turn, marked that bullet with his initials. Now, A bullet should have

---

[15] O. P. Wright was the Parkland Memorial Hospital Personnel Director of Security.

the initial of two FBI agents. (56.) On the same night, Frazier gave this marked bullet to FBI Agent Gallagher of the FBI Spectrographic Department.

Three months and two days later, March 24, 1964, A bullet is given by the FBI to Commission aide Eisenberg (57) who, in turn, gave A bullet to Mr. J. D. Nicol, an Illinois ballistic expert, to conduct tests regarding this bullet given to him by the Commission aide. Mr. Nicol took this bullet to his Illinois office and made his experiments. On April 1, 1964, he testified before the Commission, but when he returned A bullet to the Commission is not revealed in the testimony. Seventy days now elapse and on June 24, 1964, FBI Agent Odum is back in Dallas, Texas, and he shows A bullet to both Mr. Tomlinson and Mr. Wright. Bingo! Both of them refuse to identify A bullet, known now to history as Bullet No. 399, as the bullet they saw on November 22, 1963! However, cease not to wonder. FBI Agent Odum then gave A bullet to Agent Todd, who went to the U.S. Secret Service bureau, saw both Agent Johnsen and Chief Rowley, and both of them refused to accept Bullet No. 399 as the bullet they had received at the Parkland Hospital from Mr. Wright on November 22, 1963! (58.)

What happened? In law, nothing. Someone was tossing bullets around the joint. As evidence in a trial for murder, the bullet was worthless.

Bullet No. 399 is an example of how the Commission relied upon the lack of knowledge of legal procedure to deceive the people. FBI Agents testified that two of them initialed the bullet given to them by Chief Rowley. FBI Agents are taught repeatedly that they must follow legal rules for the Department of Justice to secure legal convictions. Those rules are not for the protection, as the right-wingers proclaim, of the criminal but of the average law-abiding citizen. No person is a criminal until tried and convicted under due process of law–not when the person is arrested by the police. Throughout the investigation of President Kennedy's murder, the Commission went out of its way to secure "evidence" that would convict Oswald; not to solve the murder and the conspiracy. Thus, in Bullet No. 399 there is no evidence or testimony that the Commission asked Agents Todd and Frazier if they had given the initialed bullet to Agent Gallagher. Nor did the Commission ask that agent if he gave that initialed bullet to Commission aide Eisenberg; who, in turn, was never placed in the witness chair and asked if he, in turn, gave that initialed bullet to Mr. Nicol. Mr. Nicol was never asked if he received that initialed bullet. Agent Odum never did testify that he took that initialed bullet down to Dallas and showed it to Mr. Tomlinson. It is self-evident that since both of those men and Mr. Wright refused to identify A bullet showed to them by the FBI agent as the bullet they had in their possession on November 22, 1963, that something was "fishy." When both the Secret Service agents corroborated that refusal, then something was not only "fishy" but something smelled to the high heavens. In a court of law, based on the evidence, Bullet No. 399 was a manufactured piece of evidence used by the Commission to avoid the announcement that a conspiracy murdered President Kennedy.

Bullet No. 399 was nothing more than a figment of the Commission's imagination that it went through the president and into the governor's body. The Commission never proved that the bullet was either on the president's or governor's stretcher. Mr. Tomlinson testified that "a spent cartridge or bullet rolled out that had apparently been lodged under the edge of the mat." He further said that there was a stretcher, but he had no knowledge of who had been placed on that stretcher. (59.) A hospital orderly, Mr. Jimison, who had transferred the governor from the stretcher to the operating table, testified he never saw any bullet when performing that task. (60.) Nor did any of the nurses in that operating room where his clothes were removed. (61.) If the Chairman of the Commission, Mr. Chief Justice Warren of the United States Supreme Court, had adhered to the "basic principles of American justice," he would have acknowledged that Bullet No. 399 had no bearing on the murder of President Kennedy. It was not fired from the Italian Carcano rifle and, as a matter of fact and ballistic law, was never fired from any rifle on that day.

That Bullet No. 399 was a fraud upon the American people can be readily seen in the machinations of the FBI. Mr. Nicol, the Illinois ballistic expert called in by the Commission to conduct tests to determine whether Bullet No. 399 was fired from the Italian Mannlicher-Carcano rifle, was given a bullet by that Bureau. There is no testimony by either Mr. Nicol or any agent of the FBI that this bullet was the identical one received by the Bureau from Secret Service Chief Rowley; nor did Mr. Nicol testify that this bullet had any initials upon it when he received it from Commission aide Eisenberg. Mr. Nicol admitted before the Commission that his opinion was of no value since the FBI refused to give him the Italian Mannlicher-Carcano rifle (Com. Exh. 131) so that he could make the proper legal ballistic tests and comparisons. Instead, the Bureau gave him 100 bullets which they said were fired from that Italian rifle. Mr. Nicol then simply compared that bullet, not the initialed bullet, but A bullet with the other 100 bullets, and Mr. Nicol refused to categorically admit that this FBI bullet matched the markings of the Italian Mannlicher-Carcano rifle! Mr. Nicol said that the bullet "maybe, probably, and perhaps" matched the Italian rife. (62.)

In an effort to locate the reason why this rifle expert refused to give an affirmative, positive answer the testimony revealed that the FBI informed Mr. Nicol that those 100 bullets were fired from the Italian rifle after the FBI Laboratory expert repaired the rifle! In other words, the bullet given to Mr. Nicol was nothing more than a bullet that had been discharged through the rifle barrel which had first been repaired and then a bullet from that repaired rifle was given to Mr. Nicol. He simply testified that that bullet and the other 100 bullets came from the repaired rifle. (63.)

That the rifle was absolutely worthless as a lethal weapon was thus proved beyond a reasonable doubt by the FBI. The Bureau, by admitting that it had to repair the internal conditions of that Italian rifle given to them by the Dallas police, was admitting its worthlessness. Common sense, not the self-importance of the title "lawyer," would have made it self-evident that Bullet No. 399 could not have identical markings with bullets fired through that rifle after it had internal changes. There is no ballistic expert in the world that can match any bullet to a rifle whose barrel has been changed internally after the first bullet had been fired! Therefore, since the FBI testified that Bullet No. 399 was, in their opinion, matched to those 100 bullets, the FBI was testifying that a switch had been made and that Bullet No. 399 was not the identical bullet given to them by the Secret Service and the two employees of the Parkland Hospital.

Is there any evidence that would lead to a conclusion that the bullet found by Mr. Tomlinson was planted by a member of the conspiracy? Yes, there is!

The Commission suppressed an affidavit from its "Report" concerning three attempts by four men to enter the operating room while the Parkland Hospital physicians were struggling to save President Kennedy's life. In the first instance, FBI Agent Drain and an unidentified man, who Drain said was a "doctor," attempted to enter the operating room. They were forbidden to enter and both walked away. Minutes after they departed another FBI agent, unidentified in the affidavit, with a gun in his possession, also attempted to force his way into the room. Stopped at the entrance by two Secret Service agents, this unidentified FBI agent then actually engaged in a fist fight with the two other agents and was knocked out. After recovering consciousness this FBI agent was permitted to walk away without giving his name, being placed under arrest, or being deprived of his revolver. Shortly after this affair another man was restrained from entering the operating room and, again, the Secret Service agents accepted his word that he was a "CIA" agent! Three unknown men, all with loaded guns, attempted to enter the operating room and not once did the Secret Service agents, who had sworn to protect the life of the president of the United States, attempt to obtain their names or badge number but simply permitted those men to walk away. The above (64) evidence is buried in the 18th volume of the "Hearings.

Why did the FBI attempt to "plant" an unidentified "doctor" in the operating room? Were there any assassins among the physicians, the nurses, the orderlies? Were there any "suspected" Communists in the hospital? What was the true reason why the FBI agent actually commenced a brawl outside the operating room at the exact time the president's body was under the knife? Was his job done deliberately to cause a disturbance so that if he got inside, he was to draw a gun and either shoot the president or the personnel in the hospital room? As to the "CIA" agent, was he an "agent" or a member of the conspiracy? (65.)[16]

Was the action of those men the action of men interested in the life or death of President Kennedy? Would rational, patriotic men engage in brawls and arguments at the time the president was being operated upon? Why did the Warren Commission keep an absolute silence upon those acts of violence in the Parkland Hospital? Was it because they knew that both the CIA and FBI had agents within their organizations that they knew would be happy to see the president pass from life to death? Was it because the agent, who was knocked out, was known to the Bureau to be a follower and believer in the right-wing that believed that President Kennedy should be killed because he a "follower of the communist line"? It should not be forgotten that Gov. Reagan implied, after the murder of Robert Kennedy, on a national TV broadcast, that Robert Kennedy got what he deserved because he was not a believer in "law and order."(66.)

Two other persons could have planted that bullet found by Mr. Tomlinson. In the hospital, according to evidence uncovered by Harold Weisberg of "Whitewash," was an employee and a member of the anti-Castro Batista CIA group. The other person was none other than Jack Ruby, the friend of 75% of the Dallas police force, who could enter various police stations carte-

---

[16] Secret Service Agent Andrew E. Berger (stationed with Agent Richard E. Johnsen right outside Trauma Room One) reported that he encountered the following four figures at Parkland Memorial Hospital, who each attempted to gain entry to the room: FBI Agent Drain, accompanied by a "doctor friend." An "unidentified CIA agent," who possessed credentials. And an "unidentified FBI agent," who did not possess credentials. See Vincent Palamara, *Survivor's Guilt: The Secret Service and the Failure to Protect President Kennedy* (Walterville, OR: Trine Day, 2013), pp. 271-272. Palamara concludes: "Berger's report was totally ignored by just about everyone." Author Gerald McKnight adds that the unidentified FBI agent who attempted to push his way past the Secret Service "was instantly slammed to the wall and fell to the floor after receiving a haymaker from one of the Secret Service agents. The FBI agent was later identified as J. Doyle Williams." See McKnight, *Breach of Trust*, pp. 272-273.

blanche. The same Jack Ruby who was so well-known to the staff of District Attorney Wade that he could have many of the assault and battery charges, plus other law violations, dropped from the files. The same Jack Ruby who was a gunrunner for various anti-Castro CIA groups.

An exhibit, the "Kantor" Exh. No. 7, is suppressed from the "Report," and the Commission attempted to squelch its dynamite by labelling it "Rumors & Speculations." A very clever dodge, but the Commission failed in their attempt to suppress it, for that exhibit placed Jack Ruby both inside and outside the Parkland Hospital entrance prior and after the death of President Kennedy. The "Kantor" Exhibit revealed that Mr. Kantor was an experienced police reporter for the Dallas "Times-Herald" from September 1960 to May 1962, when he became associated with the Scripps-Howard press. Mr. Kantor testified that he saw Jack Ruby at the Parkland Hospital between 1 and 1:30 p.m. He testified he saw Jack Ruby inside and outside the Hospital. However, not only did Mr. Kantor see Jack Ruby, but he personally knew Ruby, having written feature articles on Ruby's activities when Kantor worked for the "Times-Herald." Mr. Kantor not only saw Ruby but shook hands with him at the Hospital. In an attempt to cancel out this important testimony, the Commission went to Ruby's Dallas jail cell and asked him if he saw Mr. Kantor. Ruby, under the guns of Dallas police, naturally said "no." The Commission then announced that since Ruby was an honest man, a reliable person who "killed" another man under a delusion, his word was acceptable. (67.) After this denial by Ruby, the Commission asked Mr. Kantor if he had seen Ruby at the hospital; and to prove he had, Mr. Kantor showed the Commission his notebook that he kept that tragic day, and in his notes is the statement [on] how and when he saw Ruby. This did not satisfy the Commission, but instead of prosecuting Mr. Kantor as a perjurer the Commission placed his testimony in the "Rumor and Speculation" section.

Thus, a jury would have to decide who lied, Mr. Kantor or Ruby? In the "Hearings" and in Ruby's trial for the murder of

Oswald (Ruby shot Oswald; he never murdered him),[17] Ruby's background came to life. He was a pimp, ran a whorehouse, a bribe giver, a gunrunner, an assaulter of men and women, a narcotic distributor, a violator of various laws; in other words, a completely "amoral" person, but to the Commission he was a saint whose background was beyond reproach. His word was acceptable but not that of Mr. Kantor's, whose life record was impeccable. Who would the jury believe?

As previously stated, a defense attorney who can locate a witness to substantiate the testimony of another witness is living in clover. The corroborating witness was a Mrs. Wilma Tice, and the Commission desperately attempted to prevent her testimony from being accepted. If a district attorney had conducted himself in the manner used by the Commission, he would have been thrown out of the courtroom. In a trial for murder, or for any crime of felony, witnesses must be heard, not silenced! How, oh how, the Commission tried to silence Mrs. Tice. She resolutely upheld Mr. Kantor's testimony that she saw Jack Ruby outside the Parkland Hospital at approximately the same time as did Mr. Kantor. Not only did Mrs. Tice see Ruby but she was able to describe Ruby's clothes, and when the Commission "sicced" the FBI on her to see if she had committed perjury, the FBI went to Ruby's sister, who upheld Mrs. Tice's description of Ruby's clothes that he wore at the hospital! (68.)

Who was the liar? None other than Jack Ruby. He was at the Parkland Hospital, and he could have planted that bullet, for he was both inside and outside the hospital. Then, why did the Commission accept the word of a "liar"? Was it because, as Jack Ruby's smuggled letter pointed out, he was involved in the con-

---

[17] As Marks notes in *Murder Most Foul!*, from a legal point of view "Jack Ruby *shot* Oswald but did not murder him. An unknown detective straddled Oswald's body and gave him artificial respiration in spite of the fact that this treatment *pumped the blood out of Oswald body*." In addition, "An unidentified man, who looked like a doctor, was also seen over Oswald's body. This man, of twenty-three, was permitted to leave by a policeman who 'thought he was a doctor.'" See *Murder Most Foul!* Q&A #928d.

spiracy; that he knew the members of the conspiracy; that he had a cache of arms and ammunition which consisted of rifles which included German Mausers and Italian Carcano rifles; ammunition for hand guns and rifles which included those found on the 3rd and 6th floor of the Texas Book Depository? (69.) Was this the reason why Dorothy Kilgallen was murdered by slipping into her medicine a poison not known to the N.Y. Coroner's Department?

Summarizing the Commission's allegations in paragraph 1 of their indictment, it can be stated that the evidence is overwhelming that three bullets were never fired from the S.E. window of the 6th floor; that not less than 7 bullets were fired at the president of the United States, four of which struck him, and not less than two struck the governor; and that none of those bullets were discharged between 4.8 and 7 seconds. The evidence conclusively proved that the "angle of fire" made it impossible for any shots to have been fired from that 6th-floor window. The evidence proved, beyond a reasonable doubt, that the 6.5 Italian Carcano rifle, given to the FBI by the Dallas police, was never used at any time on November 22, 1963. There is no evidence, not the slightest, that Oswald ever purchased a rifle of any type from Klein's of Chicago. There is uncontradicted evidence that not less than three Italian rifles were presented to the Commission. The evidence is uncontroverted that the rifle found on the 6th floor was a 7.65-mm German Mauser with a telescopic sight that had a "brownish black" sling.

The evidence proved beyond a reasonable doubt that the 3 cartridges given to the FBI by the Dallas police never were discharged from the Italian rifle. The evidence is overwhelming and not subject to any doubt that one of those 3 cartridges never held a bullet which was discharged from that Italian rifle, for how can a bullet come from a cartridge that never held it in the first place? The evidence is conclusive that Bullet No. 399 was a piece of evidence manufactured by either the Dallas police or a member or members of the FBI. The evidence is conclusive that the FBI and CIA attempted to interfere in the surgical work being conducted upon President Kennedy in Parkland Hospital.

The evidence is overwhelming that the Secret Service was negligent in not arresting and holding for investigation the two

FBI agents, the "doctor" and the CIA agent. What law gave those two agencies, the FBI and CIA, the right to oversee, or interfere, with the medical work being conducted by the medical staff of the Parkland Hospital in their attempts to save the president's life? Did the CIA and the FBI attempt to interfere with the physicians who operated upon President Eisenhower? Was President Kennedy an enemy of his country or an enemy of the FBI and the CIA at the time he was murdered? Did some unknown persons in the FBI and CIA apparatus benefit by the president's murder? Why did not only the Warren Commission but the national media conceal the fight at Parkland Hospital? Is not the silence of the press a prelude to the creation of a dictatorship?

Based upon the evidence in the "Report," the 26 volumes of the "Hearings," and the files of the National Archives, Lee Harvey Oswald was "not guilty" of the charge of being the "sole and exclusive assassin of President Kennedy."

CHAPTER III

THE EVIDENCE THAT NEVER WAS

The second paragraph of the Commission's indictment dealt with: (1) Oswald's purchase of a rifle used in the murder; (2) his palm print; (3) fibers in a shirt; (4) a photograph; and (5) possession of the purchased rifle which he "used" on the day of the murder.

The evidence proved beyond a doubt that the trial of Oswald based upon those five allegations would prove that the Commission failed to read the testimony. There is no evidence that substantiates the Commission's charges.

Under the rules of law as practiced in an American court of criminal law, it is the duty of the prosecution to prove all five of those allegations beyond a reasonable doubt where those allegations are used to substantiate another allegation in the indictment. Generally, in a murder trial it is not necessary to prove either ownership or possession of the weapon, for it is self-evident that the accused murderer may have found, stolen, or borrowed the murder weapon. However, where the prosecution alleged the accused purchased the weapon with the future intent to use that weapon for a specific murder, then the prosecution must prove that allegation beyond a reasonable doubt. Therefore, since the Commission alleged Oswald purchased a rifle to be used for the specific act of murdering President Kennedy, they had to prove that allegation.

The Commission alleged that Oswald purchased an Italian 6.5-mm Italian Mannlicher-Carcano rifle under the name of "Hidell." His wife, Marina, made statements under oath to the FBI and Secret Service agents that she never knew or heard her husband use the name of "Alek Hidell." (70.) After she had been threatened with deportation and with her two children being taken from her, she reversed her earlier statement and said "yes."

The Commission, in its attempt to link Oswald with the "Hidell" purchaser of the Italian rifle, had to accept not only perjured testimony but also manufactured evidence. There is not a single piece of evidence that proved "Hidell" ever purchased an Italian rifle from Klein's of Chicago; there is no evidence that that Chicago gun shop ever mailed the rifle to "Hidell," and there is absolutely no evidence that proved that not only was it not delivered to the Dallas Post Office box leased by Oswald but that "Hidell" was never seen to have been given that 42-inch package by any employee of the Dallas Post Office. There is evidence that Oswald never received any size package at any time from his Dallas Post Office box.

At the onset of their problem to link Oswald with "Hidell," the Commission ran into flagrant perjury by either the Dallas Police Department or the FBI. An analysis of the evidence showed that the ever-malfunctioning Dallas police was committing perjury, but that hindered not the Commission composed of seven stalwart prestigious citizens who believed in "the basic principles of American justice." In an interview over a national TV chain, one of the arresting officers said that Oswald never gave the police his name, so the police took Oswald's billfold from his pocket, and in the billfold was a business or name card with the name of "Lee Harvey Oswald." (71.) The FBI testified that the police had lied, since this billfold and name card, which was given to them by the Dallas police, had Oswald's picture on it, but the name on the card was "Alek James Hidell." (71a.) Police Chief Curry testified that he had no knowledge of any of Oswald's aliases. As will be shown later, Oswald was known by many members of the Dallas Police Department.

In view of the obvious perjury by the Dallas police, it has become quite difficult to analyze the evidence and testimony to determine in what manner that police department came up with the name of Lee Harvey Oswald. Due to the fact that there are no legal or law notes relating to the interrogation of Oswald during his captivity in the Dallas police station, the evidence scattered in the 26 volumes of the "Hearings" revealed that Oswald informed the Dallas police of his rooming house address. The police immediately rushed to that address and found no "Alek Hidell" or "Lee Harvey Oswald." The housekeeper informed the police that the man who matched the suspect's description was "O. H. Lee" (72). The police now had three names in their possession, and they had one chance in three to pick the right name out of a hat. How did the police know at 2:30 p.m. that "Alek James Hidell" was "Lee Harvey Oswald" and not "O. H. Lee"? By his fingerprints? No, for they did not take his fingerprints until 5:30 p.m., and the Dallas police had no record of Lee Harvey Oswald in their files. The FBI did not "connect" Oswald with the "Hidell" rifle until the following midday, November 23, 1963. (73.) Lt. Day, the world's greatest fingerprint expert, never "found" Oswald's palm print until 8:30 p.m. on November 22nd; and the FBI testified Lt. Day lied. Lt. Day admitted, and he was supported by the FBI, that there were no Oswald fingerprints on the rifle. Thus, how and when did the Dallas police know Oswald was Oswald, and not "Alek Hidell" or "O. H. Lee," at the time they made their afternoon announcement, on national TV, that Oswald was Oswald in view of the FBI testimony, that the name on the billfold name card was "Alek James Hidell"? (74.)

The answer is that the Dallas police knew Oswald's name, because he had already been selected as the "patsy" by the Dallas police in association with the conspirators. Is there any substantiation of this charge? The answer is "yes!"

In Volume 4 of the "Hearings" is the testimony of Police Chief Curry, which is so astonishing that it is printed in full:

Mr. Rankin (general counsel): "When did you hear of the arrest of Lee Harvey Oswald?"

Curry: "When I was out at Parkland Hospital."

Rankin: "Do you know about what time that was, the day?"

Curry: "It was on the 22nd and the best I recall it was one o'clock or maybe a little after one o'clock."

Rankin: "How did it come to your attention?"

Curry: "Some of my officers came to me and said that they had a suspect in the shooting of our Officer Tippit."

Rankin: "What else did they say?"

Curry: "They also told me a little later, I believe, that he was a suspect also in the assassination of the president."

Rankin: "What did you do then?"

Curry: "I didn't do anything at the time. I was at the hospital, and I remained at the hospital until some of the Secret Service asked me to prepare two cars, that we were informed that President Kennedy had expired, and we were requested to furnish two cars for President Johnson and some of his staff to return to Love Field."

Rankin: "Did you do that?"

Curry: "Yes, I did."

Rankin: "What else? What did you do after that?"

Curry: "After the planes departed, I remained there I guess for an hour." (75)

The above is the complete testimony of Chief Curry, in sequence as it appears in the record, relating to the chief's idea of the arrest of Oswald. Unless the reader analyzes the chief's testimony carefully the implications will be overlooked.

(1) Chief Curry was notified of the arrest of a suspect between 1 p.m. and 1:15 p.m. There is no specific time stated, but the chief said, "I recall it was around 1:00 p.m. or maybe a little after 1:00 p.m." Now, how would a jury interpret "a little after 1:00 p.m."? Was it five, ten, fifteen, twenty, or twenty-five minutes after 1:00 p.m.? If he had been notified at around 1:30 p.m., he would have said "around 1:30 p.m."

(2) Tippit was not "logged" in the Dallas police records as being "shot" until 1:18 p.m.

(3) Oswald was not captured until 1:50 p.m. The police radio announced it at 2:05 p.m.

(4) Unidentified police officers notified Chief Curry "they had

arrested a suspect in the shooting of our Officer Tippit" between 1:00 p.m. and 1:10 p.m. when Officer Tippit was not even shot! How did those unidentified policemen know (a) Officer Tippit would be shot; (b) that he had been shot; and (c) a suspect would be arrested at not later than 1:15 p.m., unless the police knew Tippit would be murdered and knew they would capture a suspect not later than 1:15 p.m. ?

(5) The police at the Texas Theatre notified Police Hq. at 2:05 p.m. that they had arrested a suspect only in the Tippit murder–not the Kennedy assassination.

(6) Thus, when the evidence is read in the "Hearings" the following can be deduced: (a) between 1:00 p.m. and 1:15 p.m. Curry was informed that Tippit had been shot (b) between 1:00 p.m. and not later than 1:30 p.m., Curry was informed by unidentified policemen that a "suspect" had been captured. (c) Not later than 1:30 p.m. he was informed that the "suspect" was also the man wanted for the Kennedy murder. (d) All this information was given to Chief Curry a minimum of thirty minutes prior to the capture of an unnamed suspect in the Texas Theatre. Add Chief Curry's testimony to that of Roy Milton Jones, and the jigsaw becomes a little clearer–some of the Dallas policemen were involved in both murders.

It could be said that Chief Curry, under the excitement and pressure of the assassination, was violently mistaken as to the time element. Could that be possible? The answer must be a positive "no." Why?

For the reason that the chief's time schedule proved that he was on his way to Love Field prior to 2:20 p.m., when Oswald was in the police station. In his testimony the chief was positive, as can be seen, that he had also been notified that the same arrested suspect in the Tippit murder was also "a suspect in the assassination of the president." Now, as his testimony revealed, some unidentified policemen informed him, after other unidentified policemen had first notified him of the suspect captured in the Tippit murder, that the same suspect was involved in the president's murder. What time was he informed the second time? Since he had left the hospital by 2:10 p.m. and it was only "a little later" after the first Tippit notification, it is reasonable to assume that the chief was notified by approximately 1:30 when the first police radio announcement was made of the general alarm. But that police broadcast was only an announcement to hunt for a "suspect," not that a suspect had been arrested! Then how did the unidentified policemen know not later than 1:25 p.m. that a suspect had been arrested when Oswald was not arrested until 1:50 p.m., and when the news of his arrest was not flashed over the police radio until 2:05 p.m.? At 2:00 p.m. Chief Curry had departed from the Hospital to escort Mr. Johnson to Love airfield. The Only answer that can be given is that those unidentified policemen had beaten the "gun" and released the news. They were part and parcel of the conspiracy. How did those unidentified policemen know the suspect–Oswald–was wanted for the murder of the president at 1:25 p.m. unless they had prior knowledge of both murders?

As the Warren Commission has stated that Chief Curry was a "truthful" witness, and assuming that was true, then how did some "unidentified" officers know a suspect was in custody approximately 40 minutes before the arrest of the suspect? Not only for the Tippit murder but also for the murder of the president?

The only answer that can be made is that (1) Officer Tippit was scheduled to be murdered by someone in the conspiracy which included some members of the Dallas Police Department, and (2) Lee Harvey Oswald was the selected "patsy," as he shouted to the press media the day before he was murdered by the same conspiracy.

Summarizing the testimony of the Dallas police revealed the undeniable fact that the Dallas police had in their possession the "Hidell" name card prior to the arrest of Lee Harvey Oswald. The proof of this statement can be readily seen when any investigator analyzes Com. Exh. No. 2003, pages 78, 81, 91, 100; Com. Exh. No. 2160 with 7H187-188, 288; 6H438; 7 H180, 439; 10H295; 300-03. The evidence is overwhelming that the Dallas police never obtained the "'Hidell" card from Oswald's person or from his Berkley Street room. (75a.)

Neither the FBI nor the U.S. Secret Service knew of Oswald's "association" with "Hidell" until the following day after his arrest. In fact, the Secret Service did not know the connection until November 24th! (76.)

The FBI has testified that Oswald wrote the name of "Hidell" on the money order sent to Klein's for the purchase of a rifle, but their statement is self-serving since no independent handwriting experts have ever seen that signature. The FBI has admitted they removed the microfilms belonging to Klein's which contain the "Hidell" signature. Why? To prevent the overthrow of the Government? Was national security involved?

Although the Commission alleged that Oswald not only purchased an Italian Mannlicher-Carcano rifle but also received it at his Dallas leased post office box, there is absolutely no evidence to support their charge. There is no evidence published by the Commission in either its "Report" or "Hearings" that proved that Klein's, assuming they did forward the rifle to a man named "Hidell" in Dallas, Texas, ever obtained a receipt from the Dallas, Texas, Post Office which contained the box leased by Oswald. There is no receipt of such a delivery and it is common everyday practice, under post office rules, that where a package is addressed to a post office box, no person, other than the box holder, can be given mail or packages addressed to the lessee of that box. The Klein rifle package, under postal regulations, should have been returned to Klein's as "addressee unknown," and it was common practice of Klein's to enter in its business records such a return. That is the reason why the Klein's microfilms and records pertaining to the "Hidell" rifle were confiscated by the FBI. However, the FBI never confiscated the Zapruder films owned by "Life"; for "Life" is a whale and Klein's a minnow.

There is proof beyond a reasonable doubt that the Post Office officials and the FBI had positive knowledge that Lee Harvey Oswald [never] received any type of rifle from Klein's. The FBI had full knowledge of every piece of mail, every type of package, and the name of the sender, mailed to Oswald's box number, 2915, from the time he rented the box in April 1962 until the time he cancelled the lease, in May 1963. According to the Commission the rifle was ordered and delivered to "Hidell" in March 1963. However, what the Commission suppressed from the American people is the evidence that one of the men who kept that surveillance was none other than Inspector Holmes. He never testified that he ever saw any type of package delivered to the Oswald post office box. (77.) When he was not around, other

FBI informers kept tabs on what type of mail was placed in that box.

The Commission's concealment of evidence proving Oswald never purchased or received an Italian Carcano rifle from Klein's can be found in Com. Doc. No. 344 in the National Archives. This document is a statement given to the U. S. Secret Service by Mrs. Marina Oswald that her husband had a rifle in her home in February 1963; that that rifle was the only rifle ever possessed or owned by Lee Oswald. This rifle was "either on a shelf or standing up in the corner," and that rifle never had on it a telescopic sight.

Mrs. Oswald's statement was substantiated by testimony from visitors to her home where the rifle was seen in either a closet or standing up in a corner, prior to March 1963. Those witnesses testified that they had not seen a rifle with a telescopic sight attached to it. As the Commission has stated that they accepted Mrs. Oswald's testimony as being truthful and accurate, therefore it necessarily follows that the rifle in her home, the only one she had ever seen, the only one she stated was "wrapped in a blanket" in the Paine's garage, was not the rifle given to the FBI by the Dallas police. When that knowledge is supplemented by the evidence that the FBI had kept a surveillance for the entire period of Oswald's lease, then the only answer, under law, is that Oswald never purchased or received any type of rifle.

One of the hinges of the platform constructed by the Commission to convict Oswald of the murder of President Kennedy was their accusation that his "palm print" was found on the underside of the Italian rifle. There is not a single iota of evidence to support that accusation. The evidence proved beyond a reasonable doubt that there were no Oswald fingerprints or palm prints ever taken from that rifle. As a matter of fact and law, there were no prints of any kind.

The Commission has said there were prints that were identified as Lee Harvey Oswald's. The evidence revealed that one of three agencies were lying: (1) The FBI; (2) Lt. Day of the Dallas Police Department (3) the Warren Commission; and (4) a combination of 1, 2, or 3. To locate the perjurers, let the record speak!

A rifle was found at 1:22 p.m. which was first identified as a

7.65 German Mauser with a "brownish-black sling" and a telescopic sight. No officer who saw that rifle on the 6th floor disputed Capt. Fritz's statement that the rifle was a German Mauser. After handling this weapon with his bare hands, the captain worked the bolt and a live bullet was ejected from the rifle chamber. No ammunition clip was ever found by any police searcher, as proved by police statements and FBI testimony. The captain then gave this German Mauser to Lt. Day, who proceeded to take it to the police laboratory where he sought fingerprints. He retained the rifle until 11:45 p.m., when he forwarded an Italian Mannlicher-Carcano rifle to the FBI Laboratory in Washington D.C.

What occurred during the fingerprinting process is known to only one man, Lt. Day; for his accomplishments, as enunciated by the Commission, have made him the world's outstanding fingerprint expert. This fabulous expert (?) was able to locate with his naked eyesight some fragmentary nonidentifiable fingerprints on the rifle. Then, using only the most rudimentary equipment of the Dallas Police Department, he saw a palm print of sufficient clarity and size for him to identify it as belonging to Lee Harvey Oswald.

After he found those fingerprints and the one palm print, the efficient (?) police officer took only the pictures of the fingerprints but not of the palm print. (78.) That is what he said, and he was so conscious of his duty to secure evidence that he placed tape over unidentifiable fingerprints but none over the palm print seen only by himself. (79.) No fingerprints of Fritz's were ever found by either Lt. Day or the FBI despite the fact that the captain handled the rifle in several places when he was photographed by the news media.

An Italian 6.5 Carcano rifle, with a telescopic sight mounted on it, was received from the Dallas police by the FBI, who then turned it over to the Number 1 fingerprint expert, Mr. Latona–an expert of 30-plus years. Both the police and the FBI agreed that the fragments of fingerprints were worthless and could not be identified as belonging to Oswald. Thus, the controversy relates to the identity of an "alleged" Oswald palm print.

Deliberately overlooked by the Commission was the standard practice of all major police departments, including Dallas, that fingerprints on all murder weapons must be photographed for evidence in a criminal trial. (79a.) Unless the police could produce not only the latent print or seeable print on the weapon itself in open court so that they would be available for examination, no judge would accept the "latent" print as being true and accurate. If that not be the rule, then any print, at any time taken before or after the commission of the crime, would be used to "frame" the accused.

However, according to the Commission, they were not bound by the "basic principles of American justice," and one can see their interpretation of that ringing phrase when one reads the testimony of the FBI fingerprint expert, Mr. Latona. Under oath Mr. Latona swore that the rifle given to him by the Dallas police lieutenant had no identifiable prints of any kind, fingerprints or palm prints! (80.) If the reader will turn to the illustrated section, he or she will see Lt. Day carrying the rifle in his bare hands with fingers grasping the rifle barrel. Capt. Fritz can also be seen grasping the same rifle by both the barrel and the stock, but the FBI found neither Lt. Day's or Capt. Fritz's fingerprints! The Commission was now in a quandary, for someone was committing flagrant perjury. To charge the FBI with perjury was out of question, for the entire investigation was being held under their auspices; to charge Lt. Day was to admit that the Commission had no evidence to link Oswald with that rifle. (81.) The Commission therefore created out of thin air a new principle of fingerprinting. The Commission said that Lt. Day had created such a feat of fingerprinting that when he "lifted" the palm print from the underside of the rifle "there was no trace of the print on the rifle itself when it was examined by Mr. Latona." (82.)

This fabricated statement by the Commission was used by that body [to prevent anyone] from charging either party with perjury. To the distress of the Commission Mr. Latona refused to abide by the Commission's asinine theory of the vanishing "lifted" print, for he testified that not only did he fail to see a palm print on that rifle but that no "lifting" had ever been attempted by any person. (83.) Thus, Mr. Latona's testimony was in direct conflict with Lt. Day's, who testified that "even after the 'lifting' he could still see the palm print on the underside of the barrel of the gun." (84.) Who lied?

A historian must make some effort to solve this irreconcilable testimony and must render his judgment, for the palm print is the Commission's major case against Oswald. The only manner in which the Commission could tie Oswald to the murder of President Kennedy was to have Oswald's prints upon that weapon. Without it, Oswald was innocent; with it, a link, but only a link to a guilty verdict.

A superficial reading of the "Report" would lead one to assume that this mysterious "palm print" was photographed by Lt. Day and forwarded to the FBI's Mr. Latona. But, this is not so. Mr. Latona testified that he received the alleged palm-print photograph not the same night it was taken, not with the same package that contained the Italian rifle, but received it seven (7) days after Lt. Day said he took the photograph. Then why did the Lt. withhold that photograph for 7 days? Furthermore, Lt. Day admitted he withheld all information of that "palm print" for the period of four (4) days! (85.) What was the reason?

The answer can be found in Volume 4, pages 261-63 where the Lt. admitted that he could not identify any palm print or fingerprints on that rifle as belonging to Lee Harvey Oswald. (86.)

Again, let us look at the record. Buried deep, deep, deep within the numerous volumes of the "Hearings" is a statement by Lt. Day that he never made a photograph of the palm print. Lt. Day and the Commission either lied during his testimony, in his affidavits, or statements to the FBI. The testimony by Lt. Day revealed that, at approximately 8 p.m. on the night of the assassination, he made three photographs of the fragmented, unidentifiable fingerprints, but at that time he did not photograph the "identifiable" palm print. (87.) Nearly 90 minutes later the Lt. decided to photograph the same worthless prints, but again he "forgot" to photograph the "palm print." (88.) However, the time he "lifted" the palm print was at the 8 p.m. photographing session. (88a.) Thus, Lt. Day took photographs twice, and then he sent the rifle to the FBI at about 11:45 p.m. Lt. Day also swore that when the rifle was forwarded to the FBI in Washington D.C. at that near-midnight hour, he "could still see the palm print on the rifle." (89.)

Was the police officer's statement true relating to the 9:30 and 11:45 p.m. testimony? Of course not! Lt. Day swore that at 9:30

and at 11:45 p.m. the palm print was visible but, according to the Commission, when Lt. Day "lifted" the palm print at 8:00 p.m. it had disappeared. Thus, on the face of all the evidence, the Commission was calling its chief and only witness to the "palm print" a liar, a perjurer. On Page 123 of the "Report" Lt. Day made the palm print vanish by "lifting"; on the other hand, Lt. Day testified that it was still visible at both 9:30 and 11:45 p.m. when he forwarded the rifle to the FBI, who received it within 5 hours after it left Dallas, Texas. (90.) Naturally, the Commission deliberately overlooked Lt. Day's confession to the FBI that he could not identify the fingerprints or palm print. (91.)

The solution to the "palm print" leads directly to the overwhelming evidence that the Commission willfully, deliberately, and knowingly accepted evidence that was manufactured by the Dallas Police Department. For the Commission knew how the Oswald "palm print" was obtained. A study of the alleged Oswald palm print revealed it was a "plant" by the Dallas police. For Com. Exh. No. 638-40, alleged to be Oswald's palm print, revealed the fact that the palm print is absolutely flat. Any fingerprint expert worth his black ink knows prints taken from the underside of a round rifle barrel would be curved, not flat! The roundness would have distorted the image of the print and thus be unidentifiable. (See note 29, above.)

Mr. Latona's testimony, plus that of the other fingerprint experts from the FBI relating to this "palm print," definitely referred to a "flat" palm print. Not a single fingerprint expert, summoned by the Commission, testified and swore under oath that that palm print was Lee H. Oswald's–except Lt. Day of the Dallas Police Department. The evidence is conclusive that at no time prior, during, or after the murder did the Dallas police or any other police agency, local, state, or federal, photograph or lift Oswald's "palm print." Thus, the question remains: "How did the Dallas police 'obtain' Oswald's print?"

Since Lt. Day testified that he had not photographed the palm print at any time on November 22nd, then how did the Dallas police have available an Oswald palm print to mail to the FBI on November 29, 1963? The answer is self-evident, for Oswald's palm print was taken in Captain Fritz's office at 6:00 p.m. on November 22, 1963, and was retaken at 8:55 p.m. (1) It was those prints that were sent to the FBI seven days after the murder (92); (2) the police submitted to the Commission Oswald's flat palm print taken from the carton on the 6th floor.

The rifle palm print sent to the FBI was as phony as the rifle. (See note 29.)

One of the allegations in this paragraph of the indictment against Oswald was that fibers found on the rifle matched Oswald's shirt. The Commission did not say the fibers did come from his shirt but that they "most probably" came from his shirt. Under the rules of American justice, no man can be convicted of evidence labeled "most probably." There is no positive statement by the FBI Laboratory that upheld the Commission's "most probable" statement connecting the shirt fibers to Oswald's shirt. (93.)

To buttress the "evidence" against Oswald, the Commission published several photographs which they said clearly connected Oswald with the Italian rifle. The Commission accepted as authentic a photograph said to have been taken by the accused's wife on March 31, 1963. (94.) As per their custom, the Commission perverted her statement that she took only one picture of her husband and extended it to cover two pictures, for Oswald is shown in two photographs in two different poses. In her statement to the FBI and Secret Service, she stated she had never seen (1) a rifle with a telescopic sight mounted on the rifle; and (2) she had never seen her husband with a pistol. (95.) The famous, or infamous, "Life" photograph showed Oswald with a pistol on his hip and the Commission said that the pictured pistol was the one he used to murder Tippit. (96.)

This photograph published by "Life," under the principles of American law, would be branded, and it is, an outright "fake"! In a letter to the Commission, "Life" admitted that the "photograph" was a fraud, since the editor admitted that his photography department had "retouched" the original in such a manner as to destroy the picture's authenticity. (97.) Knowing that Mrs. Oswald's testimony concerning the photograph was suspect because she made that statement under coercion, the Commission summoned the FBI photographic expert, Mr. Shaneyfelt. He flatly refused to testify that the alleged Italian rifle, Com. Exh. No. 139, allegedly used to commit the murder, was the identical rifle shown in "Life." (98). Instead of summoning a few more experts to give their opinions, the Commission published a blatant lie that the rifle shown in the "Life" photograph was the "same" rifle found on the 6th floor and used to murder President Kennedy.

Here again, an investigator attempting to locate the truth must go deep into the "Hearings" and to the files in the National Archives to find it. As previously stated, Mrs. Marina Oswald testified that her husband never possessed a rifle with a telescopic sight. Her statements were substantiated by the FBI informant, Mrs. Paine, and other visitors to the Oswald home. When the Dallas police showed Oswald the "photograph," he immediately proclaimed it a fake. (99.) His denial would be expected, so the historian and investigator must proceed further.

The police officers who "found" those photographs are "known" and "unknown." The man the Commission said "found" them denied it. [As with] most of the evidence against Oswald, the police were always available to supply the ingredient that tightened the noose around his neck. (100.)

The conduct of the American newspapers in publishing this photograph was not only an act of fraud but also revealed the depth of its corruption in its interpretation of "freedom of the press." That phrase does not mean irresponsibility or license. That phrase is a two-way street, and when the two-way street is 'closed for repairs," then the press itself is responsible for the creation of a controlled press that was brought about by the same "free" press.

The method by which the Oswald "photograph" came into the hands of the Dallas police is confusing and contradictory. The "Associated Press" seems to be the culprit that supplied many of the newspapers, but they in turn said they received it from either the Detroit "Free Press" or the Dallas "Morning News." (101.) Chapter II has pointed out the various discrepancies between the "AP" photographs and the Commission's "rifle."

The admission that they published retouched photographs in the N.Y. "Times," "Newsweek," Detroit "Free Press," "Life" and other users of that photograph did not bother the Commission. Of course, the fact that in a court of law the photograph would not have been submitted to the jury because of its "fakery" was not involved, according to the Commission, since they were not operating under any established principles of law. Suffice it to say neither did Hitler or Stalin, or Franco, or Tojo, or any past, present, and future dictator. Of course, if the commissioners had accepted the advice of the editor of "Life," they would have solved the question immediately. The "Life" editor informed the counsel general to use a little "saliva" (spit) on the faked photograph and this would bring forth the original! (102.)

In this sarcastic reply to the Commission can be seen the attitude of the most powerful press lord to his peasants, to what the editor thought of the "prestige" of the commissioners, and to what he thought was the epitaph for the president of the United States:

"Use a little saliva (spit)!"

There is no dispute regarding the camera that snapped the photographs; it was not Comm. Exh. No. 137. Oswald's wife testified she never saw that camera at any time in Oswald's possession. (102a.) There is a statement by the FBI that Oswald's brother identified Com. Exh. 137, but strangely there is no testimony by Oswald's brother affirming the FBI statement. At no time did the Commission ask the brother to identify Com. Exh. 137. In a law court the FBI statement is valueless, since no legal witness identified the camera. The Commission used Oswald's wife as the sole witness to her own statement that she snapped a photograph, but she herself swore that the camera which allegedly took that photograph was not the camera she used! She further testified that she took only one picture. Thus, where did the Commission, the police, and the FBI obtain another photograph which the Commission used as part of the net around Oswald? Oswald's statement that the photograph was a "fake" has greater validity than the Commission's allegation against him. (102b.)

That photograph was a fraud, a forgery like that used to convict Dreyfus. For by accepting that forgery which was committed, as in the Dreyfus Affaire, by a government bureau to convict an innocent man as the "sole and exclusive killer" of the president, as in the Dreyfus Affaire it permitted the conspirators to go free. The French also used the same phrasing: "It would not be in the interest of the French government to establish the innocence of the accused."[18]

The final allegation in the Commission's second paragraph of its indictment against Oswald stated that the rifle was always in his possession "from the time of its purchase until the day of the assassination." This allegation is nothing more than a bald-faced lie, for the evidence is conclusive that Oswald never received any Italian rifle from Klein's. The only evidence relating to the rifle is Mrs. Marina Oswald's statement that she saw the "stock" of a rifle. (103.) This is of no legal value, for she testified that at no time did she ever see her husband ever handle, possess, or own any type of rifle with a telescopic sight. In this case, was she lying or telling the truth? If there be some witness who can corroborate Mrs. Oswald, a disinterested witness as they say in law, then a court of law would accept her statements. Therefore, is her testimony corroborated by a disinterested witness?

---

[18] Marks is perhaps indebted to Mark Lane in drawing a parallel between the "Dreyfus Affaire" and the "Oswald Affaire." For example, in a debate with Joseph Ball, Herman Selvin, and A. L. Wirin held at Beverly Hills High School on December 4, 1964, Lane was quoted as saying: "And I know that the day will come in America, as it came in France, twelve years after the conviction of Dreyfus. The whole liberal establishment and the rest of the establishment said, 'guilty, guilty, guilty,' for twelve years. Dreyfus was not guilty when the government said it. Dreyfus was not guilty when the Minister of Justice said it. Dreyfus was not guilty when the liberals in the Parliament of France said it any more than he was guilty twelve years later when the French government had the courage and the honor to reverse its position." The remarks about liberals who failed to come to the aid of Dreyfus—or to fight the good fight against the Warren Commission—were made in pointed response to A. L. Wirin, Chief Counsel for the American Civil Liberties Union in Los Angeles, who held that the Warren Commission's conviction of Oswald was somehow justified. See the *Los Angeles Free Press*, December 18, 1964, for various quotations from this debate. It's also possible that Marks' deliberations over what he refers to as the "Dreyfus Affaire," the "Oswald Affaire," and the "Tippet Affaire" led him to adopt the name "Bureau of International Affairs" for his publishing imprint.

From the testimony, given under oath to the Commission, the answer must be affirmative. The FBI testified that when they examined the blanket which was allegedly used to hide the "stock" of the rifle, the blanket had no indentations showing that a telescopic sight had been on that blanket; and also, that there were no oil stains, which should have been on the blanket since the rifle they received from the Dallas police was in a "well-oiled condition." (104.) Mrs. Paine, who kept the FBI informed of the activity of Lee Oswald, not only never saw the "stock" of that rifle in the blanket–although she, or her husband, was in and out of their garage every day–but she never saw a rifle with a telescopic sight. When Oswald's wife showed the police where the blanket was located in the Paine garage, it was discovered to be in open sight of anyone who came into the garage; it was not hidden under other garage-kept family items.

Mr. and Mrs. Paine both testified that they never saw any rifle, or shape of a rifle, or parts of a rifle, in any of the Oswald's belongings when the Paine's helped move the Oswald family from their New Orleans' home to the Paine home in Irving, Texas. The Paines testified that either one or the other handled all the cartons and duffle bags used to move the Oswalds and they saw no rifle, or parts of one. (105.) Their testimony shattered, beyond a reasonable doubt, the Commission's allegations that Oswald took a rifle from his New Orleans home to Irving, Texas.

It is a rule of the law of evidence that a prosecutor cannot accept part of the witness's testimony and reject that which contradicts his overall case against the accused. The Commission time and time again reiterated their acceptance of the truthfulness of their witness, Mrs. Marina Oswald. Therefore, the Commission, under law, is bound to accept all her testimony, especially that testimony which is corroborated by other witnesses.

Thus, in summarizing the law and the evidence relating to the Commission's allegations in paragraph 2 of the Commission's indictment, Lee Harvey Oswald would be found "not guilty." The evidence proved beyond a reasonable doubt that Oswald received no Klein's rifle known as Com. Exh. No. 139. The evidence proved beyond a reasonable doubt that there was no Oswald "palm print" on that Italian rifle. The evidence proved beyond a reasonable doubt that that rifle was never used, in any manner, as a lethal weapon. The evidence proved beyond a reasonable doubt that the "Life" photographs were fraudulent and manufactured. The evidence proved beyond a reasonable doubt that the cartridges found on the 6th floor were never discharged from that rifle.

A motion to instruct the jury to return a verdict of "not guilty" in the case of the Warren Commission vs. Lee Harvey Oswald as "the sole and exclusive assassin of President Kennedy" would be granted by any impartial criminal court judge who professed a belief in the "basic principles of American justice."

And such a motion would be upheld by the United States Supreme Court.

CHAPTER IV

THE INVISIBLE PACKAGE

As one compares the Commission's allegations with that of the testimony in the "Hearings" and the documents in the National Archives, it seems that the Commission has adopted the suicidal policy of the lemmings. At the final session of the Commission there was no doubt that Lee Harvey Oswald was innocent of "being the sole and exclusive assassin of President Kennedy." As a matter of fact and law, he was also innocent of committing the actual murder. The Commission had in its possession a minimum of eight major pieces of evidence given to them by the Federal Bureau of Investigation that Oswald was innocent. They had the official survey and report of the United States Secret Service. They had the uncontradicted testimony of the physicians from both the Parkland and Bethesda Hospitals. Yet, the Commission proceeded as a moth to the flame with the same result–its destruction.

The Commission's third paragraph in its indictment against Oswald introduced a new concept in Anglo-American jurisprudence. The age-old maxim of American law that a person must be guilty beyond a reasonable doubt was reduced to conviction by a "preponderance of the evidence." Guilt, under our law, cannot be determined by a "consensus," a "majority," or "preponderance" of the evidence. Laws cannot be changed to suit the convenience of those who govern a democracy with the consent of the governed. In other words, you cannot change the rules of the ballgame in the middle of the game.

The reason why the rules of the game were changed by the Commission is that they knew they had no evidence to support paragraph 3 of the indictment. In the place of evidence the Commission employed words. Not evidence, but mere words that suggested or implied certain activity by Oswald, and with those words, attempted to connect Oswald with the murder.

In the third paragraph, the Commission had the legal obligation and duty to prove beyond a reasonable doubt that Oswald transferred the Italian rifle, Com. Exh. No. 139, from the garage in Irving, Texas, to the 6th floor of the Book Depository. The Commission had neither witnesses nor evidence but they did have words which were used to "prove" their own statement.

The prosecution, in a trial of a person charged with murder in the first degree, may legally comment and give his own interpretation of the evidence placed before the jury; but no prosecutor has the legal right to utter statements to the jury which are not supported by the evidence. He may make inferences, but those inferences, in turn, must be supported by facts given by witnesses. Nor can the prosecutor pervert those statements. If a witness has testified that he saw no rifle in a package, or if he testified that the package was not large enough to contain a rifle, no trial judge would permit the prosecutor to say there was a rifle in that package. Thus, where the testimony of the witness is that a package carried by the accused was a brown paper bag "like you get out of a grocery store," it may not be interpreted to mean "a bag made out of wrapping paper and tape." Nor will a judge permit a prosecutor to say that a bag 26" long was, in his opinion, really 38.4 inches long. This twisting of evidence by the Commission would not be permitted under any rule of law in any state or federal court.

The testimony of the only witnesses who saw Oswald with a package on the morning of November 22, 1963, was Mr. W. Frazier, a fellow-worker of Oswald, and Frazier's sister, Mrs. Randle. The Commission said that Oswald returned to his rented room in Irving, Texas to pick up the rifle he used to murder the president. However, according to the accused's wife, Marina, Oswald came home in an attempt at a reconciliation. Naturally, the Commission decided that since Mrs. Oswald was Russian and could not understand the meaning of reconciliation, they said that she did not know the real reason why her husband returned to Irving, Texas. The night of November 21st was the night, said the Commission, that Oswald "snuck" into the garage, between 8 and 9 p.m., and wrapped up the rifle in a self-made paper bag held together by tape stolen from the Depository shipping room. There is no evidence to support those charges, and without that evidence no self-respecting American jury would accept those words.

How did this 8-lb. rifle in a package move from the Paine garage to the Book Depository? What does the evidence reveal in the "Hearings"? The sworn testimony of the only witnesses who saw Oswald with a package in his hands on the morning of November 22nd were Mr. Wesley Frazier and his sister, Mrs. Randle, Oswald's next door neighbors. (106.) Mrs. Randle, while serving her brother breakfast, looked out the window and saw Oswald crossing the street toward her brother's automobile carrying a package. Asked what type of package he was carrying, she said: "He was carrying a package in sort of a heavy brown bag, heavier than a grocery bag, it looked to me." The Commission then deceived the American people by converting her answer which related to the thickness of the paper, not to the weight of the contents of the bag. The next person to see this "brown paper bag" was her brother and Oswald's co-worker, Mr. Frazier. He saw Oswald place the package on the back seat of Frazier's automobile. (107.) During the ride to work, Frazier asked Oswald what was in the package. Oswald replied: "Curtain rods." (108.) The Commission then asked Frazier if he thought Oswald was lying and he replied: "Oswald never lied to me before, so I never had any reason to doubt his word." (109.) No severe cross-examination shook their testimony.

The cross-examination dealt mainly with the length of the "brown paper bag." Mrs. Randle, when given a paper bag which the aide said was the actual length of the Italian dissembled rifle, rejected the bag proffered to her as the actual bag she had seen Oswald carry. The aide then had her fold the bag to the size she had seen. When measured by the aide, the length was only 28-1/2." (110.) Having failed to destroy Mrs. Randle, the Commission directed its fire against her brother, Wesley Frazier. He testified that the length of the bag was between 24 and 26 inches. (111.) Thus, it was self-evident that any dissembled rifle, 34.8 inches long, could not fit within a paper bag not more than 28-1/2" long. The Commission, in their attempt to discredit both witnesses, directed the FBI to give them lie tests in the hope the two witnesses could be charged and convicted of perjury. Every state and federal court, including the U.S. Supreme Court, has ruled that a lie test is of no value in a trial. The Warren Commission admitted the same. Senator Robert A. Taft, "Mr. Conservative" of the Republican Party, on the floor of the Senate stated that he would never accept a lie test to prove or disprove a person's statement.

This "lie test" was used by the Commission on every witness who gave evidence that stated that Oswald was innocent; none were given to such "key" witnesses as: Mrs. Markham (she openly admitted she was a perjurer), Mr. Brennan, Mr. Whaley, Mrs. Bledsoe, Mrs. Paine, Mrs. Marina Oswald, Chief of Police Curry, Police Captain Fritz, Lt. Day, Detective Studebaker, Comdr. Humes, FBI Agent Hosty, District Attorney Wade, Asst. D.A. Bill Alexander, Sheriff Decker, any of the FBI and Secret Service involved in the Bullet No. 399 "episode," Billy Lovelady, Sgt. Dean, Officer McDonald, the "hero" who "captured" Oswald, Capt. Westbrook, Motorcyclist Officers Hutson and Griffin; none, not a single one of the FBI agents who were accused by the U.S. Secret Service agents of perverting the Secret Service agents' statements they gave to those FBI agents; none of FBI agents who were accused by witnesses under oath that those agents also perverted the witnesses' statements; none of the police officers of the Dallas police radio broadcasting system who submitted false transcripts of the broadcasts made concerning the President Kennedy, Oswald, and Tippit murders.

Long before Mr. Frazier gave his testimony, he showed the FBI agents the space the package occupied on the back seat of his automobile. The space was measured and the agents found the space to be 27 inches. (112.) Frazier completed the demolition of the Commission's case when he testified that the width of the package was between 4 and 5 inches. (113.) Since the alleged disassembled rifle with a mounted telescopic sight would be in excess of the width and length oi the bag seen by Mrs. Randle and Mr. Frazier, common sense, not legal knowledge, dictated the fact that the Commission's allegations were false. (113a.)

Buried in the "Hearings" is an admission by the Commission that they had manufactured evidence to support their "guilty" verdict against Oswald. This "brown paper bag" shown to witnesses had been manufactured by "special agents of the FBI Dallas Office"! Where the agents obtained the tape and paper was not commented upon by the Commission but it is known that the agents simply took it from the shipping room of the Book Depository. The FBI Laboratory testified that the "original" bag had been destroyed by chemicals used by the Laboratory when they were testing the bag. (114.) The Commission and its 26 legal aides, being versed in law, knew that the FBI had in its possession the original size of the bag in their records, but at no time did the Commission ask the Bureau to testify as to the length and width of the bag. The reason why the "bag" was "manufactured" is because the Commission had, prior to the commencement of the examination of Mr. Frazier and Mrs. Randle, the actual bag found by the FBI in the Irving Post Office! (115.)

In a court of law, the Commission's statement that Oswald carried a disassembled rifle into the Book Depository at 8 a.m. on November 22, 1963 had as much legal validity as a statement that Oswald carried a baby elephant under his armpit with the baby's right foot cupped in his right palm!

The allegation by the Commission that Oswald stole wrapping paper and tape from the Depository's shipping room was an outright lie since the only witness summoned by the Commission, Mr. West, the shipping room foreman, testified that Oswald did no such thing. In addition, Mr. West instructed the Commission in shipping room procedure by informing them that the tape would have to come through the tape machine in a wet condition. The Commission conceded that Oswald was not so stupid as to walk around the building, or Dallas, or Irving, Texas, carrying wet tape in his pockets for a period of three days. (116.)

If Oswald had remained alive to be tried for the murder of President Kennedy, his key witnesses would be the agents of the Federal Bureau of Investigation and the U.S. Secret Service. The official FBI "Reports," Volumes 1 to 5, suppressed by the Commission in the Warren "Report," and the 26 volumes of the "Hearings," contains the most significant statement regarding this "brown paper bag." The FBI reported that the rifle they received from the Dallas police was "received in a well-oiled condition." The same Bureau also received from that highly efficient (?) police department a "brown paper bag" which, the police said, had contained that rifle.

There is no mystery, today, why the Warren Commission deliberately refused to publish the 5-volume FBI report, for that report filled the Commission with dismay. The FBI tests revealed that although the rifle was received in a "well-oiled condition" the Bureau found that this bag did not have any rifle markings, rifle abrasions, or scratches either on the inside or outside of that mysteriously "found" bag. In addition, no oil stains, wet or dry, were ever found on the blanket that was supposed to have contained that rifle when it was "lying" in the Paine garage; nor were there any indentations of a rifle or telescopic sight in or on that blanket. (117.)

The FBI was taking this method to warn the Commission, prior to its issuance of the Warren Report, that the bag sent to them by the Dallas police was a "plant," a fake; for a rifle received in a "well-oiled condition," under physical science, would have to leave oil stains and markings within that bag. (118.) There being none, the Commission knew the police had lied.

This immensely important brown paper bag, according to Lt. Day was found on the 6th floor "near the window where the gun may have been fired." (119.) To obtain the truth the investigator must backtrack to the original starting point, Wesley Frazier. He testified that the package he saw Oswald carry was a package or bag as "it is right as you get out of the grocery store ... you have seen some of these brown paper sacks, you can obtain from any, most of the stores, some varieties, but it was a package just roughly two feet long." (120.) Nowhere in the testimony of either Mr. Frazier or Mrs. Randle is there a statement that the package they saw was a package made of wrapping paper and tape. Thus, the Commission's statement, in a court of law, was an outright lie.

From an investigating standpoint it is evident that the Commission willfully attempted to confuse the various witnesses concerning this "brown paper bag." In fact, unless the investigator read the testimony carefully he would not see or read the "under what shell is the pea" tactics of the Commission. The testimony revealed that the Commission constantly "used" two types of bags, namely, the one actually seen and found by various police and sheriff officers, and the unseen and unfound bag seen only by Lt. Day. What is known beyond a reasonable doubt is that Bonnie Ray Williams, an employee, ate his lunch on the 6th floor between 12 noon and 12:30 p.m. His food was contained in a lunch bag. That is the only bag ever found on the 6th floor.

Lt. Day, the Commission's key witness on behalf of the Commission, was a policeman who collected "evidence" with the energy of a magpie. When he received this bag he efficiently (?) wrote a label: "A handmade bag of wrapping paper and tape was found in the southeast corner of the building within a few feet of the cartridge case. Found next to the sixth-floor window fired from. May have been used to carry the gun, signed: Lt. J. C. Day." (121.) This paragon of police efficiency failed to (1) write the date he saw this bag; (2) the time when he was given it; and (3) the finder of the bag. In a court of law this label was not worth the ink used to write those words. (122.)

According to Lt. Day he testified that the bag was found within a few feet of a cartridge case. He did not find it but some unidentified person gave him wrapping paper with tape on it that was 38.4 inches long. It must be recalled that Lt. Day arrived on the 6th floor nearly 15 minutes after the German Mauser was found by Deputy Sheriffs Boone and Weitzman. Prior to his arrival Deputy Sheriffs Boone, Craig, Weitzman, and Mooney had searched the entire area where the German Mauser was found, and that included the space between the cartons and the windows where they found the three cartridge cases.

This 38.4 inch grocery bag was not seen by those deputies. Nor was the bag seen by Sgt. Hill or Officer Hicks. (123.) They all saw 3 cartridges each less than 4 and 3/4 inches in size lying near the cartons, but none saw that 3 foot "bag." Several officers testified that they saw a small lunch bag but no 3-foot grocery bag. Their testimony confirmed Bonnie Ray Williams' testimony that he left his lunch bag on the 6th floor after finishing his lunch at 12:30 p.m. Thus, the testimony of five experienced officers was that there was no 38.4-inch "brown paper bag" at the time Lt. Day was given this alleged bag,

Now upon the 6th floor strode, with the efficiency of an inebriated ant, Lt. Day, and a retinue of efficient (?) policemen: Det. Studebaker, the official photographer, Det. Sims, and Police Officers Montgomery and Brewer. The police photographer commenced taking pictures as fast as his finger could flick the switches but, somehow, although he took pictures of the cartridges and the cartridge by itself, his camera failed to photograph a 38.4-inch grocery bag. What a camera, what a photographer, what a farce!

Policeman Montgomery testified that "Lt. Day and Detective Studebaker came up and took pictures and everything" and that he (Montgomery) "didn't pick it up; I believe Det. Studebaker did." (124.) However, according to Montgomery's partner, Montgomery did pick up the bag, not Studebaker. (125.) To contradict both of them, Det. Studebaker said he picked up a "piece of paper, doubled over," but that when he picked it up he had no idea of its length or width, but he did dust it, and "they took it down there and sent it to Washington." (126.) The Commission did not have the common sense to ask Studebaker who he meant by "they"? Was it Lt. Day? No, for Det. Studebaker personally knew his superior officer, Lt. Day. The word "they," in English, is plural; hence, at least two policemen were involved. Why two or more police agents were necessary to carry a "piece of paper, doubled over," weighing all of three ounces, was never explained. But those two policemen were not Montgomery, Brewer, or Johnson; for Det. Studebaker knew them personally. Again, the same pattern is repeated with unidentified policemen being used to conveniently present to the Commission damaging "evidence" against Oswald.

No one knows, for the Commission could not have the members of that retinue committed for perjury. As to fingerprints, Det. Studebaker testified that "there were none, only 'smudges'." On those "smudges" Studebaker put a piece of tape, "a one-inch piece of tape over it." (127.)

It is important to note that Det. Studebaker testified that he "picked up a piece of paper, doubled over"; not a bag made of wrapping paper and tape the size of 38.4 inches by 6 inches. Since when, in law, does "a piece of paper doubled over" become a bag 38.4 inches in length? Although members of Lt. Day's retinue picked up that paper, none of their fingerprints were on that bag. Furthermore, Com. Exh. No. 628, which is the alleged paper bag, showed four creases, not two as testified to by Studebaker. Who was lying?

The most astonishing testimony was given by Policeman Montgomery, Brewer, and Johnson, who gave conflicting versions. This "bag" was discovered and seen by them prior to the discovery of the rifle, but they already knew that the bag they saw "appeared to be more about the same shape as a rifle case." (128.) However, the FBI testified that there were no indentations or abrasions of any kind on the bag given to them by the Dallas Police Department. (129.) Therefore, when the FBI experts examined that bag under the microscope and saw nothing that indicated a rifle had been wrapped in that bag, how could the Dallas police testify that the bag they "saw" had the shape of a rifle? What an imagination! What a police department!

According to Policeman Johnson, the brown bag was "right in the corner, the southeast corner." The official Commission photograph, which used superimposed dotted lines to show where the bag was supposed to have been found, revealed the fact that the "bag" was in open and full sight, but that it was seen by the Lt. Day retinue after that area had first been searched by six other police agents. It was seen not by the original six police agents, only by those whose testimony was needed by the Warren Commission. A close look at this brown paper bag published in the Report as Com. Exh. No. 628 revealed that it was truly a grocery bag. It is not a "handmade bag of wrapping paper and tape." In a court of law, Com. Exh. No. 628 is a grocery bag, but there is no evidence from the FBI, who examined that bag, that it ever contained a rifle with a telescopic sight. The FBI, as a matter of law, simply testified they received something from the Dallas police, but it was not a bag constructed of "wrapping paper and tape."

Buried in the "Hearings" by the Commission is the testimony of three Dallas policemen and one deputy sheriff, who testified that the bag they saw was a lunch bag. Their testimony was hidden because of the fact that the bag they saw was one used "normally for a lunch sack." It should be presumed that even "lawyers" know that no housewife wraps her husband's lunch in a 3-foot bag; and a lunch bag is not 3-feet long. Of course, some lawyers have never descended to carry their lunch in paper bags; they use brief cases.

The world's greatest fingerprint expert, Lt. Day, also examined the bag for fingerprints. In spite of the fact that Det. Studebaker and one other Dallas cop handled that bag, he never found their prints; nor did Studebaker find any identifiable prints when he dusted the bag, He found "smudges," but no fingerprints. This "bag" was supposedly sent to the FBI Washington D.C. Fingerprint Division and on November 25, 1963, this "same" bag was returned to the Dallas police, and on it was an absolutely legible fingerprint! (130.) Backtracking the evidence, Studebaker testified that when he gave the "bag" to the unknown "they" he saw there was "one little 'ole' piece of print on it" and some tape. However, by the time this "bag" was received in the FBI fingerprint office by an unknown "they," not only had this "little 'ole' print" disappeared but also the tape! Mr. Latona testified uncontradicted. (131.)

Neither Lt. Day nor Det. Studebaker said the bag had any "oil stains, rifle indentation marks, or abrasions"; yet the FBI said the rifle was received in a well-oiled condition. Thus, the answer to the puzzle must be that the "bag" was evidence manufactured by the Dallas Police Department. When Lt. Day examined that bag for fingerprints, he never found a single, solitary print. When the bag was examined by Det. Studebaker, he found no fingerprints, only smudges. Since the Commission accepted the testimony as being truthful, then how did the FBI locate a legible Oswald print? How did both the "little 'ole' print" and tape disappear? (132.) QED, that bag with the little "ole" print and tape was never sent, for the obvious reason that it never existed; and, since it never existed, the bag sent to the FBI was a "plant" by the Dallas Police Department.

That the above statement is true can be found in the testimony given by Dallas Police Officer Hicks. This officer was in charge of all the material evidence found on the 6th floor on November 22, 1963; and, in accordance with the Dallas police procedure, [he] entered on the official police record that evidence. He testified that on that police list record there was no long 38.4-inch brown paper bag ever found on the 6th floor. (133.) In other words, the official Dallas Police Department document relating to the evidence found on the 6th floor on November 22, 1963, called Lt. Day a liar.

Sweeping away the lies committed by some of the members of

the Dallas police it can now be stated, beyond a reasonable doubt, and supported by the Commission itself, that Lee Harvey Oswald, in fact and in law, carried with him into the Depository a grocery bag that contained curtain rods. The Commission had full and complete knowledge of curtain rods in a grocery bag, and the Commission deliberately, knowingly, and willfully concealed this fact from the American people in their efforts to brand Lee Harvey Oswald the "sole and exclusive assassin of President Kennedy."

Buried deep in the National Archives is Com. Exh. No. 205, which informed the Commission that on December 4, 1963 there was a package being held in the Irving, Texas, Post Office for Lee Harvey Oswald, for "postage due." When that package was unwrapped by FBI agents, they found a grocery bag the exact size stipulated by Mr. Wesley Frazier and that bag had indentations matching curtain rods. (134). Unfortunately, the Commission did not ask the FBI what postdate or city postmark was on the pack-age held for "postage due." Was it mailed in Dallas, or Irving, Texas?

The Commission has stated that Oswald "lied" when he informed Mr. Frazier that the package contained "curtain rods." The Commission statement was a lie, since the Commission had uncontradicted testimony that Oswald told the truth. For, buried in the 'Hearings," is the testimony that not only did a Secret Service agent find the curtain rods, but he found them in the company of a Commission aide. These curtain rods were on a shelf in the Paine garage and measured approximately 27-1/2 inches in length. Mr. and Mrs. Paine (the FBI informant on Oswald's life in Dallas) disagreed as to whether the rods belonged to the Paines or to Oswald. There was no disagreement, however, on the fact that on November 22 and 23rd every police agency in Dallas searched that garage and no curtain rods appeared on the material evidence list pertaining to objects in the Paine garage. (135.)

The solution to the "brown paper bag" is herein presented so that some future historian will not suffer a fate worse than ulcers in attempting to solve that mystery. Actually, there is no mystery for there was no "brown paper bag" ever found by the Dallas police on the 6th floor of the Depository. The bag sent to the FBI

Washington Laboratory was nothing more than a plant. Thus, several "brown paper bags" are involved: (1) the one with no fingerprints, "seen" by Lt. Day and his retinue; (2) the one that arrived in Washington D.C. upon which appeared the legible fingerprint or palm print of Oswald; (3) the one found in the Irving Post Office; and (4) the one manufactured by the Dallas FBI Bureau.

Commission Exhibit No. 628 can be one of the following: It cannot be the bag made of (1) number 3 or (2) number 4, "wrapping paper and tape," since the FBI never received any such "bag." It could be number (2), since a legible fingerprint appeared, but who sent that bag to the FBI is not known to man or beast. The only logical solution would be number 3, which is, in reality, number 2. It must be recalled that bag number 2 was received and returned by the FBI to the Dallas police on November 25, 1963. Upon receipt of that number 2 "bag," the Dallas police simply placed it in another package and mailed it to "Lee Harvey Oswald" of Irving, Texas, but deliberately failed to place any stamps on it. Thus, the Irving, Texas Post Office was left "holding the bag" for "postage due." Since this bag had curtain rod indentations upon it, then it follows that Numbers 2 and 3 were one and the same bag. The Warren Commission has kept silent as to its disposition of the Irving, Texas, bag, but the evidence is overwhelming that that "post office bag" was the one used by Oswald to contain his curtain rods.

The evidence proved beyond a reasonable doubt that the "wrapping paper and tape" bag was evidence manufactured by the Dallas police, or the FBI, and used by the Commission as part of its evidence to convict Lee Harvey Oswald. (136.)

At no time did the Warren Commission ever prove beyond a reasonable doubt that Oswald was guilty of their allegations in paragraph III. As a matter of fact and of law, he was innocent beyond a reasonable doubt.

Chapter V

Charades, Prints and Identifications

The greatest number of words used in the Commission's indictment of Lee Harvey Oswald were used in paragraph four. The only true statement in that paragraph is the first half of the first sentence, and that by itself had nothing to do with the unveiling of the president's murderers.

The first sentence in this 4th paragraph simply stated that Oswald handled two of four cartons next to the window from which the Commission asserted the rifle fired three bullets at the president. The concluding portion of that same sentence alleged that he handled a paper bag which, as shown in the previous chapter, was a lie. The evidence proved that the "brown paper bag" was a lunch bag used by a Bonnie Ray Williams, a black employee, to hold food. Thus, the Commission's statement relating to a paper bag is false.

The reference to the 2 of 4 cartons that Oswald's fingerprints were found on it meant, in law, absolutely nothing. Since Oswald was a shipping-room and stock clerk whose work consisted of selecting books from cartons on that 6th floor, there was nothing illegal or mysterious about his fingerprints being on book cartons he had to open to obtain books. The Commission's sinister allegations proved to be very nonsinister. How did the Commission expect Oswald to open cartons? With his toes?

What the Commission actually proved to themselves was that Oswald, on that tragic day, was the world's strongest human. There was a palm print on one carton and a fingerprint on another carton and, with each one of those members of his hand, Lee Harvey Oswald was able to lift a 50-pound carton of books. With the palm of one hand he lifted one 50-pound carton; with the finger of another hand he lifted another carton of the same weight! As one digs into the Warren "Report," it boggles the imagination that a body of 7 intelligent men would sign, with their honor, a "Report" publishing such incredible statements.

One can only gather that the 7 commissioners had only contempt for the intelligence of the American people.

The palm print and fingerprint, each on a different carton, was used by the Commission to prove Oswald used those two cartons for a gun rest. However, the Commission also stated that Oswald concealed himself behind a "shield of cartons" as he crouched behind that two-carton gun rest. The Commission published a picture of that "shield," Com. Exh. No. 723; and as per usual, the Commission fabricated its entire story of the "shield of cartons." The Commission had a devious reason for this "shield of cartons," since the evidence had revealed that Mr. Williams' uncontradicted testimony had him eating his lunch from 12 noon until 12:20 p.m. Oswald had to be hiding somewhere on the 6th floor, concealed from the view of any possible employee wandering onto that floor. The Commission simply created a "shield of cartons" by the use of words. The Commission said that Oswald was last seen from the sight of man between 11:55 a.m. until 12:31-1/2 p.m.

Whether or not he was actually seen at 11:55 a.m. carrying a clipboard walking toward the 6th-floor elevator is subject to great doubt. Assuming that the ex-convict who "gave" that "testimony" was truthful, it meant nothing. What is uncontradicted is that the Commission produced not one single witness who saw Oswald on the 6th floor at any time of the morning between 11:55 a.m. and 12:30 p.m. According to the Commission, not the evidence, Oswald did the following things from 11:55 a.m. until 12:31-1/2 p.m.:

(1) Between 12:22 p. m, and 12:30 he constructed a shield of cartons, consisting of approximately 32 book cartons each having an average weight of 50 pounds. (2) After constructing that "shield" to a height of about 5 1/2', Oswald went to obtain his rifle from a secret hiding place. (3) He then brought that rifle back to his hiding place in front of the S.E. window on the 6th floor. (4) He then jumped over that shield, making him the world's champion high jumper from a standing position, and assembled his rifle. (5) He assembled the disassembled rifle in 6 minutes. (6) He waited until the president's head appeared in his defective telescopic sight, which could be used only by a left-handed man, and by crossing his eyes, sighted in on the intended

victim. (7) As the rifle had no ammunition clip, the "assassin" calmly hand loaded a bullet into the rifle chamber prior to each shot, and, at the end of the 3rd shot, although the president's automobile was out of range, he also calmly loaded a fourth bullet into the rifle. Suddenly realizing that he must get away from that chamber window he (8) ceased firing and flung the rifle with such precision that it flew through the air in an upright position and landed between two cartons which embraced the rifle in the same position. (9) He "wiped" the rifle, upon cease firing, with an invisible rag thus causing his fingerprints to vanish. (10) Having flung the rifle away, Oswald, from a standing position, leaped more than 68 inches in the air and landed on the other side of the "shield." (11) Landing on his feet, Oswald dashed across the entire floor to the stairway and raced down four flights to the 2nd-floor lunch room. (12) He then reached into his pocket, took out a dime, thrust it into the slot, waited for the Coke bottle, got it, pulled the cork, and put the bottle to his mouth when suddenly he was jabbed in the belly by a gun held by a cop.

It can only be said that the 7 commissioners put the Baron Munchhausen stories out of print. As they say in Las Vegas: The Commission gave it to the Baron in spades!

The above is what the Commission would like the American public to believe. The above is what the 7 commissioners said was the truth and nothing but the truth. Yet uncontradicted evidence, both positive and negative, revealed that the Commission's truth was everything "but." The man who destroyed the Commission's theories was none other than that eminent chief of espionage, Mr. Allen Dulles, ex-CIA chief. Inadvertently, the ex-chief exposed the whole plot when he cross-examined Mr. Bonnie Ray Williams, a black employee who testified he ate his lunch on the 6th floor between 12 noon and 12:20 p.m. Mr. Dulles asked this employee four vital questions: (1) Had Mr. Williams seen anyone on the 6th floor between 12 noon and 12:20 p.m.? (2) Had he heard anyone during that period of time? (3) Had he seen anything? (4) Had he heard anything? As one can read, Mr. Dulles was covering both animate and inanimate objects. The answer to all four questions was a definite "no." (137.)

It is significant that Williams testified he left his place at the 6th-floor window "because it was so quiet there" and that from his position he could see the area near the S.E. window from which the Commission alleged the rifleman was stationed. (3H169-73.) Thus, the time limit to construct that "shield of cartons" was not, as the Commission implied, 30 minutes but less than 3 minutes. Lawyers stress the fact that a witness's testimony is immeasurably strengthened if other witnesses can corroborate that testimony. Mr. Williams had his testimony concerning the lunch and food he had eaten [corroborated] by Officers Haygood and Brewer, Dets. Montgomery and Johnson, Sgt. Hill, and Dep. Sheriffs Craig and Mooney. All were white police officers upholding the testimony of a black man. (138.)

The testimony of Williams, in law, was negative testimony; that is, he did not see any person or hear anything. Thus, it would strengthen Oswald's defense if his attorney could prove he was physically seen by other witnesses at a location where it would have been impossible for Oswald to be at the S.E. window on the 6th floor. There is a maxim of law that where a person commits perjury on a major allegation then there is a presumption that the witness's testimony was false on all other testimony. In other words, once a liar, always a liar. Did the Commission publish a statement that they knew such statement was false when it was published? The answer is "yes."

In the possession of the Warren Commission are the affidavits of three witnesses who either saw or personally spoke to Lee Harvey Oswald between 12:15 p.m. and 12:25 p.m. and immediately subsequent to the murder of the president. These affidavits were deliberately suppressed from the "Report" and the "Hearings." The first witness seen by Lee Harvey Oswald was a Junior Jarman who saw him in the lunch room. Oswald so informed Capt. Fritz that he had seen Jr. Jarman but did not know his full name, only the name "Junior." Jarman testified he was in the lunch room at that time, which was slightly after 12 noon, around 12:10 to 12:15 p.m. Neither Jarman nor Oswald knew each other personally but only as fellow employees of the Depository. (139.)

Corroborating Mr. Jarman is an affidavit that was buried deep in the National Archives and could be found only after extensive burrowing into those files. Mrs. Carolyn Arnold informed the FBI that "as she was standing in front of the building she caught a fleeting glimpse of Lee Harvey Oswald standing in the hallway between the front door and the double doors leading to the warehouse, located on the first floor." (140.) The time was approximately 12:15 p.m.

However, when the Commission was informed of Mrs. Arnold's affidavit they directed the FBI to "re-interview" her, which is peculiar to say the least. Therefore, the FBI took an affidavit which asked her if she had seen Oswald "at the time President Kennedy was shot." Naturally, she said "no," for the question before the Commission was not whether she had seen anyone shoot the president but whether or not Oswald was at the 6th-floor window at the time of the shooting. In this second affidavit the FBI did not ask Mrs. Arnold if she had seen Oswald at any time and at what place she saw him. (141.) However, the FBI outsmarted themselves, since a reading of both affidavits revealed that at 12:15 she was already "in front of the building" and at 12:25 she left that spot, but at about 12:15 she saw Oswald on the 1st floor.

The FBI should have also asked: "Did you see Supreme Court Justice Warren, Senators Cooper and Russell, Congressman Boggs and Ford, ex-CIA Chief Dulles and banker McCloy at the time President Kennedy was shot?" Mrs. Arnold's reply would be, "No, Mr. FBI agent, I did not see Supreme Court Justice Warren, Senators Cooper and Russel, Congressmen Boggs and Ford, ex-CIA Chief Dulles, and banker McCloy!" The FBI list of the people who were not seen by Mrs. Arnold would be approximately two and one-half billion. The Commission's logic revealed the limits of the Commission's brain cells.

In addition to Mrs. Arnold and Mr. Jarman there was another witness whose affidavit was buried in the National Archives, one by Mr. Edward Piper, who also saw Oswald on the first floor between noon and 12:10 p.m. His affidavit can also be found in File No. "CD-5." There is one other witness whose testimony was so damaging that it took four years of "digging" to locate his testimony. His affidavit will be discussed later in this chapter.

Thus, based on the uncontradicted testimony of Mrs. Arnold,

Mr. Piper, Mr. Jarman, and Mr. Williams, it was an impossibility of "time" that compels one to accept the fact that Oswald never committed all those acts enumerated [above]. No man or superman could have completed those acts within a time schedule of 10 minutes. Mr. Truly, the Superintendent of the Depository, testified that when he visited the 6th floor to check on his maintenance crew he saw no "shield of cartons" and that the cartons were distributed haphazardly all over the 6th floor. He saw no "shield" as portrayed by Com. Exh. No. 732. Since Mr. Truly saw none and since the maintenance crew did not construct the "shield," the Commission "blithely" assumed it was constructed by Oswald.

The Commission, assuming a fact that Americans are stupid, attempted to place upon the Oswald defense the question: "If Oswald did not construct the shield, who did?" In a law court, where the accused is on trial for murder, all allegations must be proved by the prosecution, not the defendant. Thus, the question is not "Who constructed the shield" but "Was it Oswald?" Whether he did construct that shield can be determined by the time schedule created by the Commission–not by their critics. Of course, four witnesses whose testimony was uncontradicted proved that Oswald had no time to construct any such "shield of cartons." Uncontradicted testimony of Mr. Williams revealed that no person was constructing a shield between 12 noon and 12:20 p.m., when he left his lunch window site and took the elevator down to the 5th floor. Thus, only ten minutes remains to construct the shield, etc.

However, between 12:15 and 12:25, Oswald was seen by Mrs. Arnold on the first floor. Assuming that the time was 12:15, thus giving the prosecution the benefit of the doubt, not the defendant, that left Oswald 15 minutes. However, everyone now knows that Oswald was not on the 6th floor at 12:20 nor 12:22 p.m., since Mr. Williams was leaving the 6th floor and it took him at least two minutes to walk and ride the elevator. That time is now 12:22 p.m. According to the Commission's theory, Oswald went to his hiding place of the rifle, took that rifle out of its "wrapping paper," but first stripped off the tape which was never found by any police agency and then walked (?) or ran (?) to the window. That is what the Commission would have the public believe.

Belief is not evidence in a court of law. The Commission admitted that to assemble that Italian rifle an average person would need six minutes. It is logical to assume that Oswald was not so stupid to walk from the first floor to the 6th floor (he could not use the elevator, since Bonnie Ray Williams used it to go down to the 5th floor) with a fully assembled rifle in his hands in full view of any one of the 98 employees walking around the building. Thus, subtracting the six minutes needed to assemble the rifle, the time remaining to construct the huge shield composed of 32 cartons weighing 50 lbs. each, was two (2) minutes! Would a rational jury composed of twelve impartial persons believe the concoction manufactured by the Commission? At the very moment that "Oswald" was putting the last carton in place, the president's automobile was turning the corner at Elm and Houston. "Oswald" heard the noise of the crowd, rushed to the window, hand loaded that "well-oiled rifle" in a defective condition, crossed his eyes to enable him to use the telescopic sight, and pulled the trigger. Nor did the Warren Commission ever inform the public how Oswald got in and out of that 68-inch high shield. Did he jump over it with his fully assembled rifle in his hand? How did he get out of that shield after he had fired his three bullets, one of which could not fit in the rifle chamber, by a running or standing jump? The official photograph revealed that both ends of that "shield" were closed. When and by whom that "shield" was made was not the function of Oswald's defense attorney to determine. The evidence proved it was not Lee Harvey Oswald.

The key witness used by the Commission, Mr. Brennan, said he saw a man at the 6th-floor window at 12:20 p.m. with the rifle already assembled. It could not have been Lee Harvey Oswald, since between 12 noon and 12:20 p.m. he was seen by three uncontradicted witnesses either at the lunch room or on the first floor Depository entrance. None of them saw Oswald with a rifle, assembled or disassembled. The earliest Oswald could have gotten on the 6th floor was 12:26 with a rifle in his hands. Therefore, it was not Oswald the key witness saw–if he saw anyone.

The "shield of cartons" and the events the Commission said

took place was a fabrication written by the Commission. Anyone who can absorb that fabrication can absorb the fairytale that a horse can fly because there are horseflies! By a vote of nearly 80%, the American people have rejected the Commission's fairytale.

There is a reason for the Commission's concoction of that fairytale, for it was to become a "red herring" which diverted the critics from a vital issue. By concentrating the critic's eye upon the "fairy" tale, the Commission calmly avoided the question: "How did the rifleman know the exact time the president's body would appear in his telescopic sight?" There was no public broadcast of the location of the president's motorcade. Only two persons knew the exact time: (1) The Dallas police; and (2) the conspirators. But the Commission said there was no conspiracy, so that left only some of the members of the Dallas Police or Sheriff's Department. "The Commission admitted that there were no radios in the Depository capable of hearing the police band broadcasts. Thus, if Oswald was the rifleman, then how did he know the exact time?

This time element is of major importance, for President Kennedy, according to Sheriff Decker, was shot at 12:25 p.m. (142.) Five minutes may not seem long when compared to eternity; but five minutes to Oswald is the difference between guilt and innocence. There is conclusive proof that the first bullets which struck the president were fired at 12:25 p.m. which time was recorded by the Dallas Police Department. The announcement was heard by the police reporter sitting in the police department's headquarters and forwarded immediately by him to his newspaper, the Dallas "Times-Herald," and so published by them in all their editions and never retracted! This 12:25 p.m. time was then substantiated by the "time of arrival" records of the Parkland Hospital, which stated that the president arrived at 12:38 p.m., not 12:43 as stated by the Commission. Five minutes!

In a court of law the judge would accept the time of 12:25, for that is the official time recorded at the police department which, in turn, was corroborated by an independent eyewitness, the police reporter; which, in turn, was substantiated by the editor of the "Times-Herald" city desk, who received the reporter's news and he recorded the time; which, in turn, was substantiated by the official records of the "Time of Arrival" record of Parkland Hospital.

In view of those facts, it was a physical and scientific impossibility for Lee Harvey Oswald to have fired any rifle bullets at the president at 12:25 p.m. when he was last seen on the first floor at 12:20 p.m., when he had to take a minimum of six minutes to assemble the disassembled rifle, run or walk up five flights of stairs, construct that shield, and then discharge 3 bullets.

Oswald's defense attorney would have three prime witnesses to refute the Commission's charges that Oswald was at that window when the shots were fired. (1) The U.S. Secret Service; (2) the FBI; and (3) the Altgens photograph. The testimony of U.S. Secret Service Inspector Sorrels has been overlooked by many investigators. His testimony proved that at the precise time the shots rang out he saw no person at the 6th floor S.E. window. At that time, the Inspector was seated in the lead automobile of the cavalcade looking directly at the Book Depository. His automobile was approximately 100 feet ahead of the president's and the inspector had no sun glare in his eyesight. When questioned by a Commission aide regarding what he saw at the 6th-floor window, he answered under oath: "Yes, there were at least one or two windows that were open in that section over there (the far right side of the Depository Building. I do not recall seeing anyone in any of those windows. I do not, of course, remember seeing any object or anything like that in the windows such as a rifle or anything pointing out of the windows. There was no activity, no one moving around that I saw at all." (143.) This testimony was [so] devastating to the Commission's case against Oswald that they never commented upon it at all. Why should they, for it cleared Oswald of any guilt.

The FBI and the Altgens photograph were to be intertwined with the defense of Oswald. This Altgens photograph was taken by Mr. Altgens when the president's automobile was slightly past the Book Depository's front-door entrance. This photograph was to produce another controversy regarding the identity of the "man in the doorway." The Commission admitted the man had to be either Oswald or Lovelady. To settle the controversy, the investigator need only read the testimony of Billy Lovelady and the investigations of the FBI. According to the Commission, the man was 'Billy Lovelady." The FBI evidence proved it to be Lee Harvey Oswald. (144.)

The "man in the doorway" wore a shirt with no stripes, [which] was open well down to nearly the middle of the man's body, and the shirt had long sleeves. There is no dispute concerning the clothes or the manner in which they were worn. The FBI was instructed by the Commission to conduct an investigation, and the results were so climactic that the Commission suppressed the FBI investigation from not only its "Report" but from the testimony published in the "Hearings" and buried some of it in the National Archives. The FBI submitted its report that it was not Lovelady in the picture. Since it was not Lovelady, and since the Commission said it had to be one or the other, the "man in the doorway" was Lee Harvey Oswald. He could not be in that picture and also be at the 6th-floor window. Since he was in the picture Oswald was innocent.

The identifiable part of the Altgens photograph is the pattern of the shirt and the length of the arm sleeves. Billy Lovelady informed the FBI that he was wearing a "red and white vertical stripe shirt and blue jeans." In signing this affidavit Lovelady also testified that the shirt he was wearing at the time the picture was taken was "buttoned up to the neck." The FBI, in its official letter, signed by Mr. Hoover, informed the Commission that the picture showed a man with a long-sleeved shirt; Lovelady admitted to the FBI he wore a short-sleeve one. (145.) Hoover's letter proved that the "man in the doorway" was Lee Harvey Oswald.

Mr. Hoover's letter was substantiated by an affidavit signed by Billy Lovelady's foreman: "Billy Lovelady who works under my supervision for the Texas Book Depository was seated on the entrance steps just in front of me." Signed by William Shelley, March 18, 1964. How can a man seated be a man standing in a doorway? (146.)

Six months after he gave his affidavit to the FBI, the Commission heard Lovelady's testimony which directly contradicted his statements to the FBI. Either his original affidavit or his testimony was perjurious. In Lovelady's first statement he said that after the shots were fired he immediately went to the elevator inside the Depository. In his testimony to the Commission he now stated that he immediately went to the railroad tracks. Since he was under oath, he committed perjury as a Miss V. Adams testified that he first went to the elevator, not to the tracks. His affidavit, signed on November 22, 1963, can be read in Comm. Exh. No. 3003, page 36, and this was in direct contradiction of his testimony. Furthermore, his statement that he went to the railroad tracks was contradicted by Mrs. Adams, who saw him inside the building immediately after the shots were fired. (147.) Lovelady's testimony and his perjury can be found in Volume 6, page 329-30 and 339-40. Once a liar, always a liar. What the Commission never answered was: "who exerted the pressure to compel Lovelady to commit perjury?"

Previously it was stated that a fourth witness would be named who also upheld Oswald's statement that he was at the entrance of the Book Depository when the shots were fired. There is in the National Archives a Commission Document known to investigators as "No. 354." This is a sworn affidavit which affirmed Oswald's statement that he had seen and talked to a man seeking a "phone booth" after the shooting at the main entrance door on the steps of the Depository. This witness, Mr. Allman, was a newsman for Dallas TV station WFAA. He had inquired of Oswald the location of a telephone booth so he could use it to phone in his story to the TV station. The last time he saw Oswald was when Oswald was walking into the building. Capt. Fritz, when informed of this man by Oswald, did not inform the press or the FBI that Mr. Allman had cleared Oswald. The captain was a practicing Christian, so he said. After the murder of Oswald, the Commission evidently reasoned that it would not be to their profit, or anyone else's, to remove the "guilty" stain.

Thus, the Warren Commission had in its possession, prior to the time its "Report" was sent to the printer, uncontroverted evidence from Jr. Jarman, Edw. Piper, Mrs. Arnold, Mrs. Adams, and Mr. Allman that Lee Harvey Oswald was never at the 6th-floor window between 12 noon and 12:30 p.m. when, they say, the first shot was fired. To support their testimony was the testimony of U.S. Secret Service Inspector Sorrels. To support all their testimony is the evidence submitted to the Commission by the FBI that the "man in the doorway" in the Altgens photograph was Lee Harvey Oswald.

Since the dead cannot speak, should not the living?

No one, including investigators or historians, can predict how a jury would weigh the testimony of five witnesses who saw or talked to Oswald. The only witness was Lovelady, and he destroyed his own testimony. Inspector Sorrels was uncompromising in his statement that when the shots rang out he was looking directly at the S. E, window of the Depository and he saw no one. He saw no smoke, he saw no rifle, he saw no person. An investigator and a Historian can safely say that a jury has the common sense to say "not guilty."

As a last resort, the Commission produced their key witness whose testimony was so weak that the Commission was reduced to a phrase that earned the contempt of any lawyer who had pride in the profession called "law." That phrase: "most nearly resembled the man" would not be applicable in any Western nation, including the United States. However, the Commission needed this witness, Mr. Brennan, so desperately that they accepted his testimony in spite of the fact he admitted he perjured himself when he gave his statements to the FBI agents. But the need for that testimony permitted the Commission to prostitute their integrity.

The Commission was to publish two statements regarding this "witness." In fact, their own "Report" revealed the fact that they did not know how to handle this perjurer. Mr. Brennan admitted that he had seen Oswald's picture on a television station prior to his trip to the police lineup in the late afternoon of November 22, but he failed to select Oswald in that lineup. On December 17, 1963, he informed the FBI that he could identify Oswald but, three weeks later, in another statement to the same agency, reversed himself. (148.) The Commission, in despair, confronted their "yes, I can; no, I can't" witness with the statement he made to the FBI on November 22 and again, under oath, Brennan testified that his November 22nd statement was his true one and that he could not positively identify Oswald as the man he "saw" at the window. In spite of this testimony reaffirming his FBI statements, the Commission calmly accepted Brennan as their "key" eyewitness. If Brennan had thus "purged" himself of perjury, then the perjurers were none other than the commissioners in informing the American public that Brennan had identified Oswald under "the basic principles of American justice."

A reading of Brennan's testimony revealed that he never made the statement that he had "positively identified Oswald." (149) Police Chief Curry, in a national TV statement on the 22nd, stated that the police had no eyewitness to the murderer, and this statement was made after he knew Brennan had visited the police lineup and had not selected Oswald. The Commission published their perjured statement regarding Oswald in spite of the fact that they had the testimony of Inspector Sorrels that he saw no one at that window when the shots rang out. The Commission published that statement in spite of the fact that four witnesses testified they saw Oswald either on the 2nd floor, the first floor, or outside the building when those shots were fired. Oswald was not the liar, it was the Commission that lied to the American people.

Other vital evidence which supported Oswald's innocence was suppressed by the Commission. In a letter buried deep in the "Hearings" is a statement by Mr. Hoover of the FBI that the Italian rifle given to them by the Dallas police emitted "white smoke" when discharged. (150.) Brennan testified that when he saw the rifleman fire that rifle he made no claim that he saw any "white smoke." Nor did this "eyewitness" see any telescopic sight although he "saw" 70 to 80 percent of that rifle protruding out of that window. (151.)

Further evidence that Mr. Brennan lied can be found in the affidavit he made to Sheriff Decker the day after the murder. In line 4 from the bottom there is a statement in which Brennan had the rifleman "stepped down out of sight," which, under normal usage of the English language, would mean that the rifleman was standing on some object. In the middle of the same affidavit, Brennan had the rifleman sitting down waiting for the president to arrive. Brennan stated that he "could see the whole body of the rifleman from the hips up," but when he was firing the rifle "he could see from the belt up." At the time of the shooting he saw the rifleman shoot at the president "standing up." (152.)

Again, assuming the Commission was correct in their statement that Mr. Brennan's veracity was perfect, then Brennan was testifying that he saw the rifleman shoot through two panes of window glass! The Commission admitted that the window was open approximately 12 inches. Thus, the Commission was asking all the world to accept as a fact that, after the shooting, those two panes of glass repaired themselves since no shattered glass was ever found on the 6th floor and no spectator on the street level was struck by shattered glass. Oh, what contempt the 7 commissioners had for their citizenry! (153.) By this time, Brennan had committed four lies: (1) He saw between 70 and 80 percent of the rifle but saw no telescopic sight; (2) he saw no smoke emitted from that rifle; (3) the rifleman was standing up when he fired those 3 shots; and (4) after firing those three shots he "stepped down," avoiding the glass he had shattered when the bullets came from the rifle when the trigger was pulled.

As the Commission proclaimed Oswald the world's greatest marksman on that day, it is impossible for any person with common sense to accept the fact that that kind of rifleman would endanger his face and eyes by shooting through two panes of window glass. Of course, the commissioners were not men of common sense; they were "lawyers"!

The perplexing element in the "Report" of the Warren Commission is its determination to persist in accepting perjury as the basis for convicting Oswald. Brennan's affidavit and testimony stated that "he saw a man standing up and resting against the left window sill, take positive aim, and fire his last shot,"(154.) The Commission's "'Report" called him a liar when they stated that the rifleman used the cartons near the window as a gun rest. (155.) The Commission admitted Brennan was a liar when he said he saw the man "sitting down," because "a man sitting down could scarcely be seen from the street." (155a.) Secret Service Inspector Sorrels testified he saw no one and no object at that 6th-floor window. (156.) Capt. Fritz admitted that no person standing on the street could tell whether a man was tall or short when that man is 6 floors above the street level. (157.)

Who was lying? Brennan? The Commission? Or both? Both!

The Commission did prove one thing by their "eyewitness"; that he was consistent. The Commission also used his testimony as the basis for the original police signal pertaining to the murderer. According to the Dallas police radio tapes, the first alarm was broadcasted at 12:45 p.m., which consisted of a conversation between Dallas [Secret Service] Inspector Sawyer and the police radio announcer: "The man wanted is a slender white male, about 30, 5 ft. 10 inches, carrying what looked like a .30-30 type of Winchester." Hq. Radio: "Any clothing description?" Sawyer: "Current witness cannot remember that." (158.) This was the only description broadcasted by the police!

Without any investigation, a person reading the "Report" would have assumed that Brennan was the man who gave that description to Inspector Sawyer. But Brennan denied he gave any information to Sawyer and said he gave it to U.S. Secret Service Inspector Sorrels. However, Inspector Sorrels denied Brennan's statement that he received from Brennan the following description: "To my best knowledge and description, a man in his early 30's, fair complexion, slender but neat, possibly 5' 10" weight 160-170lbs." Again, an investigator must determine who was telling the truth; Brennan or the Secret Service inspector. The testimony revealed that the inspector was telling the truth, for he proved that when Brennan alleged he gave that description to someone Inspector Sorrels was riding from the Hospital back to the Depository. (159.) Thus, Mr. Brennan's eyesight was so "excellent" that he could clearly see a man 6 floors above the street level but could not identify a man 6 feet tall, standing between 2 and 3 feet from his eyes. A person can be farsighted but Brennan's eyesight bordered on the ridiculous.

Under the stress of the murder it could have been possible that Inspector Sawyer's description was given to him by Brennan, who wore a construction worker's steel helmet. But Sawyer, under oath, said he never saw Brennan at any time during that tragic day. In fact, Inspector Sawyer, being trained by the highly efficient (?) and intelligent (?) police force, said he forgot to obtain the name of the "white man" who gave him that information used by the Dallas police. But the Dallas police were to "forget" more than the name of the "white man" who gave them a description that matched every "white man" who was 5' 10" tall, weighed between 160-170 lbs., and was carrying a .30-30 "Winchester rifle." A Winchester .30-30 rifle is not a 7.65 German Mauser military rifle nor a 6.5 Italian Mannlicher-Carcano military rifle. (160.)

Naturally, Brennan's statement in one of his affidavits was

that the man on the 6th floor was wearing a "light" jacket, so the Commission evaded the fact that Oswald was wearing a dark tan long-sleeved shirt. (161.) The Commission went a long way from the "basic principles of American justice" to protect their perjuring witness.

In their effort to tighten their "net" around Oswald, the Commission decided to trace his movements from 11:55 a.m. until 1:40 p.m., when he was arrested in the Texas Theatre. As usual, the "net" was supported by perjury. The Commission assumed that its veneer of perjured testimony would be overlooked in the same manner of its statement that it was not a German 7.65 Mauser that was found on the 6th floor but an Italian 6.5 Carcano rifle. Operating under the Nazi-Communist theory that if a lie is constantly repeated people will accept it as the truth, the Commission traced Oswald from "somewhere he had never been to somewhere he never was"!

In a criminal trial for murder, it is not necessary to trace the movements of the accused. However, the Commission violated the number one rule of cross-examination: "Never ask question when you do not suspect the answer." In other words: "Leave Pandora's Box alone." When the Commission sought Oswald's movements they opened up the door to the conspiracy, for the Craig and Jones affidavits had to be exposed to the light. (162.)

The first crystal-clear indication that Oswald was the prime "patsy" and the first open break in the "Ring of Conspirators" surrounding the murder of President Kennedy was the Commission's deathly silence regarding the uncontradicted testimony of Deputy Sheriff Craig. Dep. Sheriff Craig was the first person to see Lee Harvey Oswald from the time he left the Book Depository until the time, 1 p.m., when he was seen by his rooming-house keeper, Mrs. Roberts. Strangely, or pathetically, the first man to crack under the strain was Police Captain Fritz, who opened the eyes of the world to the existence of a conspiracy.

On November 23, 1963, Deputy Sheriff Craig signed an affidavit in the sheriff's department. In his affidavit Craig swore that at 12:45 p.m. he saw a "white man running down the hill from the Texas Book Depository, and I saw what I think was a light-colored Rambler station wagon with [a] luggage rack on top pull over to the curb, and this subject who had come running down the hill get into the car. The man driving this station wagon was a dark-complected white man ... I reported this incident at once to a Secret Service officer whose name I did not know." (Note: this "officer" was one of the conspirators, as will be proved later by the U.S. Secret Service.) "Later I heard the city (police) had a suspect in custody, and I called in [that] I had reported the information about the suspect ... to Capt. Fritz and was requested to come at once to the City Hall ... I went to the City Hall and identified the subject (Lee Harvey Oswald) as being the same person I saw running down the hill and get into the station wagon and leave the scene." (163.) One need not now wonder why the Commission deliberately buried this affidavit nineteen volumes, and one million words, away from their 888-page "Report"!

As previously stated, in a law trial a lawyer is in clover when he can find a witness who can substantiate the testimony of another witness. But the Commission, knowing that there was another witness to Dep. Sheriff Craig's affidavit buried in the 19th volume of the Hearings, buried the corroborating witness's testimony not in the 'Hearing" but in the National Archives, Washington D.C. Substantiating the deputy's affidavit is one under File Code No. "CD-5," where a Mr. M. C. Robinson testified to the FBI that between 12:30 p.m. and I p.m. when "he was in front of the Texas School Depository Building, a light-colored Nash station wagon suddenly appeared before him ... stopped ... and a white male came down the grass-covered incline between the building and street and entered the station wagon after which it drove away in the direction of the Oak Cliff (Oswald lived near that section) section of Dallas." (164.)

Craig's description of the white man he saw get into that station wagon was a man "in his twenties, five feet eight, about 140 or 150 pounds, with blue trousers and a light-tan shirt." (165.) An exact description of the clothes worn by Oswald. After Craig had reported to Capt. Fritz and identified Oswald as the man getting into the Nash station wagon, Oswald's first words were: "Don't involve her. She knows nothing!" The "she" was none other than Mrs. Paine, the FBI informant! Oswald, according to the inestimable Capt. Fritz and Dept. Sheriff Craig, never denied getting into a station wagon and never denied that the station wagon was owned by Mrs. Paine. Nor did Capt. Fritz, that paragon of police efficiency, ever question Mrs. Paine to elucidate (1) was that station wagon her station wagon; (2) who was the driver; (3) where did that "'dark complected white man" take Oswald? In his testimony before the Commission, the captain swore that "he (Craig) was telling me things (at 5:30 p.m. on November 22nd) I knew would not help us ... His (Craig's) story didn't fit in what we knew to be true."

With that testimony the captain was admitting the existence of a conspiracy!

The captain opened the door to the hallway leading to the conspiracy, for the Warren Commission knew:

1. Captain Fritz testified that he was at Parkland Hospital from 12:45 p.m. and returned at 12:58 p.m. to the Book Depository.

2. The 7.65 German Mauser rifle was not found until 1:22 p.m.

3, No palm print of Oswald's was ever found on the switched Italian rifle.

4. No fingerprints of Oswald's were ever found on the same rifle.

5. At the 4 p.m. identification lineup Brennan did not identify Oswald.

6. At the 4:30 national TV and radio broadcast Policy Chief Curry admitted the police had no eyewitness to the identity of the rifleman.

7. Oswald denied killing President Kennedy. Since the police had absolutely no evidence of any kind at 5:30 p.m. in their possession as seen in 3, 4, 5 and 6, Oswald was legally and morally innocent. Thus, in view of those elements, how did Capt. Fritz "know" Oswald was "guilty"?

8. Therefore, at 5:30 p.m., when Dept. Craig made his identification of Oswald, how did Capt. Fritz, in spite of the above six elements, "know" that what Craig was telling him "would not help us" and "didn't fit in with what we knew to be true." (166.)

Capt. Fritz's standard of morality is subject to doubt when he testified before the Commission. At that time he used a shroud of silence to conceal Oswald's statement that Oswald had talked to "a man or Secret Service agent" who sought directions to a telephone booth while Oswald was near the front entrance of the Book Depository when the shots rang out (Com. Exh. 354). If the dead cannot speak, should not the living?

What did Police Captain Fritz know that no one [else], including 197,000,000 Americans, knew? What did Capt. Fritz "know" and why did the Warren Commission refuse to demand that he inform the American people? Why did the Warren Commission refuse to ask Captain Fritz why he failed to question Mrs. Paine? Why did the Commission fail to ask her when she appeared before them? Or did the Commission know that she was an FBI informant and that the driver of that station wagon was also a person in the same position? Of course they did.

In an attempt to overcome the Robinson and Craig affidavits, and to draw the public's eyes from the conspiracy testimony given by Capt. Fritz, the Commission invented a "cock and bull" story of Oswald's alleged movements. In that episode the Commission denied the sworn testimony of one witness, suppressed further evidence of a conspiracy, and accepted the "identification" of two witnesses who collapsed under a friendly cross-examination by an aide.

According to the self-serving statements of the Commission, Oswald left the Depository Building at 12:32 p.m. and walked 7 blocks from that building away from his rooming house. Then he hopped on a street-car bus and rode back toward the Depository, left the bus, took a six-block walk to the Greyhound Bus Depot, became tired after murdering the president, hired a taxi-cab which drove him 6 blocks past his rooming house; jumped out of the cab, walked back 6 blocks and entered his room at 1 p.m. The only truth in their own statement was the Commission's statement that he arrived at his rooming house at 1 p.m. when he was seen by Mrs. Roberts, the housekeeper.

Oswald, according to this Commission theory, got on a bus whose driver identified a 16-year-old boy as Oswald. At the lineup, bus driver McWatters identified a Milton Jones, whose physical attributes were as close [to Oswald] as a fish to an elephant. The Commission did admit that the driver's identification was "too vague," but they accepted a Dallas police exhibit which said that the bus driver made a "positive identification." On the witness stand McWatters denied making that statement, but his moral courage outweighed the Commission's physical. The Dallas police statement was an outright lie, and the Commission knew it was a lie when they refused to place on the stand the police stenographer who typed and submitted that "positive identification." (167.)

With the bus driver admitting that he never saw Oswald on the bus, the Commission now accepted the "testimony" of a Mrs. Bledsoe, who was assisted in her testimony by the United States Secret Service. This was a new concept in promoting the "basic principles of American justice." This woman, whose testimony showed that she hated Oswald, mainly because she owed him $2.00, swore that Oswald "looked like a maniac, his sleeve was out there, his shirt was undone, his face distorted, with all the buttons off and a hole in the right elbow." In this manufactured bus episode, the Commission had selected three witnesses. Mrs. Bledsoe, Mr. McWatters, and Mr. Jones. The two men never saw any man described by the aged Mrs. Bledsoe. Neither did Mrs. Bledsoe, for she admitted that she had to have an attorney to assist her to read her notes; that was the excellency of her eyesight. The two male witnesses never saw any man on the bus wearing the clothes described by Mrs. Bledsoe. However, to assist her memory, the Commission, although chaired by the Chief Justice of the U.S. Supreme Court, permitted the Secret Service inspector to show her Oswald's shirt, but by a whim of the Gods he showed her the wrong shirt, which Mrs. Bledsoe identified as the one she saw Oswald wearing on the bus. (168.) Nor did Oswald's shirt, which he had taken off in the rooming house, have a hole in his sleeve. When Oswald was murdered, Mrs. Bledsoe probably was one of the happiest old women alive–now she did not have to pay him the $2.00.

As stated in the previous chapter, there was evidence that the Dallas police instituted the search for Lee Harvey Oswald within fifteen minutes after they broadcasted the 12:25 p.m. alarm that the president had been shot. The Commission also failed to publish in their "Report" the fact that the police were searching the street-car buses within minutes after the shooting, although the description of the suspect was not flashed over the police broadcasting system until fifteen minutes after the shooting! In suppressed Document No. 2641 is the sworn statement of Milton Jones that the bus he was on, the McWatters bus, was stopped on Elm St., four blocks from Houston St., at approximately 12:30 p.m., and was boarded by two policemen who searched the passengers to see "if any were carrying firearms." (169.) In this same document, Jones described a man who had boarded the bus six blocks before the bus reached Houston St. as a white man, 30 to 35-years old, weight 150 pounds, receding dark-brown hair wearing a light-blue jacket and gray khaki pants. The age was not Oswald's and neither the clothes. The bus driver identified Jones as the man who got on the bus.

As to the Commission's key witness, Mrs. Bledsoe, neither Jones nor McWatters saw Mrs. Bledsoe on the bus during that period of time when the bus was stopped and searched. Nor did Mrs. Bledsoe recognize them. Since her testimony relied upon a "hole in the sleeve," and since the Commission never stated that Oswald's shirt had been torn or had a hole in any sleeve he had worn to work that morning, then it is obvious that she was mistaken. According to the "Report," Oswald, at his rooming house between 1 p.m. and 1:04 p.m., changed his pants and his shirt, and the shirt he took off had no holes. (170.) Although there were about fifteen passengers on the McWatters bus, the Commission heard two, McWatters and Jones, and they refused to uphold any of the Commission's statements. Mr. Jones did not see Lee Harvey Oswald, nor did Mr. McWatters for the reason [that] Oswald was never on that bus. Mrs. Bledsoe never saw Oswald, for her statement was not supported by the other two eyewitnesses. But the fact does remain that, within minutes, less than 10 minutes after the shooting, the Dallas police were seeking Lee Harvey Oswald.

There is no testimony that the FBI, who received the Jones affidavit, made any attempt to check the police radio broadcast or to have Jones attempt to identify the two policemen.

When the Jones affidavit is compared with the testimony of Chief Curry, and when both of their testimonies are combined with the testimony of Capt. Fritz, then it is self-evident that some of the Dallas police were deeply involved in the conspiracy of the cold-blooded murder of President Kennedy. How they were involved will be discussed in a later chapter.

The Commission's final witness that "supported" the Commission's fantasy was a taxi driver who said he picked Oswald up at

12:45 p.m. at the bus station and drove him six blocks beyond the address he had been given by Oswald. Some taxicab driver. To substantiate his "trip," the cabdriver produced his "trip ticket." However, the time on the "trip ticket" automatically disproved the Commission's theory, as they blithely said the driver was "mistaken"–which is a new rule in American law: if the proof conflicts with the theory, discard the proof and adhere to the theory! Shades of Hitler and Stalin.

In addition to the "trip ticket," the cabdriver's identification of Oswald as his passenger was completely demolished by one of the Commission aides. Cabdriver Whaley identified an 18-year-old boy at the lineup as his passenger. He also had his passenger wearing not one jacket, but two jackets. When this passenger was in Whaley's cab, the passenger sat in the front seat beside driver Whaley. Oswald was not identified at any time by the cabdriver. Then why did the Commission overlook Whaley's testimony? Why did they pervert it and say that he "identified" Oswald? The Commission relied upon a written statement submitted to them by the Dallas police which said that Whaley signed a statement identifying Oswald as his passenger. Thus, in law, Whaley had committed perjury and the Commission could have cited him for such act.

The reason why the Commission refused to have Whaley charged with perjury was due to the legal theory that Whaley was compelled by the Dallas police to sign that statement prior to identifying an 18-year-old boy. Whaley, when on the witness stand, informed the Commission that he signed the police statement prior to going to the lineup, and he signed the statement which was written by a Dallas policeman prior to his selection of the boy. Here again is an exquisite example of the Commission's practice of "the basic principles of American justice." (171.)

In summation of paragraph IV of the Commission's indictment against Lee Harvey Oswald, there was uncontradicted evidence that Oswald was seen getting into a Nash Rambler station wagon at approximately 12:45 p.m. He was next seen at 1 p.m. by an unbiased witness, his housekeeper, Mrs. Roberts, between 1 p.m. and 1:04 p.m. The evidence is conclusive that Lee Harvey Oswald was never at the 6th-floor window at 12:30 p.m., for positive evidence of four witnesses showed him at either the

2nd-floor lunch room or at the Book Depository entrance. Positive evidence, produced by the Federal Bureau of Investigation, conclusively proved Oswald was standing at the Depository entrance at 12:30 p.m. The Warren Commission "proved" Oswald was at the 6th-floor window as if they had also "proved" that the moon is made of green cheese.

CHAPTER VI

ANIMATE AND INANIMATE WITNESSES– THE TIPPIT AFFAIRE

Until the conspiracy that murdered President Kennedy is revealed to the American people, the murder of Officer Tippit will remain the subject of controversy. Not because he was allegedly murdered by Oswald but [because of the question of] whether his murder was coincidental, a part of the conspiracy, or a successful attempt by some members of the Dallas Police Department to "rid" themselves of a man who "knew too much." From the testimony and documents there is no question that he was a pawn, a patsy, like Oswald. Did Tippit, who had a job moonlighting for a high executive of the John Birch Society,[19] see and hear too much for his own good? There is no question that Tippit was scheduled to die on November 22, 1963.

The Commission alleged that Oswald was positively seen shooting Tippit by two eyewitnesses and his flight from the murder site was witnessed by seven more. The Commission also alleged that the cartridges "found" near the Tippit murder were all discharged from Oswald's revolver, and that the revolver "found" in his possession at the time of his arrest was the revolver that fired those bullets. Finally, the Commission alleged that a jacket found along the path of the killer's flight was Oswald's, which he discarded as he ran from the murder.

---

[19] Tippit moonlighted as a security guard at Austin's Barbecue. His boss, Austin Cook, was involved in business dealings with mobster Ralph Paul, who financed Jack Ruby's nightclubs. According to journalist Seth Kantor, Ruby used Paul as a "money supplier." "Over the years Ruby 'borrowed'" Paul "remained a mysterious, silent partner behind clubs fronted by Ruby," and he "held fifty percent of the stock in Ruby's Carousel but rarely went there." Seth Kantor, *The Ruby Cover-up* (New York: Kensington Publishing Group, 1978), pp. 212-213.

This fifth paragraph is an excellent example of an indictment, for it tells all without equivocation of words. The accused was seen to fire those bullets into Officer Tippit, and he died as a result; the cartridges matched the weapon used in the murder of Tippit, and the killer discarded a jacket worn during the murder. The only difficulty the Commission had when it acted on behalf of the State of Texas in its role as prosecutor was the fact that there was absolutely no evidence that proved, beyond a reasonable doubt, that the killer, in fact and in law, was Lee Harvey Oswald. As in the previous discussion of the first four paragraphs in the Commission's indictment, the proverb "where there's smoke there's fire" had no validity in the Oswald-Tippit Affaire, since the evidence revealed that it was the Commission who made the fire and then blew their own fire smoke upon their selected "patsy," Oswald.

By using both positive and negative testimony Oswald's defense attorney would have destroyed the Commission's case against his client–Oswald. The uncontradicted testimony of Oswald's rooming house manager, Mrs. Roberts, stated that she left the rooming house at 1 p.m. and that she saw him standing at a street-car bus stop at 1:04 p.m. Her evidence is positive evidence since she saw him at that bus stop, and it is interesting to note that the Commission made no indication that Mrs. Roberts was mistaken or lying. (172.) Since Mrs. Roberts gave positive evidence, the burden of proof remained upon the Commission to prove that, from 1:04 p.m., Oswald could, and did, walk to the Tippit murder site within 4 to 5 minutes.

The Tippit murder site from the rooming house was nine-tenths of a mile. The Commission therefore had one of their aides make a walking test to determine the length of time it would take a normal walking man, crossing all streets without attracting attention, to arrive from the Oswald bus stop to the Tippit murder. The time was 17 minutes, 45 seconds. (173.) By positive testimony of their own, the Commission proved Oswald was not at the murder site when Tippit was killed. With this evidence in their possession, the Commission resorted to the hat trick and, with the use of words, informed the American people that Tippit was not murdered between 1:06 and 1:08 p.m. but at 1:16 p.m.

A true addict of the art of detection is always fascinated by the method used by writers of detective novels to "tie in" the threads of their murder story. A true addict can always spot where the thread breaks, and a good writer never permits that thread to break prior to the solution given to the reader. The "Oswald-Tippit-Commission" Affaire was a detective story where the thread broke and the solution offered was falsified.

With the use of words, not evidence, the Commission informed the public that Tippit was shot at exactly 1:16 p.m. The Commission arrived at this time schedule by willfully and deliberately overlooking the sworn testimony of two witnesses whom the Commission said gave the truth and nothing but the truth. When the testimony of those two witnesses was read and analyzed, it revealed the fact that one witness was a liar and the other never said what the Commission said he said!

Mrs. H. Markham was the prime witness for the Commission relating to the identity of Oswald as the killer, and she committed perjury several times during her testimony. Again, as in the Brennan testimony, the Commission impaled itself on the horns of a dilemma. Her testimony was the "testimony" used by the Commission in their attempt to place Oswald at the Tippit murder site. Their dilemma occurred when she testified that she saw "Oswald" shoot Tippit at exactly 1:06 p.m. However, Mrs. Roberts' testimony placed Oswald at a bus stop at 1:04 p.m. and the Commission's expert walker took slightly more than 17 minutes to walk from the Oswald room to the Tippit site. Thus, the Commission, by Olympian fiat, concluded that Oswald was the world's fastest human being on November 22, 1963! According to the Commission, Oswald could have given Man O' War or Kelso a hot race before Oswald faded in the stretch.

Realizing that they could not afford to have Mrs. Markham's testimony impeached, they decided to solve their dilemma by fabricating an entirely new time schedule but overlooked their tester's walking time. In police circles it is well known that the vast majority of hard-core criminals use the same "modus operandi." The Warren Commission, according to the Dallas police records, was no exception, since they adopted the identical pattern when the Commission determined the time of the president's murder by moving the clock ahead, from 12:25 p.m. to

12:30 p.m. In that murder, they used five minutes; in the Tippit murder, 10 minutes. The Commission decided "in the interests of national security" that their chief witness, Mrs. Markham, was mistaken. Her 1:06 p.m. time was really 1:16 p.m. It was flabbergasting that the Commission should have stated that the time of the killer was between 1:17 and 1:18 p.m., for their own tests revealed that "Oswald" could not have reached the Tippit murder until 1:17:45 p.m. Where did "Oswald" pick up one and three-quarters minute? In the Tippit murder, the Commission proved that not only were they liars but poor liars, and that is unforgivable to readers of detective stories. What proverb has said that a liar manufactures the web by which he is caught? (174.)

This time element never bothered the Commission, as they never took the time to refute it. What is important to Oswald's defense is whether or not there is any evidence in the "Hearings" or the National Archives which would substantiate a time closer to Markham's time of 1:06 p.m. than the 1:16 p.m. false time created by the Commission, 1:16 p.m. If there be any evidence corroborating the 1:06 p.m. time, then Oswald must be found "not guilty." (Mrs. Markham's affidavit to Dist. Att. Wade, notarized by Robert Wisdom.)

On page 202 of the 24th Volume of "Hearings" is corroborating testimony that Mrs. Markham's time of 1:06 p.m. was correct. A Mr. Bowley testified that at 1:10 p.m. he was driving his automobile when he approached the Tippit murder site and saw the body of Officer Tippit "next to the left-front wheel of the squad car, on the street." (175.)

He further testified that he got out of his automobile and called the police on the squad car radio. The Dallas police radio log recorded his message: "A policeman has been shot. He is lying out there in the street. I think he is dead." The police then "logged" this conversation as to the time when they received the Bowley message, not the time of the murder but the time of the message, as 1:16 p.m. (175.)

In law, there is no discrepancy between Mrs. Markham's time, Mr. Bowley's, or the police log. The police recorded the time of Mr. Bowley's message. Thus, when the police received the Bowley message, Officer Tippit was already dead or dying. Since Mr. Bowley, at 1:10 p.m., never witnessed the shooting or even saw the murderer flee from the scene, time had elapsed. Mr. Bowley's uncontradicted testimony revealed that he had looked at his wristwatch which showed 1:10 p.m. Therefore, since the act of murder had been completed and the murderer had fled, common sense, not legal mumbo jumbo, proved that Mrs. Markham's time of 1:06 and 1:08 p.m. was correct. In law, in spite of the fact that she committed perjury on other substantive matters, her time of 1:06 p.m. is lawful testimony when that same testimony was upheld by an impartial witness.

What must be remembered is that without Mrs. Markham's testimony the evidence of Mr. Bowley was sufficient to absolve Oswald of being the killer of Officer Tippit. Oswald could not be at the bus stop at 1:04 p.m. and also be the killer of a police officer killed nine-tenths of a mile away from the bus stop at 1:06 or 1:08 p.m. Add the Commission's own tests to the time element, and Oswald was proved innocent by the Commission.

The Commission willfully deceived the American citizen by implying that the police "logging" of 1:16 p.m. was the actual time of the Tippit murder. The Commission's reasoning would be the same as if saying the time of a murder is identical to when the police received information that a murder had been committed. The stupidity of the Commission's reasoning is easily pierced, for to use that reasoning would mean that a dead body found ten hours, ten days, or ten years after the police were informed of the finding of the body would, ipso facto, also be the time of death. The Commission published their fabricated statement because they knew that the general public had little knowledge of law.

Since the Commission accepted Mrs. Markham's veracity as being above reproach, then her time of 1:06 as the time the shooting commenced must be accepted. With the time no longer an issue, the Warren Commission then proceeded to attempt to prove that the death of Officer Tippit was caused by bullets fired from a revolver used by the accused, which caused the death. However, in the Tippit Affaire, there is no legal cause of death! He may have died of the common cold, galloping cancer like Jack Ruby, T. B., a strep throat, mumps, scarlet fever, or other ailments. There is absolutely no legal statement regarding the cause of Tippit's death. President Kennedy's autopsy "report" is published but not Tippit's. Why?

The two important questions that the Warren "Report" has refused to answer are: (1) What caused the death of Officer Tippit?" and (2) How many Tippit bodies are involved?" The reason "why" the Commission suppressed the answers can be read in a suppressed Secret Service document now in the National Archives under a code number 87. In file no. 87 is a strange, mysterious, and foreboding document, code number M63-352, authenticated by the United States Secret Service, dated November 22, 1963, and signed by a Dr. Rose. Not less than five (5) "Tippit" bodies are involved; the FBI added a sixth!

Secret Service Agent Moore, whose name is signed to the report, wrote that Dr. Rose informed him that 3 bullets penetrated Tippit's body and the 4th bullet merely "hit a button on the officer's coat." Body No. 1.

Agent Moore continued: "Three bullets hit Tippit in the chest and one in the head." Body No. 2 has 4 penetrating bullet holes.

The agent continued further: "Officer R. Davenport informed him that 'a .38 caliber bullet was taken from the stomach of Officer Tippit.'" Body No. 3 has a stomach wound.

One would now believe that the Commission had sufficient bodies to prove that Officer Tippit died as the result of bullet wounds. But, no! Inspector Kelley of the U.S. Secret Service testified that "Tippit was shot once in the head and twice in the chest." Body No. 4 has only 2 chest wounds.

The Dallas police now became involved and furnished the Commission with a body that "was shot 3 times, one each in the hand, chest, and head." Body No. 5 has a hand wound. (177.)

For the finale, the FBI testified that a bullet carried part of the button on Tippit's jacket into the body. Body No. 6 has part of the button going into Tippit's body. (178.)

Thus, according to the testimony, Tippit was struck by 3 chest bullets, 2 head bullets, 1 hand bullet, once in the stomach, and one bullet carried part of the button into his chest. These reports given by the various police and federal agencies revealed the contempt they had for the Commission and the dead officer. With six different bodies involved, not a single eyebrow was raised by the upholders of the "basic principles of American justice." Not an eyebrow was lifted at the outright perjury being committed by some of those police agents.

In view of the conflicting statements given under oath by the two federal agencies and the Dallas police, one can honestly raise the question: "Was Officer Tippit's cause of death the result of bullets fired into his body?" If the autopsy report authenticated by the U.S. Secret Service is true and correct, then what does the Tippit death certificate state? Only that he was dead? Is the death certificate true and honestly correct? It is a certainty that five bodies are not in one casket, but the legal question is: "Whose body?" Any attorney defending Oswald in the Tippit Affaire must ask that question, for no man can be convicted of murder when the prosecution selects five bodies.

The duty therefore devolves upon any person who is investigating the Warren Commission as to the reason why the Commission acted in the manner it did in the Tippit murder. There must be a reason and perhaps an investigation will reveal it. Thus, an investigation must relate back to the time the murder occurred.

The Tippit Affaire had its starting point when Code 3 was flashed on the police broadcast: All squad cars were to be on the lookout for a "slender white male, about 30, 5' 10", weighing about 165 lbs., carrying a .30-30 Winchester." The Commission admitted that Oswald's name and description were never used by the police in any broadcast. (179.) The Commission admitted that the Dallas police and the district attorney's office lied to the press media when they announced Oswald was "wanted" because he missed a roll call and that the "found" rifle was known to be Oswald's. There was never any roll call, and the rifle was not found until after the murder of Tippit. (180.) However, the Commission did conceal the fact that a rifle with no telescopic sight was taken from the Depository at 1:00 p.m., and that rifle was found on the 3rd floor where a police executive also found 3 cartridges which disappeared from the police station. (181.) The Inspector Sawyer announcement to the police broadcaster also stated that the wanted man was carrying a .30-30 Winchester rifle, but his announcement carried no clothing- or facial description of any person. Thus, the question never answered by anyone was: "How and why did Officer Tippit stop a white male at 1:06 p.m.?"

After stopping his squad car, Officer Tippit, according to the Report," got out of his car and approached the "white male" with his gun remaining in his holster. Would an experienced police officer approach the suspected murderer of the president of the United States with his gun in his hand or in his holster? Then, as Tippit approached this man, he was shot 3, 4, 5 or 6 times, depending upon the testimony of the police, the Secret Service, or the FBI. The Commission would state that Tippit was shot five times although they had no evidence to support their statement. Why? The answer will be uncovered by the testimony. In view of the autopsy report and the number of bullets taken from "Tippit's" body, no one in Dallas or Washington, D.C. legally knows how many bullets either struck Officer Tippit or were recovered from his body,

The only lawful evidence given to the Warren Commission is that the FBI received four bullets from the Dallas police and none of these four bullets came from the Oswald revolver which the FBI received from the police.

The Commission stated that they had two eyewitnesses to the Tippit shooting who could identify Oswald as the murderer. The Commission's key witness was Mrs. Markham, who informed the police at the murder scene that the killer (1) was a white man; (2) had bushy hair; (3) wore a white shirt; and (4) wore a white jacket. She then reiterated this description for the benefit of a CBS television and radio audience. To the FBI, Mrs. Markham gave an affidavit to Agent Odum that the killer was a "white male, about 18 years of age, black hair, red complexion." (181a.) On page 167 of the Commission's "Report," the Commission summed up their judgment of Mrs. Markham: "reliable." (182.) At the identification parade, the Dallas police admitted that Mrs. Markham was too sick to view the lineup, was in a state of shock, and was unable to give the police any physical description of the man she saw as the killer. (183.) She reiterated her statement [that] she could not and did not recognize Oswald at the police lineup. (184.) Oswald, when he left his rooming house, was wearing a tan shirt and a dark jacket, never had bushy hair. This has been admitted by the Commission, the Dallas police, and the FBI. What more would Oswald's defense attorney need?

The Commission's second witness was Mr. Benavides, who described the murderer as a white man who had "curly hair" and was "dark complexioned." In fact, the police used his description in one of the police broadcasts. (185.) When the police questioned him at the scene of the murder, he informed them he could not identify the killer, so they did not ask him to go to the police lineup. Of course, the fact that he admitted he could not identify the killer did not obviate the fact that if he had gone to the lineup he could have testified that it was not Oswald. This is what the police did not want, a positive identification of Oswald as the man not seen by Mr. Benavides! Yet, he was only 15 feet away from the killer when he witnessed the murder.

With their allegations concerning the identify of Oswald as the killer collapsing, the Commission was reduced to summoning a taxicab driver whose identification was assisted by various police agencies. In his testimony the cabdriver admitted that he never saw the killer's face nor was he able to select Oswald's face when FBI agents showed him photographs. (186.) Nor did he see Mrs. Markham at any time when he viewed Tippit's body near the squad car. (187.) The Dallas police also admitted that at no time did they regard the cabdriver's description of any value since he could furnish no physical or facial description of the killer. However, in a lineup loaded with fraud, the cabdriver selected Oswald as the killer when he had already informed the police that he could not describe the killer.

The Commission dwelt a long time with this unexpected witness, but what the Commission failed to inform the American people of was that this same witness testified that the killer was left-handed, as the killer fled with the gun in his left hand. (188). Oswald was right-handed. (189.)

With their identification charade being destroyed, the Commission decided that the only way to connect Oswald to the murder was to allege that during his "flight" from the murder scene he became hot and dropped his jacket. In its "Report" the Commission stated that Police Captain Westbrook was the finder, and, as usual, the Commission lied since the captain denied finding any jacket. (190.)

Not a single person, not one witness who testified before the Commission, ever identified this jacket, Com. Exh. 162–a grey jacket which the Commission said belonged to Oswald–as the jacket they saw the killer wear. Mrs. Markham absolutely denied it was the jacket she saw the killer wear (191); Mr. Benavides identified a blue jacket (192); the cabdriver said "no" (193); as did the Davis sisters (194); nor did Ted Callaway (195); nor did Mrs. Roberts, the only witness to see Oswald and the jacket he wore when he left his rooming house at 1:00 p.m. (196.) Finally, Wesley Frazier, Oswald's next door neighbor and fellow employee, testified that at no time did he ever see Oswald wear the jacket. (197.)

The Commission's contortions in their attempt to associate an unknown jacket to Oswald was clearly seen in their fraudulent attempt to conceal the fact that the Commission did not know how or when that jacket was found. Capt. Westbrook testified he did not find the jacket; that it was given to him by an "unknown" policeman who, according to the police radio log, wore Badge No. "279." There is also a statement by an Officer Hutson that it was not Capt. Westbrook who picked up the jacket but another officer and, unfortunately, Hutson did not know the name of that officer. (198.) In Dallas, the presumption must be that any person who wants to be a Dallas policeman simply goes into an Army-Navy retail store and purchases a Dallas police uniform. This is not as funny as it reads for the activities of the Dallas police made the Mack Sennett "Keystone Cops" look serious. The testimony revealed that Badge No. 279 was worn by an Officer J. Griffin who, in turn, was a police officer in a 12-man motorcycle squad of which both Hutson and Griffin were members! (199.) Yet, Hutson testified he never knew Badge No. 279 belonged to his friend in his own motorcycle squad. Who was committing perjury? Was that jacket, Com. Exh. No. 162, found or was it a plant by the police in the Dallas Police Headquarters?

The evidence proved, beyond a reasonable doubt, that no jacket was ever found in the Tippit murder area. It was a plant made by the Dallas police.

What the Commission had concealed is that both Griffin and Hutson testified that the jacket they "found" was "white" not grey. (200.) No police officer ever admitted he located or picked up the Commission's grey jacket; nor did any officer admit he picked up a jacket and gave it to another policeman. Thus, the question never answered by the Warren Commission was: "If no police officer admitted finding or handling that jacket, how did it get into the hands of the police department?"

Now reduced to an absolute zero in their efforts to have that jacket belong to Oswald, the Commission summoned their most expert witness on the life of Lee Harvey Oswald: his wife, Marina. Knowing that she would lose the custody of her two children, and facing deportation, Mrs. Oswald promptly acceded to their "request" that she identify Com. Exh. 162 as belonging to her husband. (201.)

This Commission jacket, when given to the FBI by the Dallas police, had attached to it a laundry code number "B-9738." The jacket was a "medium" size and Oswald always wore a "small" size. The FBI, the Dallas police, and the Secret Service visited every cleaning and laundry shop in the Dallas; Irving, Texas; and the New Orleans area, and they never located, out of those 600 shops in those areas, any shop that used that code number. Mrs. Oswald, prior to her statement to the Commission, informed the FBI and Secret Service that she never took her husband's clothes, at any time, to any dry cleaning or laundry shop during their married life! (202.)

After the arrival of the police upon the Tippit murder site, they attempted to obtain witnesses for the description which they could broadcast. Upon analyzing the radio logs, it seems clear that the original police broadcast used the information given to them by Patrolman Summers: "I got an eyeball witness to the getaway man. He is a white male, age 27, 5' 11", black wavy hair, fair complected, wearing a light Eisenhower-type jacket, dark trousers, and a white shirt, apparently armed with a .32 dark-finish automatic pistol, which he had in his right hand." (203). Oswald, when captured some 20 minutes after that broadcast of 1:33 p.m., was wearing a tan shirt and did not have black wavy hair. The Commission admitted that Oswald wore a tan shirt at the Depository and at the Texas Theatre!

In addition to the description that did not match Oswald, two other facts appeared: (1) the police, as per its custom, failed to obtain the name or address of the "eyeball witness," and (2) the killer was armed with a .32 automatic pistol, not a revolver allegedly taken from Oswald when arrested. Furthermore, Sgt.

Hill, immediately after Summers' talk to the radio dispatcher, also informed his radio contact that the killer was armed with an automatic .38, as indicated by a discharged shell left at the murder site. (204.) Thus, both policemen informed the radio dispatcher that an automatic gun was used, or was one of the weapons used, to murder Officer Tippit. Another indication that two killers were involved was the testimony of cabdriver Scoggins, who saw the killer flee with the gun clutched in his left hand.

In summation relating to the identity of Oswald as the "killer," the Commission had no witness who identified Oswald as the murderer; the Commission had no evidence that not only was the jacket "found" under mysterious circumstances but that no witness identified the jacket to the man they saw flee from the actual scene of the murder; and at no time was the jacket associated with Oswald under any circumstances in spite of the testimony of Mrs. Marina Oswald, who admitted that at no time had she ever sent Oswald's jackets to a dry cleaning or laundry shop.

Of course, the perversion of the time of the murder from 1:06 p.m. to 1:16 p.m. was conclusive proof beyond a reasonable doubt that Oswald was never at the Tippit murder site.

The Commission, having failed in its endeavors to link Oswald as the killer, was now reduced to relying upon (1) an unknown pistol; and (2) bullets allegedly recovered from one of five bodies in the Dallas morgue. Within twenty minutes after the police broadcast of the Summers description, Oswald was arrested in the Texas Theatre. What occurred during his arrest is not known, as the Dallas police carefully screened approximately 10 to 15 patrons and selected only two–who promptly gave contradictory statements regarding those events. Why those, and only those two witnesses, were selected was never asked by the Commission; although the captain-in-charge testified that he directed his lieutenant to make a list of all of the patrons. What happened to that list, if taken, is unknown. The Commission never subpoenaed that list. Why? Could the answer be that the uncalled witnesses would reveal the fact that Oswald never drew a revolver from his waist belt? Thus, an investigator of the Tippit Affaire is reduced to analyzing the testimony of the Dallas police, many of whom gave perjured testimony.

The policeman who was given credit, "in the face of death,"

was Patrolman McDonald. His activity on that day revealed the type of conduct practiced by the Dallas Police Department and accepted, as normal, by 7 commissioners and 26 lawyer aides. In an earlier chapter a distinction was made between a liar, in law, and a perjurer. In one instance, McDonald was a liar; in the other a perjurer. On November 24, 1963 this "heroic" patrolman gave his personal story to the Dallas "Morning News" wherein, according to himself, he showed great initiative when he heard a tip while at the Depository. Leaping in his trusty squad car a la Hop-along Cassidy, putting his foot down hard on the gas pedal, he sped to the theater, rushed into it, had the lights turned on, but received another "tip" from an unknown patron who told him the "suspicious" character was not in the balcony, as the first tipster had informed him, but on the first floor. How the "tipster" on the first floor knew that the suspect was now on the first floor instead of in the balcony, McDonald did not explain. Of course, it could be interpreted that a conspirator was the "tipster," but the Commission said there was no conspiracy.

Did McDonald, the intrepid, go directly to the man pointed out by his unknown tipster? Of course not. He jumped off the stage and proceeded down the aisle where he first passed a short time-of-day by talking to two patrons with his back toward the suspect. But he first took his pistol out of his holster in spite of the fact that it would be pointing the other way. He then ceased his conversation with the two patrons, approached Oswald, a struggle ensued, with McDonald using three hands to subdue this man who had "snuck" into the theater, and Oswald was overpowered by this 10-ft. tall patrolman. McDonald also claimed that Oswald fired at him but the "primer was dented and it didn't fire." And with a blare of bugles, McDonald signed the news story.

Now, proceeding to point out the lies. At the time of the shooting of President Kennedy, McDonald–as were many other police squad cars–was instructed to go to the Book Depository to render assistance. (He was not cruising around.) He arrived at the Depository at 12:40 p.m. and remained there until 1:16 p.m., when he said he heard the police radio flash that a policeman had been shot. Without notifying any of his superior officers he got into his squad car and drove toward the Tippit murder site.

On the way there he testified he heard that the man suspected in the Tippit murder was "a white male, 5' 10", 27 years old, wearing a white shirt." Note that the suspect is wearing a "white" shirt. He never heard the Summers description, he admitted. (205.)

Although McDonald admitted that "at the time of Oswald's arrest he (Oswald) was wearing a dark brown shirt, a T-shirt, and dark trousers, the Commission never asked McDonald how he reconciled a "white shirt" with a "dark tan" one. (206.) Nor did the Commission ask the patrolman how his theater "tipster" knew that he was looking for a man on the first floor instead of a man in the balcony. Now can be seen the reason why the police lieutenant never submitted the list of patrons he was ordered to take by the police captain. The "informer-tipster's" name would be on it.

McDonald, upon hearing that there was a suspect in the Texas Theatre, then hurried to that place. Although there were some 20 to 25 police at the theater, McDonald rushed into the theater accompanied by the shoe salesman and manager. The lights were put on and Mr. Brewer pointed out Oswald. He went down the stairs, conversed with the two patrons (what they said was not told by McDonald to the Commission), then approached Oswald with his cocked pistol in his hand. This "suspect" then got up from his seat, and despite the fact that McDonald already had a cocked pistol pointing at him, deliberately drew from his waist a revolver, but did not fire, only struck out at McDonald. McDonald used one hand to hold the gun, another one to grab Oswald's gun which did not fire because "the primer was dented," and with his third hand grabbed Oswald around the body. While all this was going on, Special Detective R. Carroll "jerked" a gun from someone's hand. (207.)

McDonald's "epic" story never answered pertinent questions: (1) Since when does any police department send 15 to 20 policemen to answer a call to apprehend a man "sneaking" into a theater? (2) Since Oswald's description in no shape, manner, or form matched the suspect in the only description given over the Dallas police broadcast, why did the Dallas police send that many men to arrest a man for a misdemeanor? (3) How did the police rationalize that overwhelming force when no one saw

Oswald enter the theater with a gun in his hand or clothes? (4) How did McDonald rationalize the only description he received was that of Oswald?

The only answer with any common sense applied to it would be that Oswald was ordered to the theater by his fellow-conspirators and they, in turn, believed that Oswald would, in panic, seek to escape and be shot down by the police stationed in the rear of the theater.

What actually occurred can be placed together after the reading of all of the testimony. The commissioner who destroyed the Commission's case regarding the question of whether or not Oswald had a revolver in his possession when arrested was Senator Cooper. In his cross-examination to establish the legal requirement that the weapon "taken" from Oswald was the identical weapon before the Commission, Senator Cooper asked Det. R. Carroll from whom did he "jerk" the revolver. To the consternation of the other commissioners and aides, the special detective calmly testified he "jerked it" from someone's hand but he did not know whose hand. (208.)

Previous to Carroll's testimony, McDonald testified that he had put his "mark" upon the weapon he had "taken" from Oswald; but on cross-examination the patrolman admitted that he had put his "mark" on a weapon given to him by an "unknown" policeman at the police station. Thus, in fact and in law, McDonald was admitting that he had not recognized Oswald's weapon since the weapon he identified was given to him at the police station. Again, one is impressed by the tremendous number of policemen who do not know their fellow-policemen in Dallas, Texas. Unidentified "cops" float all over Dallas and all over the head of the Commission. Whenever the Commission desired "evidence" needed to draw Oswald into their net, the Commission was always able to locate the essential "unidentified" policeman right at their elbow.

In view of the testimony of McDonald and Carroll, the only implication that can be made, based upon their testimony, is that the Dallas police had Oswald's revolver in their possession prior to his arrest and prior to the murder of Officer Tippit. Which, in turn, implies that Officer Tippit was primed to be murdered with the knowledge of some Dallas policemen.

Perjury was immediately presented to the Commission for (1) McDonald testified that when he "took" the revolver from Oswald's hand after he had been subdued, McDonald immediately opened up the revolver chamber and put his "mark" upon one of the six bullets in that space. He lied, for he put his "mark" upon a revolver given to him at the police station. (208a.) (2) But Det. Carroll testified that when he "jerked" the revolver from an unknown hand, he immediately gave the revolver to Sgt. Hill, who in turn, while seated in the squad car outside the theater, opened the revolver, saw six bullets in the chamber, and made his mark upon the bullets. (209.) (3) A revolver was then taken to the police station and that is all those two men know about a revolver. (210.) This scenario is the exact duplicate of the one enacted over Bullet No. "399." A bullet is found; a revolver is found, and in both cases no legal identification can be made in a court of law. Thus, one of the questions to be answered is: "Was a switch made?" Of course, the question could also be asked: "Since no one except McDonald testified that Oswald had a revolver when he was arrested, and he had committed perjury and had also lied, his credibility was under a severe strain. Was the revolver at the police station a plant?"

The evidence supporting both a "switch" and a "plant" of the revolver was admitted, by error or mental strain, by Capt. Fritz. After the arrest of Oswald and his booking by the police, the Captain held a press conference and, in addition to his comments concerning why Oswald was the killer of President Kennedy, announced that Oswald was "guilty" in the Tippit murder, because Oswald's gun had "two empty shells in it." According to McDonald, Carroll, and Hill, six live shells were in the revolver but the revolver that the Captain had in his office, which was given to him by Sgt. Hill, had only 4 live shells and two empty ones. QED the revolver taken or "jerked" by Carroll from an unknown hand was not the revolver in the possession of the Dallas police, which they said was the one used by Oswald to kill Tippit.

In a further attempt to connect Oswald with that "revolver," the Commission accepted the "word" of the police that they found a gun holster on Oswald's bed when they illegally searched his room after his arrest. Mrs. Roberts, whose testimony was never contradicted, testified that at no time as long as he had lived in her home did she ever see Oswald have a revolver or holster. She testified that she cleaned his room and changed the sheets. (211.) The police again "found" the evidence which the Commission needed to draw the "net" a little tighter around Oswald.

McDonald as previously mentioned, testified that Oswald attempted to murder him when Oswald pulled the trigger of his "gun" and the "primer misfired because it was dented." It was this testimony which led the Commission to accuse Oswald "of attempting to kill a police officer while resisting arrest" (Commission Conclusion No. 5). The reason why they made this charge is absolutely baffling, for they had the testimony of the FBI ballistic bureau that said McDonald was mistaken. McDonald testified that he heard the "click" and the revolver misfired, not that he put his finger or part of his hand between the trigger and the chamber. The FBI testified that when they examined the shells given to them by the Dallas police they found that "none of the cartridges found in that revolver bore the impression of the revolver firing pin." (212.) That disposes of the Commission's 5th Conclusion. Oswald never pulled that trigger and it casts further doubt on the credibility of Patrolman McDonald.

What did the FBI seek to achieve by using the language: "none of the cartridges found in that revolver bore the impression of the revolver firing pin"? The only logical answer is that the FBI was warning the Commission that that revolver was never used in any murder on November 22, 1963! "Oswald" was supposed to have reloaded 6 bullets in that revolver when he fled. Capt. Fritz testified that that revolver had 4 live bullets and 2 expended shells. Now, the FBI was saying that none of the cartridges had any impression of the revolver's firing pin. Then what force compelled the two bullets to leave the cartridges?

During the entire investigation conducted by the Commission in the Tippit murder, they never produced a scintilla of evidence that the theater revolver was ever taken from Oswald or that he had one in his possession; or that the revolver sent to the FBI by the Dallas police was the identical revolver "taken" from Oswald. Thus, in a court of law, the Commission only proved that Oswald "owned" a revolver known as Comm. Exh. No. 143, but they never legally proved by the evidence published in the "Hearings" that that revolver was "used" in the Tippit murder.

With the evidence blowing up in their collective faces regarding the revolver, the Commission was reduced to the bullets and cartridges given to the FBI by the Dallas police; for, in a court of law, those bullets and cartridges must match the bullets taken from "Tippit's body(s)," and the cartridges must also match the Tippit revolver. From a legal point of view, to this day, no one knows the exact number of bullets used to kill Officer Tippit, if, in fact, he was killed by bullets.

That the Commission willingly and knowingly accepted perjured testimony from the Dallas police is seen by their statements that only three (3) bullets were fired in Officer Tippit's body. Det. Leavelle and Capt. King swore there were only three bullets. (213.) In view of their sworn testimony, the ballistic expert for the FBI, Mr. Cunningham, testified: "For the record I would like to state these 4 bullets, C251, C252, Q13, and C253 were recovered from the body of Tippit."(214.) Here the Dallas police was being charged with perjury by the FBI, yet the Commission said nothing and did nothing, Thus, who was committing perjury? Did the Commission know for a certainty who was committing the perjury, the FBI or the Dallas police? The Commission knew that the police were committing flagrant perjury since a Commission aide directly informed the Commission in response from Commissioner Boggs: "How many bullets were recovered?" Aide: "Four were recovered from the body of the Officer ... that does not mean four bullets were found, because there is a slight problem here." (215.)

Slight problem? What a problem! That should have been the answer.

It was a problem that was taxing to the brain. For, in the development of attempting to reconcile the testimony of the Dallas police with that of the U.S. Secret Service suppressed autopsy report, which revealed the existence of five (5) different Tippit bodies, and with that of the police testimony of only three bullets while at the same instance, right on the top of the Commission's table, were 4 bullets, was the "slight problem." With these four bullets on the Commission's table, to what did the aide think Agent Cunningham was referring? Cats and dogs? Why did the police commit this obvious perjury, and why did the Commission agree to accept their perjury?

As the investigator digs into the "Hearings," he becomes amazed at the duplicity practiced by the Commission. In the "slight problem" enunciated by the aide, the problem was stated but never solved. The Commission's fourth bullet on its table was none other than a bullet from a .38 automatic which could not be discharged from the revolver "taken" from Oswald at the theater. Two policemen, as has been stated, found an automatic shell, recently fired, at the Tippit murder site. (216.) Thus, either the killer was a "two-gun" man or there were two killers. Yet the two key witnesses, Mrs. Markham and Mr. Scoggins, only saw one killer. One killer, one gun. Oswald's weapon was not an automatic pistol. Using common sense, the automatic shell proved Oswald was not the killer.

There is now no doubt that the Dallas police never proved Oswald had a revolver in his possession, nor an automatic; in addition, if there was a pistol taken from him, it was not the weapon used to murder Tippit. Therefore, the police switched that weapon for another weapon in the police station. When the FBI asked the police for the bullets that killed Tippit, they gave the FBI a bullet and a statement that only one bullet was recovered. That was on November 23, 1963, but as rumors swept the country that more than one bullet was involved the Commission demanded that the police surrender the other ones. Lo, and behold, after searching their "dead" files, the police "found" three bullets. The FBI did not testify that these 3 bullets came from a specific revolver, just that the Dallas police gave them those 3 bullets.

Upon an examination in the FBI Laboratory, the Bureau knew that they were being asked to act as the "fall guys" for the Dallas police. In the FBI's testimony they said: "It is not possible from an examination and comparison of those bullets to determine whether or not they had been fired–those bullets themselves–had been fired from one weapon or whether they had been fired from Oswald's revolver." (217.) The meaning of that testimony was loud and clear, for the Bureau warned the Commission that the police were involved in (1) switching revolvers; (2) planting false evidence; (3) suppressing evidence connecting someone in the Dallas Police Department with the Tippit murder. In the "Hearings" the FBI testified that "(a) three of the four bullets given to them by the police were manufactured by the Winchester-Western Corp.; (b) the fourth bullet was a Remington-Peters; (c) only two shells of the three bullets were found; and (d) two shells of one bullet were found." (218.)

"How can," asked the FBI, "one bullet be discharged from two shells?"

Damaging evidence from the FBI was suppressed by the Commission, but it can be found in FBI File No. 87, Dec. No. 774, in which Mr. Hoover wrote: "that the bullets sent to the FBI Laboratory were too mutilated to be tested. That three of the four bullets may have come from the revolver given to the Bureau by the police, from Oswald's pockets, or the U.S. Secret Service." In a court of law, a judge would have given a "not guilty" verdict to Oswald. Since none of the bullets could be matched to that "Oswald" revolver, the prosecution had no case. Having relied upon the FBI as its only witness and agency to test the bullets, the Bureau's answer was a complete clearance of Oswald. True, the chief's letter is an amazing one in that he impliedly implicated the U.S. Secret Service, but the fact remained that the FBI said those bullets could not be ballistically tested, so that the Bureau could not, beyond a reasonable doubt, say those bullets did in fact and in law come from the alleged Oswald revolver given to the FBI by the Dallas police. Mr. Hoover knew that no revolver could discharge a .38 automatic bullet from that "Oswald" pistol, and he was not going to place his head on the chopping block when the Oswald Affaire was to be examined by historians as the years passed.

The evidence is overwhelming that, as with the rifle cartridges, the Dallas police were submitting "faked" cartridges to the Commission. According to FBI Agent Cunningham's testimony, the bullets given to him by the Dallas police as being discharged from the "Oswald" revolver were too small a caliber to fit properly within that revolver. As to the 4 cartridges, two of them were found by the man who could not identify Oswald as the killer, Mr. Benavides, and one each by the Davis sisters.[20] Benavides's two cartridges were taken by Patrolman Poe, who marked those two with his initials "JMP." (219.) He then gave them to Sgt. Barnes, who also placed his initial "B" upon those two plus the other two cartridges. What happened at the Hearings? As usual, both policemen refused to identify the cartridges shown to them by the Commission as coming from the "Oswald" revolver! Their initials had disappeared. In a court of criminal law, no respecting judge would convict a man accused of murder on the cartridges, which had been either "planted" or "switched" by the Dallas police. In law, those four cartridges given to the Commission were outright fakes. (220.)

One of the most intriguing questions in the Tippit murder is: "How did the Dallas police know Tippit was to be slain approximately 30 to 40 minutes prior to its occurrence?" The reader is advised to read Com. Exh. No. 2003, No. 78 to 85 inclusive. No. 79 is a police statement that a Dallas policeman was stationed at the Trade Mart where the president was to give his luncheon address. At 12:40 p.m., after the announcement that the president was shot, the policeman was ordered to go directly to the Book Depository to render assistance. The Depository is less than 4 miles from the Trade Mart. The officer immediately left at 12:45 p.m. to go to the Depository, but then this officer, between the Trade Mart and the Depository, heard the police announcement that a policeman had been shot in the Oak Cliff district. The time? Not later than 1 p.m.! Tippit was shot at 1:06 p.m., but no announcement was made, according to the Dallas police, until 1:20 p.m., when it was flashed over the Dallas police radio band.

This same officer, although the president of the United States was dying from gunshot wounds, and although being ordered by a superior officer to assist in the investigation of the shooting of the president, decided to investigate a shooting of a fellow officer, although no police radio call had summoned any police from the Trade Mart or Book Depository to go the Oak Cliff murder site. The same officer, violating his instructions, contin-

---

[20] Barbara Jeanette Davis and her sister-in-law, Mrs. Charlie Virginia Davis.

ued on the way to Oak Cliff, but on the way he heard on the police radio that a suspect was being sought in a Dallas branch public library some 5 miles away from the Tippit murder site. Therefore, to assist his competent (?) fellow police to search the library, this police officer dashed to the library. Arriving there, he was informed by a man representing himself to be a "U.S. Secret Service agent" that it was a false alarm and to go to the Texas Theatre! This patrolman then drove to the Texas Theatre.

Thus, in this Com. Exhibit No. 2003 can be seen (1) a statement that can only be labeled "perjurious," for if that policeman left the Trade Mart at 12:40 p.m.–and since the Book Depository is less than 7 minutes by siren-sounding police radio squad car–how did this patrolman hear the shooting of Officer Tippit at not later than 1 p. m.? (2) Who was the "U.S, Secret Service agent" at the Dallas branch public library that notified this patrolman that the library "tip" was false, and the alleged killer of Tippit was somewhere else? (3) Why did the Warren Commission fail to cross-examine this officer who heard the Tippit alarm some 40 minutes prior to its occurrence, and why did they fail to ask him about the "Secret Service agent?"

In the same Exhibit, No. 2003, #83, a Lt. Cunningham was also at the Trade Mart. He also heard of the Tippit shooting at the same time the first policeman said he heard the announcement. Lt. Cunningham also said he heard that the suspect was in the Texas Theatre. He hurried to that place and entered it, where some unidentified officer notified him that the suspect was in the balcony. While searching the balcony, Lt. Cunningham heard someone shout that the suspect was on the first floor. Another Exhibit, #81, was signed by Special Detective Carroll, the man who "jerked" a revolver from an unknown person during the Oswald "struggle." When Carroll entered the theater, an "unknown white female" informed him that the suspect was in the balcony, so he went to the balcony. While in the balcony, Carroll heard another "unknown" voice shout that the suspect was on the first floor! Who was the unknown "tipster" that knew that Lee Harvey Oswald was wanted for the Tippit murder? Who knew that Oswald was on the first floor and not in the balcony? The only answer must be a conspirator.

The outstanding feature of the police affidavits in Com. Exh.

2003 is the salient fact that the police at the Trade Mart were informed by some voice over the police radio band that Tippit had been shot 30 minutes prior to the actual statement made by Mr. Bowley from Tippit's radio squad car. The police radio announced the shooting of President Kennedy at 12:30. Between 12:30 and 12:45 p.m., the police at the Trade Mart were instructed to go to the Book Depository to render assistance. The Trade Mart police said they left immediately and, on the way to the Depository, a mere 5 miles away, they all heard the police radio announce the shooting of Officer Tippit. Therefore, the absolute maximum time they heard that announcement was 12:55 p.m.

This time element was substantiated by Police Chief Curry's testimony that he was notified "a short time after 1 p.m." that an "officer had been shot" in the Oak Cliff area. He was informed by "unidentified" policemen at the Parkland Hospital. This notification was also prior to the time of Tippit's death!

Now it can be seen why the Dallas Police Department submitted false transcripts of their radio tapes between 12 noon and 2 p.m. This falsification was so obvious that the Commission asked the FBI to attempt to obtain the truth, but the police so garbled the original tapes that the FBI had no success. Of course, what could have occurred was the same situation in the Dr. King assassination when the conspirators intervened on the Memphis, Tenn. police radio band and directed the Memphis police away from the killer's automobile. However, in the Dallas murder, the conspirators directed the police toward their "patsy," Lee Harvey Oswald.

Further evidence that Tippit was also slated to be murdered is the undisputed fact that fake Secret Service agents were "assisting" the Dallas police in seeking Oswald, both at the Public Library, at the Texas Theatre, and at the Book Depository. Yet, the Commission said "no conspiracy."

Summarizing the testimony in the "Hearings" and the National Archives, a court of law, ruled by an impartial judge, would instruct the jury of impartial Americans, to bring forth a verdict of "not guilty" if Lee Harvey Oswald had lived to face trial for the murder of Officer Tippit. Capt. Fritz testified that Oswald never admitted that he killed the police officer. He did admit owning a revolver but he never admitted, according to the same police captain, that he ever used that weapon to kill anyone. Oswald never admitted that he had any revolver in his possession when he was arrested in the Texas Theatre. In fact and in law, there is no evidence that proved any policeman took a revolver from him in that theater. McDonald was proved to be both a liar and a perjurer and his testimony that he saw Oswald with a revolver in his possession and that Oswald attempted to shoot him was not verified by any police officer in that theater, or by an FBI examination of that gun.

The evidence proved that the jacket "found" near the murder site was not worn by Oswald; nor did the evidence reveal the finder of that jacket; nor did the evidence show that that jacket fit Oswald. As a matter of fact, although the police had that jacket for the two days while they were interrogating Oswald, the evidence revealed that not once did the police ask of or show Oswald that jacket. The evidence revealed that the jacket label was "medium" when all of Oswald's clothes bore a "small" label.

Oswald was never legally identified as the man fleeing from the Tippit murder site nor was he identified by the two key witnesses used by the Commission as the man who fired bullets into Tippit's body.

No legal authority knows how many bullets were fired into Tippit's body. No legal authority testified that he died from bullet wounds in the body. There is no legal autopsy report as to the cause of death, therefore Tippit could just as well have died from natural causes, poison, knife wounds, or bullets. At no time did the Commission summon the ambulance drivers who placed Tippit in the ambulance. Was he alive? Was he bleeding? Did he have bullet wounds? Where were those wounds, in the head, chest, hands, legs, where? No one knows. What is known, in law, is that there were five different "Tippit" bodies involved. Which was the "real" Tippit?

The Warren Commission's allegations in paragraph 5 and its "Conclusion No. 5" was never proved with the slightest aroma of legal evidence. QED Oswald was innocent and a verdict of "not guilty" would be upheld in any court of this land.

CHAPTER VII

ODDS AND ENDS

Probably the most asinine conclusion arrived by the upholders of "the basic principles of American justice" was the Commission's "Conclusion" No. 7 that Oswald attempted to murder ex-Maj. Gen. Walker. The testimony of every Dallas police officer who investigated the attempt admitted that at no time was there the slightest evidence that connected Oswald to the crime. The only witness who did make the connection was his "ever lovin' wife." She admitted that though Oswald never admitted making that attempt, she believed he did because he acted peculiar. Of course, the fact that the slug recovered from the Walker home was found to be a .30-mm bullet which cannot be discharged from a 6.5 Italian Mannlicher-Carcano rifle proved Oswald innocent.

In the official FBI Report, Vol. I, is the statement by the Bureau which proved that the Italian rifle was a "plant." This sentence, overlooked by many critics and supporters of the Commission, said, on page 21: "because of the mutilation of this (Walker) bullet and because the gun barrel may have been changed since April, 1963, it was not possible to determine whether or not this bullet was fired from Oswald's rifle." Extraordinary language! The FBI was warning the Commission that the Italian rifle given to them by the Dallas police was manufactured evidence. Where could anyone purchase the barrel of a 1941 Italian rifle? Why would the purchaser change the barrel? Furthermore, a .30-mm slug cannot be discharged through a 6.51-mm carbine. A .30 bullet has the dimensions of a 7.65 bullet and it cannot be discharged through a 6.5 rifle barrel! The FBI should not be held responsible for the stupidity of the Commission aides.

The validity of the Commission's accusation against Oswald relating to the Walker murder attempt is as valid as making a statement that the moon is made of green cheese. An impartial judge would have thrown the case out of court–and the prosecutor with it.

One of the major allegations in the Commission's indictment was that Oswald was guilty because he lied to the police concerning important substantive matters. This was the Commission's "Conclusion No. 6." Under the "basic principles of American justice," to establish the legal fact that a person lied two factors must be proved: (1) legal notes must be taken by a competent stenographer who can interpret those notes in open court and be subject to cross-examination concerning the translation; or (2) witnesses who were in the interrogation room and who heard both the question and answer to the specific question.

This rule of law was recently involved in a New York federal criminal case where the defense attorney for the accused successfully raised the point that the notes taken by the prosecution stenographer were transcribed improperly from the stenographer's notebook to the original typewritten record. The federal judge ruled that those notes were inadmissible to both the court and the jury. (221.) The Commission, under its own interpretation of the "law," buried in the "Hearings" the fact that they relied heavily upon the evidence given to them by Capt. Fritz. The Commission stated that the learned captain relied upon his "rough" notes. The Commission, however, being "outstanding" members of the American Bar, knew very well that no court of law would accept the captain's testimony to convict Oswald of murder. The Commission either lied on page 180 of the "Report," where on one page he kept "no notes," or on page 611, where he kept "rough notes."

If no valid notes were taken then how could the Commission prove that Oswald was lying on substantive matters? The Commission made no comment to the fact that the Dallas Police Department in one of the wealthiest cities in the United States could not afford (1) a stenographer; or (2) a tape recorder. Nor could that same police department request a stenographer from District Attorney Wade's office, or ask for his tape recorder; (3) nor did the Police ask any county office for a stenographer or tape recorder. Of course, the fact that a conspiracy was involved and in that involvement were some low and high members of the Dallas Police Department, the sheriff's office and the district attorney's office, meant that what was said would not be heard by persons who should not hear what was said. But, as in a conspiracy, the threads start to unravel when men start to lie and some cannot maintain the facade of truth very long. Thus, we see the thread holding the conspiracy together commencing to unravel in the testimony of Capt. Fritz relative to the testimony of Deputy-Sheriff Craig; and the startling testimony of Police Chief Curry receiving notice that Officer Tippit was shot before he actually was shot; or the "palm print" of Oswald vanishing after lifting," and then "reappearing," and then vanishing on its way to the FBI Washington Bureau. Of such is the stuff of which conspiracies are made!

Oswald was interrogated verbally, with no stenographer and tape recorder present by: (1) The Dallas police; (2) The FBI; (3) The Texas Rangers; (4) The U.S. Postal authority; (5) The Immigration and Naturalization Department of the U.S. Department of State; (6) The Secret Service. After everyone had been examined by the Commission, the only legal fact was that the notes of all those groups were in conflict with each other. After reading those "notes" submitted by the various agents, it is a wonder that Oswald did not become insane. So inept were those agents in taking notes that a court of law would not permit any of those notes to be read to a jury, for some of those agents were committing perjury when the notes of the other agents were compared together.

The evidence is overwhelming that Lee Harvey Oswald was arrested for the murder of President John F. Kennedy and not Patrolman Tippit. An examination of the Report, pages 598-636, revealed an absolute lack of "notes" for three interrogating sessions on Friday, November 22, 1963. How, then, did the Commission know Oswald was lying? Because he was accused of something which he denied? Every major question asked of Oswald dealt not with the murder for which he was arrested but for the murder of President Kennedy! Did the Dallas police and the FBI have "inherent wisdom" that Oswald was the murderer of President Kennedy at 1:50 p.m. despite the evidence that those two agencies theoretically had no fingerprints, no palm prints, and no identification of Oswald at any time on the day of the murder? Why did FBI Agent Hosty, at 3 p.m. on the afternoon of the murder, one hour after Oswald was arrested for the murder of Officer Tippit, inform Lt. Revill of the Dallas police that Lee Harvey Oswald was (1) a communist; and (2) "killed President Kennedy." (222.) How did FBI Agent Hosty know Oswald was the murderer of President Kennedy when the interrogation of Oswald did not commence until 4:20 p.m.? The Commission stated Oswald was arrested only for the Tippit murder. How did Agent Hosty make the transition from Tippit to President Kennedy at 3 p.m.?

The Commission admitted that the Dallas police willfully lied to the Press when they said Oswald was suspected because he "missed a roll call." There was never any roll call made; in fact, more than 75% of the employees never returned to work after the murder. As the police radio tapes revealed, the only radio broadcast for a suspect working in the Depository was for Charles Givens, not Oswald. It was Givens who was the only person working on the 6th floor with a 5-man maintenance crew that "saw" Oswald at 11:55 a.m. The other maintenance crew members did not see Oswald, only Givens, who, as the evidence revealed, was a black employee and an ex-convict subject to police control! Out of every employee who visited the 6th floor on the morning of November 22nd, only Givens saw Oswald. No one else. Was Givens "used" by the police when they put out a 'pick up" for a suspect C. Givens so that they could control his sighting of Oswald at 11 a.m. on the 6th floor?

Lee Harvey Oswald was not classified in the FBI files as a member of the U.S. Communist Party nor as a secret member of the USSR Communist Party at any time during his lifetime. As a matter of fact, there is a suppressed document in the National Archives written by the Intelligence Division (on subversives) of the Dallas Police Department that the FBI considered Oswald "all right!" (223.) What was "all right" for Oswald? That he was an informant for the Bureau and an agent for the CIA?

The Commission, not its critics, put their "honor" on the block when it convicted a man because he "lied." However, let us look at the record!

Was Oswald a liar when he denied killing President Kennedy? No.

Was he a liar when he denied killing Officer Tippit? No.

Was he lying when he denied trying to kill ex. Gen. Walker? No.

Was he lying when he denied trying to kill Officer McDonald? No.

Was he lying when he said he saw TV announcer Allman? No.

Was he lying when he said he saw Jr. Jarman eating lunch? No.

Was he lying when he said he was standing on the steps? No.

Was he lying when he said he was not at the 6th-floor window? No.

Was he lying when he said the rifle was not his? No.

Was he lying when he said he purchased "curtain rods"? No.

Was he lying about the package containing "curtain rods"? No.

Did he admit owning a revolver? Yes.

Did he see a 7.65 German Mauser on the 6th floor? (223a) Yes.

Was Oswald lying when he admitted visiting Mexico City? No.

Did he deny getting into a station wagon at 12:45 p.m.? No.

The above are the "substantive matters" relating to the Tippit and President Kennedy murders. On what matters did Oswald lie? The evidence proved he told the truth. If the American people believe that "1984" has arrived, then they can accept the Commission's accusations against Oswald. The evidence proved he told the truth; the Commission did the lying.

The Commission concluded its eight accusations or "Conclusions" by stating that Oswald had the capability with a rifle to commit the assassination. This presumed the evidence that on November 22nd Lee Harvey Oswald was the world's greatest rifleman; although the FBI testified that the rifle given to them by that paragon of police departments, Dallas, was proved to be an absolutely worthless rifle, incapable of discharging a bullet through its barrel until the barrel was repaired by the FBI firearms laboratory.

The issue of whether or not Oswald had the capability of firing that defective rifle, equipped with a telescopic that could be used only by a cross-eyed left-handed rifleman, and then only if three shims were used, was not proved by the Commission. There was no rifleman's association in the world that upheld the Commission's contention. Of course, riflemen are not lawyers and many lawyers have been proved capable of only shooting off their mouths.

The burden of proof lay upon the shoulders of the Commission to prove that their statement relating to Oswald's capability was of such a degree that he could hand load that defective rifle in the period of time stipulated by the Commission. Since Oswald was dead, with the connivance of some civilians and police in Dallas, the Commission first resorted to tests that were fraudulent, then to theory, and then to Oswald's Marine Corps record.

The U.S. Marine Corps, through Col. Folsom, quickly disposed the Commission's theory that Oswald had the capability with a rifle to hit the president. Oswald's record as a marksman after basic training was 212; when he was discharged his capability had deteriorated to 191, which is a mere 1 point above qualifying. (224.) The Marine Corps flatly stated the Corps considered Oswald "a poor shot." (225.) Since the Corps rejected the Commission's theory by their records and appraisal, the Commission rushed to the records of the USSR. In a suppressed document now in the National Archives, under Doc. No.434, is the statement by a defected USSR Intelligence agent that when Oswald went hunting in Minsk he was so poor a rifleman that his companions had to shoot the game and give Oswald the credit. (226.) The Commission admitted that upon his return to the United States Oswald used only a .22 rifle.

Blocked by both the U.S. Marine Corps and the records of the USSR that Oswald could not hit the hind quarters, forequarters, or the head of a deer, the Commission instituted a new concept in marksmanship. As a matter of fact this new concept, if proven, would revolutionize the art of rifle marksmanship. Oswald became "proficient" by working the bolt of a rifle! (227.) The Commission not only had contempt for the common sense of the American people but damned their intelligence. One of the oldest languages in the World, Hebrew, has a word for the Commission's statement. It is called "chutzpa!" This is the same as a lawyer saying that the court should have mercy upon his client because his client is an orphan–on trial for the murder of his mother and father! "Chutzpa!"

The Commission ran into a trap of its own making when they selected the time the shots were fired: not less than 4.8 seconds and not more than 7 seconds. They carefully refrained from publishing in their "Report" any mention of the internal and external condition of the Italian rifle foisted upon the FBI by the Dallas Police Department. The following testimony of the FBI proved beyond a reasonable doubt that that Italian rifle was not the weapon from which came the bullets that struck President Kennedy:

(1) The Commission's own experts testified that during the "dry run" the trigger was not pulled because they feared it would break. (228.)

(2) The telescopic sight was mounted for a left-handed man. (229.)

(3) The telescopic sight was "structurally defective." (230)

(4) The firing pin was worn down with rust on pin and spring. (231.)

(5) Three shims were necessary to support the sight. (232.)

(6) No shims, or scratches, or abrasions were on the rifle. (233.)

(7) No bullet could be fired through a barrel corroded and worn.

(8) The barrel had to be repaired internally because of (234.)

(9) No ammunition clip was used with that Italian rifle thus (235)

(10) the FBI proved no 3 shots could be fired within 7 seconds. (236.)

QED: The FBI unequivocally proved Oswald innocent.

After the Italian rifle had been completely overhauled and new parts installed the Commission instructed the FBI and experts from the American Rifleman's Association to conduct tests to prove to the world that "any 'ole rifleman" could hit the target. Of course they could. After all, the tests were as phony as plastic baloney. But even with those fraudulent tests not one single rifleman got off the three shots in the time scheduled and hit the target like "Oswald." The test-firing pattern revealed that the height was only 45 feet but the 6th-floor window was 60-feet high. In the second test round, the height was now reduced to 30 feet. Some test! (237.) In spite of their own tests the Commission calmly published their statement that in their "inherent wisdom" it was a simple task for Oswald to hit the president in the head, when, in the USSR, he could not hit the broadside of a deer at 50 paces but in the U.S. he could hit the head of a person at 275 feet.

Thus ends the case of the Warren Commission versus Lee Harvey Oswald in their charge that he was the "sole and exclusive killer of President Kennedy."

The intriguing questions remaining to the historian is why, and how, the Commission reached its conclusion that Oswald was the "sole murderer." For the answers, one must delve into the background of the Commission's methods used to attain their false "Conclusions."

It is therefore necessary to investigate the rumors concerning a conspiracy, and to see if there is more to the rumors than just rumors. Thus, if there is evidence to support the rumors by facts in the "Hearings" or the National Archives, then the Oswald phase has ended but the conspiracy lingers on. The balance of this small volume now attempts to enter the "dark world" that is slowly, oh, so slowly, being lit, although full light may take until the year 2038–if the "basic principles of American justice" have the strength to remain as principles guiding this long-suffering nation.

CHAPTER VIII

THE METHODOLOGY OF THE WARREN COMMISSION

A lie rewritten twenty times does not equal the truth written once! Six days after the murder of President Kennedy, on November 28, 1963 President Johnson announced that he had issued Executive Order No. 11130, creating the commission now known to history as the "Warren Commission." President Johnson stated that the purpose of the Commission was "to ascertain the truth and evaluate the evidence so that the truth would be exposed to the world."

As had been said, the Commission never ascertained the truth, never evaluated the evidence, and the truth was never exposed to the world.

A historian of the Commission has the responsibility to inform those interested in the reasons why the Commission, having spent nearly three million dollars and taken nearly nine months of labor, conducted an exercise in futility. Was there a reason for "their" madness? Why did seven distinguished men put their "honor" upon a "Report" that became a subject of contempt, not only in their own country, but throughout the civilized world? What is the reason why this august body of seven prestigious men deceive, defraud, and practice duplicity upon their own citizens?

When an analysis of the attendance record of those seven men was conducted, it revealed that Mr. McCloy really practiced "banker's hours," for he attended 33 out of the 94 witness sessions. However, he should not be greatly admonished, for Senator Russel heard a mere 6 witnesses and Congressman Boggs increased that figure to 20. The chief justice attended all the 94 sessions; while Senator Cooper heard 50 witnesses; ex-CIA Chief Dulles, increased that by 10; and Congressman Ford to 70. However, those figures for partial attendance and the transcript revealed that few, if any, attended for the full session of an individual examination of witness. Thus, what each commissioner heard was only a mere portion or fragment of the testimony. How the "whole truth" can be obtained by listening to a fragment of it has never boon explained.

Another interesting facet of the Commission was the composition of that "august" body. Since the chief justice of the United States Supreme Court is impartial in matters political, he must be granted that impartiality. As to the other members, the congressmen and senators, Republican and Democrat alike, their affinity to the martyred president, on a political level, was nil. Thus, Senator Russell's interest in the "who, what, when, where, and why" of the answers to the president's murder was seen in his condescending to attend six sessions. He was an "Et tu" Democrat. The selection of banker McCloy remains a mystery; and the appointment of Allen Dulles, who would lead a witness up the path pointing to the conspiracy but then lacked the courage to open the door, was strange in view of his dismissal by President Kennedy in Dulles' attempt to override the president in the Bay of Pigs disaster.

It can be honestly stated that what the commissioners saw and what they heard was the "partial" truth, not the whole truth and nothing but the truth. This fact is based on their 888-page "Report," which published some of the truth but not all the truth. It is a fundamental principle of law that no accused person in a criminal case can be convicted by the jury who has been given the 'partial" truth. In the Lee Harvey Oswald "trial" before the Commission, they were the judge and the prosecution; the American people was the jury.

It was Allen Dulles who upheld Oswald's statement that he was not on the 6th floor at the time the president was shot when Dulles, in his cross-examination of Bonnie Ray Williams, obtained the fact that the witness saw no one and heard no one from 12 noon until 12:20 when he left that floor, walked to the elevator, and rode down to the 5th floor. Having opened that door to the conspiracy, Mr. Dulles refused to enter. It was Mr. Dulles who expressed great incredulity concerning Allen Specter's "Bullet No. 339," yet he did nothing. Why?

Senator Cooper was the one who demolished the Commission's case against Oswald in the Tippit murder. His cross-examination of Patrolman McDonald brought out the fact that the witness never knew whether the gun in the Commission's possession as the murder weapon was the identical weapon McDonald said he "took" from Oswald. The Senator obtained the admission from McDonald that the "mark" on the Commission's weapon was made on a revolver given to the patrolman at the Dallas police station. When Det. Carroll testified that he "jerked" a revolver from someone's hand but he did not know from whose hand, both Mr. Dulles and Senator Cooper knew, as men with legal backgrounds, that no court of law would accept the Commission's statement that the Commission's revolver was the weapon used to murder Officer Tippit.

Congressman Boggs was the commissioner who, with raised eyebrows, asked the Commission aide "How many bullets are involved in the Tippit murder?" But none of those commissioners raised a single question when the obvious perjury of the Dallas police was given in respect of obtaining 3 bullets from 4 or 5 bullet holes! Why did Congressman Boggs accept this police perjury?

For reasons known only to themselves, the seven commissioners decided that they had the competency to "interpret" and "evaluate" the facts surrounding the murder of the President. The "Report" now reveals that their attitude was either the height of arrogance or the height of contempt for the intelligence of their fellow citizens; and, as the "Report" revealed, it was both.

If ever a profession earned the accolade: "It smelled like a dead fish rotting in the moonlight on a dank dismal shore," the legal profession earned it with the "Report."

The powers of the Commission, as approved by a Joint Resolution of Congress on December 3, 1963, were as broad as possible. The Commission was given the power of granting immunity to any witness who desired it and to subpoena all documents and physical evidence the Commission deemed necessary for its search to locate the truth. However, the power of subpoena was carefully applied to only the fishes, not the whales. When it came to subpoena the original "Zapruder" film from "Life," the Commission scurried from the field. Although the U.S. Secret Service had the X-Rays of President Kennedy taken during the autopsy, the Commission blatantly lied when they said those files were in Robert Kennedy's possession. The Commission refused to subpoena the radio and television tapes from the stations who offered to sell them those tapes at cost. However, under the power of subpoena, the Commission simply had to go to a court of law and demand those tapes–at no cost.

Many citizens do not understand the power of subpoena and believe that once the property is given to the court, who, in turn, gives it to the applicant, the owner loses possession. Nothing is further from the truth, for once the property has been used in the function under the subpoena the property is returned to its legal owner. The fact that "Life" purchased the "Zapruder" films from Zapruder, who gave the entire amount to Tippit's family,[21] did not give the right of that publication to refuse to grant the Commission the right to examine those films in [their] original state. Under the Constitution of the United States, the Commission could have subpoenaed those films, examined them at their leisure, and then returned them to "Life." No nation can long survive its heritage if the law is applicable in different degrees to the fishes and the whales.

The FBI, the Secret Service, and various police agencies of the State of Texas not only unlawfully seized films taken by the individual citizen but refused to return the film and the picture to the rightful owner. Do they have rights lesser than those granted to "Life"? However, the sole reason why the Commission refused to subpoena the Zapruder film was not due to any property right but due to the fact that certain persons would appear in that film who would be recognized as being agents for several federal and state police agencies. In a suppressed Commission Document in the National Archives, No. 962, is an appeal by the Secret Service for the Commission to purchase, for a mere $450.00, the tapes of assassination from the moment the president turned onto Elm Street until his automobile sped away toward Parkland Hospital. The only reason is that those tapes show the steps of the Book Depository Building where Lee Harvey Oswald stood; where the spectators ran when they heard the

---

[21] The film was sold for $150,000, plus royalties. Mr. Zapruder donated the first $25,000 to Tippit's widow.

shots; if Jack Ruby is on the film near the Depository; whether or not a rifle did appear on the second floor of the Dal-Tex Building; and if certain identifiable persons went in and out of the Book Depository between 12:25 and 12:40 p.m. That is the reason why those television tapes and films were not purchased.

The essential photograph that was not purchased by the Commission was the Hughes photograph which was analyzed by the FBI. The Bureau revealed the fact that, at the exact time the president was struck, it was impossible for any rifleman situated at the S.E. corner window of the 6th floor to strike the president with a bullet discharged from any rifle. The location of the president's automobile prohibited a bullet coming from a 6th-floor rifle to penetrate his head or body. The "angle of fire" that hit the president, according to the FBI and Secret Service Survey, was between 40 and 60 degrees; the Commission admitted that the "angle of fire" was between 17 and 18 degrees from the window. No nondeflected bullet can change course in midair. Not even the prestige of the seven commissioners can change the law of science. The FBI letter to the Commission can be found in the National Archives, not in the "Report," The Hughes photograph revealed that at the exact moment the shots were fired there was no person at that window, and no rifle barrel is seen poking itself through two panes of window glass. This photograph upheld Secret Service Inspector Sorrel's testimony "that he saw no person, no rifle, and no activity" when the shots rang out.

The president's Executive Order No. 11130 also committed an act that was never analyzed by the critics of the Commission. That order effectively removed the attorney general of the United States, Robert F. Kennedy, from any supervision of the activities of the FBI headed by the arch foe of the Kennedy family, Mr. Hoover. The person who pointed that fact out to me was Senator Kennedy and it was placed in my book, "Murder Most Foul." At the time the "Report" was issued, Mr. Kennedy was no longer the attorney general. Thus, at a stroke of the pen, President Johnson removed the one man who would have gone through hell and high water to capture the conspirators who murdered his brother, the President of the United States, John F. Kennedy.

At the first meeting the Commission appointed J. Lee Rankin as the general counsel and, at the same time, selected 14 assistant counsels or aides, and 12 staff members. The selection of the general counsel and the 26 staff members brought forth "a strange breed of cats." The slanting of the Commission's objective can be readily seen in the fact that the Commission had already chosen its course of action: to accept only the evidence that would prove Oswald guilty and that no conspiracy existed. The aides who held the key positions were Mr. Joseph Ball, .Mr. W. Liebeler, Mr. D. Belin, and Mr. A. Specter. Specter parlayed his "experience" in the investigation by becoming a turncoat Republican and winning the District Attorney Office of Philadelphia and then running for mayor when the citizens of "Brotherly Love" slammed the door in his face. If Specter conducted his district attorney office in the same manner he conducted his various activities on the Commission, the only thing that can be said is "God help the accused!"

Mr. Liebeler, now a professor of law in California, admitted that he thought so poorly of the "Report" that, as a class assignment, 22 law students were involved in a project to locate evidence in the "Hearings" to uphold the "Report." Liebeler is an optimist, for he could cube the number 22 and never find any evidence to support the "Report." (238.) The professor and his students are still searching. If the "Report" is true, why are any students needed, Mr. Liebeler?

Specter, now the "D.A." of Philadelphia, was the "Rube Goldberg" of the Commission. It was he, and he alone, that Invented a bullet, No. 399, that did what no other bullet in the history of bulletry has done. This Bullet No. 399 was nothing more than an exercise of his imagination and used by him, and the commissioners, to "prove" a conspiracy did not exist. The Specter concoction was conceived by him in a statement made to Allen Dulles that Specter "would locate" the evidence after he gave birth to Bullet No. 399. In other words, the mother first gave birth and immediately after the birth became pregnant with the same child just born! Specter did go to Dallas to "find" his evidence and then "convinced" the seven commissioners that he was right. Bullet No. 399 did just what Specter said it would do. Unfortunately, Bullet No. 399 could not answer in the manner in which it was conceived.[22]

Nearly two full years passed after the assassination, and not quite a year after the "Report" was published, Specter admitted that his bullet, No. 399, was nothing but a figment of his imagination. In an interview with the "Greater Philadelphia" magazine of August, 1966, he admitted that Bullet No. 399 was not indispensable to the Commission's theory that one bullet struck the president and then continued into the governor's body. Thus, Specter was now admitting he was lying [either] when he said in the Report" that one bullet did all the damage or in his statements to the magazine. Both cannot be correct. Lee Harvey Oswald was convicted by the Commission on its theory that one bullet, and one bullet alone, entered both bodies. If Bullet No. 399 was an independent bullet, then a conspiracy, in fact, did exist, and the Commission willfully concealed it. If that theory is not now indispensable, then the Commission published a deliberate lie. (239.) Professor Liebeler in a public statement also admitted that the "one bullet theory" is "simply incorrect." (240.) Was the professor thus not also conceding that a conspiracy existed?

One of the statement's in Epstein's "Inquest" is an account of the work done by two Commission aides, Mr. A. Goldberg and Mr. N. Redlich.[23] Those two aides had the responsibility of writing a "Report" that did not conflict with the testimony and evidence in the "Hearings" and the National Archives. Epstein stated that some of the chapters were rewritten a minimum of twenty times. A child could have informed the aides that a lie rewritten twenty times is not the truth written once!

Today, it is a foregone conclusion that the Warren "Report"

---

[22] It was for this reason that researcher Ray Marcus dubbed it "the bastard bullet"–as an item of uncertain provenance. See his privately printed monograph of that title from 1966, which features the amusing subtitle: *A Search for Legitimacy for Commission Exhibit 399.*

[23] Pentagon historian Alfred Goldberg served as advisor, co-author, and co-editor of the Warren Report. Norman Redlich, appointed by J. Lee Rankin to serve as special assistant on the WC, played a key role in developing the so-called single bullet theory.

should never have been printed or published. What is known today is the fact that, at the very first meeting of the Commission, as an organized body, the Commission had in its possession the facts that Lee Harvey Oswald was innocent beyond a reasonable doubt in both the murders of President Kennedy and Officer Tippit. They knew, from that evidence, that a conspiracy involved high persons in the economic and government structure of our nation. With that knowledge, the Commission decided that its "inherent wisdom" compelled them to conceal the truth. They knew that Oswald was not the "sole and exclusive killer."

In the possession of the Commission were (1) the official reports of the FBI; (2) the official reports of the United States Secret Service; (3) the official survey of the location of the president's automobile when the president was struck by each bullet; and (4) the official statement by the Dallas Sheriff's Intelligence Division that Lee Harvey Oswald was an FBI informer and on that Bureau's payroll with a code number.

The FBI "Reports," two of them issued not later than January 13, 1964, impliedly state that, in the Bureau's opinion, Oswald was not the murderer. As previously stated, the pictures taken by the FBI of the president's clothes revealed that a bullet struck him in the back, not the back of the neck, and the "angle of fire" of the bullet's path into the president's back proved a bullet was never fired by a rifle held by a man positioned at the S.E. window of the 6th floor. Furthermore, the language used by the Bureau in its "Report" was such that a person with common sense would know that Oswald was not the killer since that said repeatedly Oswald only "owned" the rifle: never the word "used." In the FBI reports they refused to accept Brennan's statement that the man he saw was "Oswald," for the Bureau had in their possession Brennan's affidavit given to FBI agents and the Dallas police where he said he could not identify Lee Harvey Oswald. The Bureau thought so little of Brennan that his name does not appear in the FBI's original or supplemental report! (Dec. 1963, Jan. 1964.) Yet, Brennan was used as the Commission's key witness. A strange interpretation of the "basic principles of American justice."

In the hands of the Commission, with the FBI reports, was the official report of the U.S. Secret Service, Code No.2-34-030, dated November 28, 1963. The report, signed by Inspector Kelley, stated that the president was struck by one bullet, another one hit the governor, and the third bullet hit the chief executive of the United States. Three bullets, three hits! With that report was attached the official Secret Service Survey, made by Mr. R. West, [24] which positioned the president's automobile out of the range of any bullet being fired from a rifle held by a gunman at the S.E. corner window of the sixth floor of the Depository. The official reports by both government bureaus were withheld from both the Warren "Report" and material published in the "Hearings." Both repose, like a finger pointing, in the National Archives.

The federal agency that is the paradox, the Chinese puzzle, in the entire investigation is the Federal Bureau of Investigation. As has been stated in previous chapters, that Bureau overwhelmed the Commission with evidence that proved Oswald innocent in both murders. What is the puzzle is the fact although the Bureau time and time again warned the Commission that its "conclusions" would not stand the scrutiny of the light of day, that agency then turned right around and conducted itself in a manner implying they had something to hide–to conceal their possible involvement in the assassination. The Bureau was involved in suppressing the same evidence they had originally uncovered and exposed to the world!

In the previous chapter, ten major elements of Oswald's innocence with the rifle were uncovered by the FBI. They also proved Oswald was the "man in the doorway" of the Book Depository, not Billy Lovelady. It was the FBI photograph that showed the bullet hole in the president's back. It was the FBI that proved that there was no Oswald palm print or fingerprints on the rifle. It was their testimony that proved no ammunition clip was with that rifle. FBI agents proved that the rifles had been switched and planted to secure Oswald's guilt. It was the

---

[24] Marks is referring here to Dallas City Surveyor Robert West, who worked under the supervision of Secret Service Agent Elmer Moore. West provided the survey plat of Dealey Plaza for the December 5, 1963 reenactment of the assassination.

FBI testimony that refused to authenticate the "Life" photograph. It was the FBI that supported the Hughes photograph that proved no rifleman was at the 6th-floor window when the shots rang out. It was the testimony of three FBI agents that exposed the differences in the rifle sling–one being made out of rope or string. The Bureau exposed the perjury of the Dallas police concerning the "bullets" taken from "Tippit's" body.

Yet, in spite of all their evidence, it was the agents of the FBI that were accused, under oath, by U.S. Secret Service agents, and other witnesses, of perverting the statements given to the FBI by those other persons. It was the FBI that evaded and avoided answering pertinent questions asked by the Commission, and it is to the disgrace of the Commission that they lacked the moral courage to demand that the Bureau answer those questions. Why they acted in that manner is open to supposition, but the Bureau's conduct can only lead to a conclusion that the Bureau was operating on both sides of the fence in the slim hope that any investigation of the "Report" would not be undertaken by a serious investigator of that "Report." "Heads or tails," the FBI could prove that they had given evidence, or uncovered evidence, disproving the Commission's accusation that Oswald was the "sole and exclusive killer of President Kennedy." What is perplexing is Mr. Hoover's defense of the Commission in the face of that evidence, and his various statements, which were obtuse or contradictory, that did nothing to add to the honor of the FBI.

The attempt by the FBI to prevent the disclosure that Agent Hosty's name was in the Oswald notebook proved that the FBI knew more than what they said they knew about Oswald. (241.) Not only did the FBI keep Oswald's p.o. box in Dallas under surveillance, but they had another informer in Oswald's home in Irving, Texas: Mrs. Paine, who also kept the FBI informed of his various places of employment. (242.) Thus, the Commission's statement that Oswald and his place of employment was unknown to the Bureau in Dallas was false. The "denial" by the FBI that Oswald was not an FBI informant meant nothing in a court of law since the Commission admitted that, at no time, no commissioner or aide ever read the FBI's dossier relating to Oswald. To add to the above must be the statement made by

Agent Hosty to Dt. Lt. Jack Revill at 3 p.m., that Oswald was a Communist and he "killed President Kennedy." (243.) Very strange that an FBI agent, who was the Oswald "contact" on behalf of the Bureau, knew at 3 p.m. that Oswald was the "murderer."

The Commission's method of investigating the "dirty rumor" that Oswald was an informer and on the FBI payroll showed the extent to which the "Report" distorted the law pertaining to the rule of "hearsay." In a suppressed document in the National Archives, Code: Secret Service Co.-34-030; 736, signed by Secret Service Agent Bertram,[25] is the fact that Oswald was an FBI informer. Not only was he an informer; he was on the FBI payroll, paid monthly, not just for tips. In that document is a statement that a Mr. Hudkins, a staff reporter for the Houston "Post"," was informed by the Chief of the Criminal Division of the Dallas Sheriff's Office that Oswald was paid $200.00 per month under a code number "S172."[26] In an effort to discredit the Hudkin's affidavit, the Commission issued a childish statement that they could not investigate the facts in the affidavit because of Mr. Hudkin's right to claim "freedom of the press"! This was the

---

[25] Lane Bertram, the Secret Service agent in charge of the Houston office, was never called as a witness before the Warren Commission. In his book *Breach of Trust* (2005), author Gerald McKnight suggests that the reason for this may be because Bertram's testimony might have revealed Oswald's role as an informant for the CIA.

[26] Oswald may have been an FBI informant, but it later emerged that "S172" was a fictitious badge number and part of a hoax played upon the Bureau. Dallas County Assistant DA William Alexander suspected that the FBI was tapping his phones, so he decided to play a trick. He arranged a conference call with his friends Lonnie Hudkins and Hugh Aynesworth, reporters who also suspected that their lines were bugged. (They were said to be investigating the possible connection between Oswald and the FBI.) The trio had prearranged to discuss Oswald's "payroll number": was it S172 or S179? "Within half an hour" of the call, "FBI agents, flashing their badges, showed up at the offices of all three of these marplots asking what they knew about Oswald's government payroll number." Gerald D. McKnight, *Breach of Trust* (Lawrence, KS: University Press of Kansas, 2005), p. 139.

greatest barrel of hogwash thrown over the American people and the Commission knew it. Nor was the legal rule relating to "hearsay" involved. (Judy Garland vs. Torres.) As Mr. Hudkins had stated that his information came from the Chief of the Sheriff's Criminal Division, Mr. Sweatt, the Commission only had to do two things in a law court. The Commission only had to place Mr. Hudkins on the stand and ask him to answer, under oath, if he received his information from Chief Sweatt. If Hudkins answered in the affirmative, then the Commission would swear in Chief Sweatt and ask him if he had informed Mr. Hudkins. If the Chief again replied in the affirmative, then the Commission could have asked the chief how he obtained his information. It was as simple as that, but the Commission had no desire to arouse the antagonism of the Chief of the FBI, Mr. Hoover. The FBI office in Washington has never legally denied that Oswald was not an informer and not on their monthly payroll as Informant Number S172. Further evidence that Oswald was associated with the Bureau is the fact that Oswald successfully appealed to the New Orleans FBI Bureau for assistance when Oswald was arrested for "disturbing the peace" when he was circulating "Pro-Castro" leaflets.

Finally, the Commission knew that there existed in the Dallas Police Department's Criminal Intelligence Division a memorandum dated February 2, 1964, in which the Dallas police were informed by the FBI that "Oswald was alright." Of course Oswald was "alright"; he was a paid FBI informer.

The role of the United States Secret Service in protecting the life of President Kennedy was one of either willful and deliberate negligence or one that was involved in the attempt upon his life. Instead of acting as a protecting shield, the Service lowered it. The chief of that service admitted to the Commission that seven of the nine agents assigned to protect the president went out on a "beer bust" the night before the murder. On the premurder night, the service thought so much of his life that they assigned only 2 of the nine to guard his hotel floor. This, in an area where the night edition of the Dallas "Morning News" carried a full-page advertisement stating that, since President Kennedy was a "red," he should be done to death as all "reds" are traitors and all traitors should be murdered without a trial.

Rage and anger cannot be used as evidence, as an investigator must attempt to locate evidence in either the "Report," or in the "Hearings," or in the National Archives to determine whether or not the Secret Service was negligent in its protection of the president; whether or not they had evidence that Oswald was innocent; and whether or not they had evidence of a conspiracy.

The "Report" has stated that the Secret Service had no information at any time that Oswald was considered a potential assassin. (244.) But this is not true, for Agent Kellerman expressed amazement that, in view of the attempt to lynch Ambassador Stevenson a month prior to the trip to Dallas by the president, there should have been some names on the list. However, the Protective Research Section of the Secret Service (PRS) had no names to give the Secret Service Bureau in Dallas (245.) By comparing Mr. Kellerman's statement to that of the Commission's, one can immediately see that, by limiting their question to "Oswald," they were attempting to prohibit any evidence of a conspiracy. The agent's statement was applicable to any potential assassin; that is, the PRS was negligent in not informing the Dallas bureau of any potential assassin in the Dallas area. Has that agency adopted the philosophy that fascism is now "Americanism-in-action"?

Vital information relating to a conspiracy was quickly hushed up by the Commission when the testimony of Agent Lawson was analyzed. This agent testified that, during the interrogation of Oswald, the agent received a phone call in which he was informed that the caller "gave us some information on people who it might have been–a case that wasn't Oswald!" As seen as that statement was uttered, the Commission aide interrupted the agent and refused the agent permission to finish the agent's complete statement. But the Commission stenographer did obtain the conclusion of the original sentence: "a case that wasn't Oswald." (246.) The aide did not request "an off the cuff" interview with the agent in spite of the fact that the Commission permitted their aides to conduct such off the record interviews when the witness gave testimony in favor of Oswald. Why the distinction? Were the aide and the Commission in fear of their lives if they received information concerning the names of the conspirators? What were the names of those "people who it might have been"? The same people who were behind the scenes, the puppeteer pulling the strings on his puppets who nearly lynched Ambassador Stevenson?

The conduct of the Secret Service agents at Parkland Hospital when three unidentified men, with guns, tried to force their way into the operating room where the medical staff was fighting to save the life of the president was reprehensible. Their failure to obtain, at the minimum, the names of those three men, was gross negligence. But a far greater crime was morally committed when the Secret Service kept silent. Of course, after the event, silence was golden, for the public would have also asked why those agents refused to disarm those men and keep them under arrest until they proved what they claimed to be–FBI and CIA agents. (247.)

It must be granted to both the FBI and the Secret Service that they presented the Warren Commission with sufficient proof that Lee Harvey Oswald was not the "sole killer of President Kennedy." That record cannot be erased.

The final problem relating to Lee Harvey Oswald was whether or not he was an official agent for the CIA. Once again the only way to answer "Yes" is to delve into the official records available to the general public. The CIA, by letter, informed the Commission that they had searched their records and their soul, and upon their "honor" Oswald was never an agent for the CIA. Accordingly, the Commission accepted the word of the agency that had investigated itself and found to their surprise the CIA was as "white as sheep"–but some sheep are black.

The former head of the CIA, Mr. Dulles, raised an interesting point of law concerning a state of fact as to whether or not Oswald was an official or nonofficial employee of the CIA. The former head of that clandestine bureau posed the question: "When does a person become an agent?" The Commission never answered the question raised, but any attorney, and the Commission had 26 of them, could have provided them with the proper answer. Is a person an agent if he supplies the CIA with information never requested by them? No. Is a person an agent if he supplies the agency at their specific request although the informer received no payment? Yes. Is a person an agent if he accepts both command, direction, and pay from that agency? Yes. In the legal sense, whether or not a person is an agent is dependent upon one of those three questions and answers. There is no need for a person to be on the payroll of CIA to be an agent for the CIA. Where the CIA uses a "front" for that purpose of securing information, then the person who acts in that "front" for the agency is an agent.

Since the CIA investigated itself and found they had no dirt on their cuffs, it is necessary to "look at the records."

At the conclusion of his basic Marine Corps training, Oswald was shipped to Japan where he received additional training in radar and codes at the Atsugi CIA U-2 Air Base. He was also taught Russian by various Marine Corps and CIA instructors. It is well known in the Armed Forces that they do not spend money training soldiers in a foreign language for the edification of the soldier's own brain. Oswald was given classified information under his Class A Security Clearance by the Marine Corps and the CIA relating to all U-2 flights. An officer of the Marine Corps testified that Oswald, during his enlistment, not only had a Class A Security clearance, but he was taught and had full access to all U.S. codes relating to radar, radar ranges, and all radio codes. (248.) The Marine Corps admitted that Oswald received this secret Security Class A clearance in spite of the fact that, in public, and to his Marine buddies, he was always spouting his love for "communism." This conduct was not for a day, or a week, but during his entire service in the Corps; yet the Corps gave this word-spouting "Communist" a Class A Security Clearance, taught him Russian, and gave him complete access to all our military codes! But, on the "honor" of the CIA, Oswald was not an agent.

After his tour of duty, Oswald was shipped back to the United States, and he suddenly applied for a "hardship" discharge. While waiting for that discharge, Oswald applied for a passport to Europe, which included the statement that he was going to visit the Soviet Union "as a businessman exporter-importer"! He had never been in business. Now, a young kid of twenty, and he was in the import-export business! It is incredible that the CIA would believe that the Soviet counter-intelligence would accept Oswald's "cover" story. One of the most difficult businesses to learn is the export-import business; yet a "kid" of 20 was posing as an expert! Oswald had no education, no background, and no training, for he went from his high school studies directly into the Marines. Speculating, was the CIA planning a long-range mission for Oswald where they could use him as an "expendable" for or against his own country? Thus, the U.S. Marine Corps had full written notice from their "Class A Security" Marine "Communist Lover" that he was going to visit the USSR. Six days after his application on September 4, 1959, he received his passport through the U.S. Marines.

Then, an inexplicable thing happened. Although Oswald was now going to the USSR with all the top-secret knowledge he had acquired, the Corps transferred him from the active Marine Corps status to that of the "Inactive Reserve" list but with his Class A Security Clearance intact! On the day of his discharge, Oswald formally swore that he would not give any secret information to any person or nation. In that form is the penalty which he would have to pay if he violated that discharge–5 to 10 years in the federal penitentiary. He had also obtained his "hardship" discharge on the fraudulent basis of supporting his mother, whom he never supported or saw after he donned his civilian clothes and went aboard his ship to Europe.

In October, 1959, this 20-year-old "kid" made a public renunciation of his nation at a public press conference in Moscow, and, at the same time, announced that he was giving all the military secrets of which he had knowledge to the Soviets. (249.) Upon receipt of this information from the State Department, the CIA and the FBI opened up an "Oswald Dossier." (250.) Thus, every major federal agency had an "Oswald is a traitor" file, including the Office of Naval Intelligence, which forwarded the information to the U.S. Marine Corps and its Counter-Intelligence Department.

Since the Soviets knew all about Oswald when he ["renounced"] his citizenship and the knowledge that Oswald had been transferred to the inactive Marine reserves while still retaining his Class A Security rating, the Reds sent Oswald to Minsk, which is a long way from Pinsk, which is a long way from any Soviet military base. With nothing to do Oswald wed a Soviet citizen, and after a long wrangle between the State Department and the CIA Oswald returned, with his wife and child, to the United States in May, 1962.

Legally, Oswald was subject to immediate arrest the moment he stepped on U.S. soil. In an effort to obtain the answer "who protected Oswald from arrest," the Navy, the FBI, the CIA, and the State Department, the Commission only saw that "hot potato" question tossed around with no one catching it. In a suppressed document in the National Archives is a sworn statement by the FBI that when the Bureau examined the official files of the Marine Corps relating to Oswald there was no derogatory information. The State Department testified that the FBI was satisfied that Oswald had meant no harm to the United States. The FBI also stated that the Office of Naval Intelligence contemplated no action against Oswald. The State Department testified that when Oswald requested a loan to return to this nation, the State Department did not believe he was a "loyal" citizen. (251)

Based on the documents in the National Archives there was no question that, in view of Oswald's admission that he had given secret military codes and radar secrets to the Soviets, Oswald was subject to imprisonment. The records of the U.S. Marine files and the Office of Naval Intelligence can only lead to the conclusion those agencies were instructed by another agency in the federal government to overlook "Oswald's treason." The only agency that had that power was the Central Intelligence agency.

To close this chapter on the Commission's methodology and to summarize the Commission's "Report," the overwhelming evidence proved that the Commission deliberately and willfully:

Manipulated and distorted the facts present to them.

Issued false and misleading statements.

Refused to accept testimony contrary to their pre-conceived theory.

Accepted false photographs.

Accepted perjured testimony with the knowledge it was perjury.

Permitted in excess of 200 "off-the-record" interviews between the witness and the Commission aide in violation of the Commission's rules.

Accepted perjured testimony identifying Oswald as the Tippit murderer.

Accepted false testimony which identified Oswald as the Kennedy killer.

Accepted, with full knowledge, the perjury of Mrs. Oswald.

Refused to investigate the activity of the Dallas police, prior, during, and after the murder of President Kennedy.

Refused to subpoena the Zapruder films from "Life."

Refused to subpoena the X-Rays from the U.S. Secret Service.

Refused to interrogate the FBI agents who were accused by witnesses and agents of the Secret Service of deliberately perverting statements made by the witnesses and given to the FBI.

Issued statements that the Commission had read vital documents when, in fact, they never read those statements, thus lying to the people.

Refused to purchase the TV films and radio tapes taken by that media relating to the activity prior, during, and immediately after the shots struck the president. These tapes showed (1) the grassy knoll; (2) the persons on the steps of the Book Depository; (3) persons on the fire escape of the Dal-Tex Building; and (4) persons on the roof of the Book Depository, the Dal-Tex Building, and the Dallas County Building.

Accepted from the CIA and the FBI those agencies' own self-serving statements when the truth of the statements made by those agencies were under attack.

Suppressed the Hughes photograph proving Oswald's innocence.

Refused to investigate the infamous "double detour."

Suppressed the Allman affidavit which upheld Oswald's statement that he directed a man to a phone booth at the Depository entrance.

Suppressed Inspector Sorrels' testimony.

Suppressed the FBI Reports in both the "Report" and "Hearings."

Suppressed the official U.S. Secret Service Survey proving Oswald innocent.

Suppressed the fight between a "CIA" agent, an FBI agent, and Secret Service agents.

Suppressed the finding of the curtain rods by its own aide.

Refused to read the FBI dossier on Oswald.

Refused to investigate Hudkin's report to the Secret Service by refusing to obtain testimony from Chief Sweatt of Dallas.

Refused to investigate the Secret Service testimony that "Oswald was not the man."

"Lost" the Lt. Day memo relating to the actual rifle found on the 6th floor.

Refused to investigate the official Dallas police report that 3 cartridges were also found on the 3rd floor at 12:45 p.m.

Refused to investigate the rifleman captured by deputy sheriffs "on the grassy knoll."

Refused to investigate the man captured in the Dal-Tex Bldg. who was later mysteriously released by Dallas police agencies.

Refused to investigate the "brown paper bag" found in the Irving, Texas, Post Office.

Refused to investigate Sheriff Decker's 12:25 p.m. announcement to his _department, via his radio, that the president was shot.

Refused to investigate the police statements in Com. Exh. No. 2003, No. 78-85.

Refused to publish the autopsy report on Officer Tippit.

Suppressed the proof that the Dallas police knew Oswald's secret hideaway on Elsbeth Street; and sent a police squad to arrest him there.

In conclusion, the Warren Commission in its unanimous "Report" admitted that a conspiracy murdered President Kennedy! On pages 95, 105, and 111, the seven commissioners agreed that the president was struck in the back; not in the back of the neck. Many adherents and critics have overlooked this vital feature of the 888-page "Report." Since the language used by the Commission is concise, then a conspiracy in fact and in law murdered President Kennedy. QED Lee Harvey Oswald was not, in the opinion of the Commission, the "sole and exclusive killer of President Kennedy."

In brief, the "Report" was written more than twenty times in an attempt to negate the truth.

The subtitle to the Warren Commission's "Report" should read: 'Here "Truth" Lies.'

CHAPTER IX

THE CONSPIRACY THAT MURDERED PRESIDENT KENNEDY

The most contemptuous statement ever issued by a member of any governmental commission investigating the murder of the head of his government was issued by Allan Dulles in "Look" [magazine]: "If they've found another assassin, let them name names and produce their evidence!"[27]

The Warren Commission, all "honorable men," did not come to praise the martyred president; no, they gave him a funeral and used his shroud to conceal the murderers.

It was not, and is not now, the duty of any American citizen to discover the assassins; that duty and responsibility was assumed by those seven men who gave their bond and honor that they would conduct an impartial investigation and "let the chips fall where they may."

Based upon the testimony, affidavits, and records in the "Hearings" and the National Archives, the overwhelming evidence is that Lee Harvey Oswald murdered no president, no policeman, wounded no governor, and never made any attempt to murder another policeman and ex-general. Lee Harvey Oswald was guilty of only the assumption that the agency he was employed by would protect him. As the evidence proved that he was not the "sole and exclusive assassin of President Kennedy," then that same evidence proved beyond a reasonable doubt that a conspiracy and conspirators murdered President Kennedy.

It is not necessary for the critics of the Warren Commission to produce "their" evidence; it is only necessary that Commissioner Dulles read the evidence published in this book which his Commission produced. Therefore, for the benefit of the commissioner a review of the evidence, which proved Oswald was not

---

[27] See Fletcher Knebel, "A New wave of doubt; concerning *Inquest* by E.J. Epstein," *Look* magazine, July 12, 1966: 60-72.

the "sole and exclusive assassin of President Kennedy" and the evidence which revealed a conspiracy is now presented,

If Mr. Dulles had taken the time to discuss the murder of President Kennedy with his staff attorney, Mr. Specter, the staff attorney would have informed Mr. Dulles that Bullet No. 399 did not "tumble" through Governor Connelly's wrist and then "tumble" into his thigh. (252.) Mr. Dulles should have listened to his Staff aide when he said that bullet No. 399 was "not" indispensable to the Commission's Theory. (253.) Thus, Mr. Dulles: Who lied, the Commission or the Staff aide? If the Staff aide is correct, then a conspiracy, in fact and in law, did murder President Kennedy.

Where were you, Mr. Dulles, when this same aide admitted that the back wound was not a wound in the back of the neck? Or do you contend that there is no distinction between those two types of wounds? Did you listen when Comdr. Humes admitted that that back wound was in the identical location given in the official FBI reports? Were your ears or your mind closed? That testimony, by itself, proved the existence of a conspiracy.

Mr. Dulles, your own cross-examination of Bonnie Ray Williams proved that Oswald was not on the 6th floor between 12 noon and 12:30 p.m. when your Commission said the bullets were fired at President Kennedy. Mr. Commissioner, in regard to the Tippit murder, how many bodies are involved? The evidence revealed the existence of not less than five "Tippit" bodies and from those "bodies" the Dallas police say they extracted only three bullets. Do you believe that, when your own aide admitted that four bullets were taken from the Tippit" body and five shots were fired? Was not the fourth cartridge the one that was discharged from a .38 automatic which was not Oswald's weapon? Is that not additional evidence that a conspiracy existed? Where were you, Mr. Dulles, when Commissioner Senator Cooper proved that Patrolman McDonald lied regarding his "mark" on the alleged Oswald weapon?

Where is the Commission's proof that Oswald had a revolver in his possession when he was arrested? There is none, Mr. Commissioner. You need not say it, but the evidence proved he had no revolver, There were 15 to 20 patrons on the first floor when Oswald was arrested, Mr. Dulles. Yet, no patron testified they saw Oswald with a revolver, only the Dallas police. Why was the police list of witnesses never submitted to the Commission so that the Commission could examine their story? Why did the police select the two witnesses who contradicted each other? Who were the mysterious "informers" in the theater that knew Oswald was on the first floor and not sitting in the balcony? When he entered the theater, it was completely dark, so how did they know where he was seated?

Be not so contemptuous of your fellow-citizens, Mr. Dulles, for although many of them may not be blessed with your intelligence, you should not forget that Abraham Lincoln placed common sense above intelligence.

The Dulles statement made to "Look" was one he knew impossible for anyone except the CIA, the FBI, and other federal agencies to fulfill. The only element that can be proved by any citizen or investigator of the "Report" is that a conspiracy did murder the president but no individual can "name" the conspirators except those federal agencies. The conduct of the commissioners in the manner which they investigated the murder can only lead to the conclusion that they too had knowledge of the conspiracy. It is no excuse by any of those members that they did not have the time to read all the evidence and affidavits and thus they relied upon their aides. That is the cowards' way out, for the "Report" was signed unanimously; there were no dissenting opinions. When each member signed the 888-page "Report," each of them was stating that the evidence in the "Hearings" and the affidavits in the National Archives supported the statements in the "Report." If the aides of the Commission were morally dishonest, if they became intellectual prostitutes who sold their integrity for the "prestige" of being aides, the responsibility for their selection and their character belonged solely to the commissioners who appointed them.

The historical verdict of the Warren Commission is that the Commission proclaimed a precedent whereby it is now permissible for the president of the United States to be murdered by men who believe that the vice president, who becomes the president upon the death of the president, would be more amenable to the philosophies of the murderers.

What was the result of the murder of President Kennedy?

The overthrow of the government by an invisible coup d'état!

Without investigating any statements given by various persons concerning the possibility of a conspiracy, and remaining strictly within the confines of the testimony given to the Commission, to the documents now available in Washington, D.C., the following pages will prove, beyond a reasonable doubt, that a conspiracy murdered President Kennedy.

There is an official statement, never denied by the Federal Bureau of Investigation or the United States Secret Service, that both of those agencies knew, prior to the murder in Dallas, that a conspiracy was in existence which would murder President Kennedy in Dallas, Texas, on either November 22 or 23, 1963.

The full report was published in the Miami "News" on February 2, 1967, written by a Bill Barry, under the headline: "Assassination Idea Taped Two Weeks Before JFK Was Killed." The Miami, Fla., police then gave a copy of the tape to both the U.S. Secret Service and the FBI. On November 17, 1963, the FBI sent a "Tel Fax" message to its Dallas office that the president of the United States would be under the guns of the murderers. (254.) Yet, the Dallas FBI office did nothing! As to the Secret Service, who had the direct responsibility of protecting the president, the testimony of Agent Kellerman [shows] that the Dallas Secret Service Bureau and the PRS division did not give the presidential security detail a single name of a potential murderer. But when Agent Lawson also testified that he received information during Oswald's interrogation that some other person killed the president, and the Commission refused to investigate this testimony, the conclusion must be drawn that the Secret Service and the FBI were grossly negligent. (255.)

The above statement does not mean that the agents of those agencies were involved directly in the assassination of President Kennedy but, rather, from a legal point of view, those agencies were involved, since it was their obligation, responsibility, and duty, under the laws of the United States, to act affirmatively. They had the duty, and they failed to exercise it.

By contrast, the Miami, Fla., Police Department, upon receiving the information from this informer, immediately took all precautionary methods, including the helicoptering of President Kennedy from the airport to downtown Miami.

Both the FBI and the U.S. Secret Service admitted the receipt of this tape recording from the Miami Police Department, and the only statement they made to the mass communication media after the Miami "News" broke the story was "no comment." Why did those two federal agencies fail to protect the president? "No Comment!"

Although the information gave the names of those persons and organizations, the FBI–under the federal code relating to felonies, attempts to commit murder, or murders of any employee or official of the federal government–failed to arrest or interrogate those named persons or organizations prior to President Kennedy's murder. The president of the United States is both an employee and an official of the federal government. There has been no report that any federal district attorney in Tennessee, Florida, or Louisiana convoked any federal grand jury in those states to investigate the allegations in the Miami, Fla., police tapes. Why? Under federal law, a conspiracy to murder a federal employee or official is a federal crime. States' rights are not involved. There is a provision in the federal code passed in the late 1870's-1880's making an assault upon a federal officer a criminal offense. The president of the United States is a federal officer. There was one person who could have compelled the U.S. District Attorney to act–Attorney General R. Clark.

The essential elements in the possession of the FBI and the Secret Service were: (1) the president would be shot with a high-powered rifle from an office building; (2) the gun would be disassembled, taken into the building, and then reassembled; (3) to throw the public off, they will pick up somebody within hours afterwards; (4) the organization behind the conspiracy was the KKK of the State of Tennessee; (5) other right-wing organizations were involved; (6) the murders and bombings against Civil Rights groups and persons were made by those same men and organizations.

Five days after the assassination, the man who gave the information to the Miami police and the FBI was interrogated by the FBI. That man has now disappeared. Conveniently, for whom? Why did the FBI wait until after the murder?

The manner in which the Secret Service heeded the Miami, Fla., police warnings can be seen in the mysterious selection of the president's motorcade through downtown Dallas. In spite of the fact that the Secret Service had a minimum of thirteen-days' notice that the president would be shot by a high-powered rifle held by a murderer hidden in an office building, the Secret Service approved the selection of a route which led President Kennedy directly into the ambush of three assassins!

Under the regulations laid by the Secret Service relating to the protection of the president of the United States, it is stated therein that under no circumstances shall the president's automobile take a parade route which will decrease the speed of that automobile to below that of 25 miles an hour. Furthermore, where the Bureau has the belief that the president may be under attack in an unfriendly city or area, an agent must ride on the step platform which is directly behind the president. On that day in Dallas, there was no agent at any time on that platform which guards the rear of the president's body. Why? Was Dallas, after the attempt to lynch Ambassador Stevenson, regarded as a "friendly" city? Did the full-page advertisement in the Dallas newspapers calling for the "murder" of this "traitorous president" make Dallas a "friendly" city?

The first glimmer of a conspiracy was told to the world by the Dallas "Times-Herald" and the Dallas "News" when both newspapers published statements that the shots were fired at 12:25 p.m. not 12:30 p.m. A vital five minutes! The time was corroborated by a newspaper reporter who heard the news flash while sitting in the police station listening to the report of the progress of the president's motorcade as it proceeded through Dallas. The reporter's story is substantiated by none other than the police tapes of the Dallas Police Department. (256.)

The voice on the police tape instructing his men to get up on the railroad tracks, at five minutes prior to the shooting, was none other than Sheriff Decker, the chief of the Sheriff's Department of Dallas! Why did Sheriff Decker, five minutes prior to the time the shots first rang out, use his radio to say that shots were being fired at President Kennedy? The Commission emphatically stated the first bullet was fired at 12:30 p.m., yet the sheriff notified the sheriff's department that the shots were being fired at 12:25 p.m. Who was lying? The sheriff or the Commission? The police radio tapes support the sheriff! The Parkland

Hospital records also support the sheriff, for those records state the president arrived at the hospital at five minutes earlier than what is published in the "Report." Why? If the Commission's "truth" was accepted, then the Commission was implying that the sheriff was involved in the conspiracy; if the sheriff's radio tapes are correct, then the Commission is deliberately involved in a vast "cover-up" of other federal, state and local government personages. Why?

The second thread to the conspiracy can also be found in the "Hearings," when the testimony of the selection of the route of the motorcade is discussed–or rather, deliberately confused by the Commission. The Commission, out of invisible cloth, concocted a story that Oswald knew the motorcade route the day prior to the murder. The Dallas police conveniently found a map in Oswald's room with "x's" on it, and the police said that proved Oswald had previous knowledge. However, the Commission admitted that those map "x's" were places Oswald was seeking employment. (257.) The Commission also admitted that the route "eventually selected ... passed through a portion of suburban Dallas, through the downtown area along Main St. and then to the Trade Mart via Stemmons Freeway." No mention was made, as can be seen, of the motorcade turning onto Houston St. and then again making an abrupt left turn onto Elm St. and thence down to Stemmons Freeway. (258.)

What the testimony did prove was that the U.S. Secret Service permitted, in violation of their own rules and regulations, the Dallas police to guide the president into a perfect ambush site where he could be hit from (1) the direct rear; (2) the side; and (3) the front of his body. The Secret Service permitted this ambush route in spite of the fact that the Bureau had thirteen-days' notice that the president would be under rifle fire from "a tall office building by a man using a high-powered rifle"! Yet, this Bureau did nothing.

The Commission stated that this "double detour" route was necessary because of a traffic street obstruction on Main Street near the triple underpass to Stemmons Freeway. Was this the truth? It was a deliberate lie. The Dallas traffic patrolman who had the duty at that "obstruction" testified that the "obstruction" could not deter the president's automobile, or the motorcade, from crossing Main St. onto Stemmons Freeway under the triple underpass. (259.) This detour, now known in history as the "double detour," was an essential ingredient to the murder of President Kennedy, for it compelled his automobile to reduce its Secret Service speed from 25 miles per hour to between 10 and 12 miles per hour. The "double detour" also compelled a further slowing down when the president's automobile turned onto Houston, travelled a short block to Elm St., came to a complete stop to make that turn from Houston to Elm which led to Stemmons Freeway under the triple underpass. This "double detour" brought the president right into the line of fire from a rifleman stationed in the Dal-Tex Building; another rifleman's telescopic sight stationed on the County Building; and, as the president's automobile proceeded down toward Stemmons Freeway, right in front of the wooden fence on the "grassy knoll." And Mr. Dulles, you say there was no conspiracy?

Unfortunately for the Commission, photographs snapped prior, during, and after the murder are in existence. Unfortunately for Mr. J. Edgar Hoover, there are not and never were any trees on Houston Street which prevented a rifleman stationed in the Book Depository on the S.E. corner window from hitting the president. A rifleman so stationed would have a clear, unhampered view of the president for more than 90 seconds when he travelled from the corner of Main to Elm on Houston St. (260). The common sense reason why the president was not shot when on Houston St. was the fact that there was no rifleman on the 6th floor but there was one in the Dal-Tex Building. Nor was the Commission's case helped by photographs taken of Main St. near Stemmons Freeway, where there is no street cement obstruction.

One of the most important questions whose answer was concealed and suppressed by the Commission was the fact that the president's automobile came to a complete stop before the shots rang out at 12:25 p.m. To protect someone, or some persons, the Commission flatly stated that his automobile never came to a complete stop. However, eyewitnesses, who testified that the automobile did come to a complete stop, had their testimony either buried in the "Hearings," the National Archives, or were never summoned before the Commission. A few of them were: United

States Senator from the State of Texas, Mr. Yarborough, Mrs. Woodward, Mr. Truly, Patrolman Brown, and Motorcycle Officer Chaney, who was riding "flank guard" to the automobile. (261.) Of course, if the Commission had found some overlooked funds in the U.S. Treasury they might have purchased the television tapes that showed the president's automobile at a complete halt in violation of Secret Service Regulations. But then that would have revealed the faces of persons on the Depository steps, and Oswald might be in those pictures, as well as Jack Ruby, and as well as a rifle poking out from a window, near a fire escape, in the Dal-Tex Building. These are the reasons why the Commission permitted those tapes to be destroyed.

There is absolutely no answer given by the Warren Commission to the question: "What agency, the Dallas Police Department, the Sheriff's Department, or the U.S. Secret Service, selected the route known to history as the 'double detour'?"

The Commission said that it was general knowledge of the people of Dallas that the "double detour" was to be used on November 22, 1963. To support their statement the Commission published a photograph, reduced to about 1/8 of the original, showing the map of the route in the Dallas "Morning News." Upon examination of the map as published in that newspaper, there exists no double detour! The Commission's statement is a lie. The presidential motorcade is shown driving straight down Main St. and crossing over into Stemmons Freeway.

Thus, Mr. Dulles, who guided President Kennedy into that "double detour"? The police, the sheriff's office, or the Secret Service? All of them or a combination of them, or one of them? Is there an answer? Can one be found?

The answer to that question may be found in a statement by that eminent (?) Dallas chief of police when he informed the Dallas "'Morning News" after the murder: "THEY had to bring him through town ... A Secret Service man told me they didn't want that either." Common sense would have led the Commission to ask the chief to interpret the word "they." It could have been someone in the presidential party, but "to bring him through town" does not [refer] to the "route" selected, and that is the key to the question: "Who selected the 'double detour' which violated the U.S. Secret Service regulations?" Nor did the

Commission ask any Secret Service official why the bureau permitted the use of that "double detour" when, according to Police Chief Curry, the Secret Service did not want to bring the president into the downtown area. Chief Curry, although still alive, has retired, but some enterprising reporter might ask the former chief the above questions. (The author's letters remain unanswered.)

The testimony has revealed that the driver of the lead automobile was none other than Chief Curry. In that automobile were Inspector Sorrels of the Secret Service and Sheriff Decker. According to his statement to the N.Y. "Times," Chief Curry stated that the shots came from the Book Depository; to the Commission he said: "get some help in the railroad yards and check these people." (262.) How the chief, who was 100-125 feet ahead of the president's auto, knew the shots came from the Depository is slightly more than extraordinary. What is more extraordinary is the fact that at no time did the Commission ever ask the chief that since he was the driver of the lead automobile why did he make that "double detour"? Why did Chief Curry use a route that was not published in the official map release of the police department, which can be seen by anyone reading the November 22, 1963 issue of the Dallas "Morning News"? Who ordered Chief Curry to use the "double detour"? Was the chief acting as the "Judas" goat?

It was "in the interests of national security" that the Commission was under an obligation to destroy any testimony regarding the possibility of shots not coming from the Book Depository. In view of the uncontradicted testimony of every physician in the Parkland Hospital that the president was shot in the front of his throat, which includes now the admission by Specter that Bullet No. 399 did none of the things he attributed to it; and in view of the admission by Comdr. Humes that the president was struck in the back, the front of the throat, and twice in the head, the Commission serenely "overlooked" all the testimony that the president was hit by riflemen in ambush behind the fence on the "grassy knoll."

The following police agent witnesses, some of whom heard five shots, testified or signed affidavits that the shots came from the "grassy knoll" were: Smith (263); McCurley (264); Oxford.

(265); Mooney (266); Inspector Sorrels (267); Agent Landis, Jr. (268); Chief Sweatt. (269.) Their testimony was upheld by the following civilian witnesses: Mr. Newman (270); Mr. & Mrs. Hester (271); [Mr.] Chism (272); Mrs. Woodward (273); Mr. Miller (274); Mr. Price (275); Mr. Newman (276); Mr. Truly (277); Mr. Reilly (278); and Mr. Holland. (279.) The above is only a partial list of witnesses, both police and civilian, that testified they heard shots come from the "grassy knoll." Are you stating, Mr. Dulles, that all of them are mistaken? Then what about the Zapruder film, and the other suppressed films, which the Commission admitted revealed the vast proportion of witnesses running to the "grassy knoll"? Do those films also lie, Mr. Dulles?

The chief of the United States Secret Service not only informed the Commission of a conspiracy but also proved it was a conspiracy. What happened to the men who identified themselves as "Secret Service" agents to the various witnesses and collected evidence from those witnesses and then those "agents" disappeared with the evidence? The chief of the Secret Service admitted that every Secret Service agent went either to Parkland Hospital or went on to guard Vice President Johnson immediately after the bullets ceased to fire. Then, Mr. Dulles, who were those "agents" seen near and behind the "grassy knolls" when policemen and deputy sheriffs approached them and those 'agents" flashed "credentials"? Who were those men discussed in Com. Exh. 2003, No. 79-83? Secret Service agents or conspirators? Uncle Remus and his friends? Or members of the conspiracy? (280-81.) No conspiracy, Mr. Dulles?

Further evidence that a conspiracy murdered President Kennedy can be found in the statement made by Sheriff Decker when he instructed his men, at 12:25 p.m., that "all available men from the jail and office go to the railroad yards off Elm Street near the triple underpass." This was the Decker announcement, at 12:25, that can be heard on the Dallas police radio tapes. Now, Mr. Dulles, why would the sheriff instruct all his men to search the railroad yards off Elm St? If you accept the sheriff's statement as being honest and truthful, then the sheriff believed the shots came from behind the "grassy knoll." Sheriff Decker was 100-125 feet in front of the president's automobile, beyond the building confines of the Book Depository and the Del-Tex Building, so that the sound and reverberations of the shots would not misguide the sheriff's sense of sound and direction, and he instructed all his men to go to the railroad tracks. If the sheriff was lying, then he directed his men away from the conspirators, thus permitting them to escape capture. Whether or not the sheriff was truthful or lying, the fact remains that under either category a conspiracy was proved by his statements!

And you, Mr. Dulles, now have the gall to say no conspiracy existed!

To assist your recollection, Mr. Dulles, your Commission's method of operation concerning evidence proving a conspiracy was to bury the proof in either the "Hearings" or the National Archives. There is uncontradicted evidence that witnesses also heard shots fired from the Dal-Tex building and from the County Records building or the County Jail buildings, which abut each other. A Mr. Mudd testified he heard shots from the Dai-Tex Building, as did Miss Dorman (282); while Mr. Williams testified that some of the shots came from the County Building (283.) The lead article in the Dallas "Morning News" after the murder of the president stated that the shots "came from a building beyond the Book Depository." That building is none other than the Dai-Tex Building in which Dallas deputy sheriffs arrested a man and took him to jail for investigation. To this day no record exists of the name of that man and the questions and answers given and taken in the "Hearings," the records of the Dallas Sheriff's Office, or in the National Archives. Why? He is mentioned as an unknown. (284.) This man had a rifle in his hands when arrested. Another man, within 15 minutes after the shooting, was arrested by a Patrolman Barker. He was held, incommunicado, from November 22, 1963 until December 10, 1963, and then mysteriously released. His fingerprints are not on file, and why he was held after the murder of Oswald on November 24th until December 10th is not known. (285.)

If two men, both carrying rifles, were not suspicious to the Commission, then the arrest by the sheriff deputies of a man on the "grassy knoll"–who was identified by two witnesses to the shooting that the man was seen firing at the president–should have created a little concern by at least one commissioner, Mr.

Dulles. Yes, what happened to this man, Mr. Dulles? Sheriff Decker? (286.) Was he one of the assassins?

In attempting to seek a solution to the question: "Did a conspiracy murder President Kennedy," the persons involved may be unnamed but that does not prevent an investigator to obtain facts that prove the conspiracy. The evidence surrounding the 6.5 Italian Carcano rifle is a perfect example that locating the evidence can prove a conspiracy but not the persons involved in it. Although the finder of that rifle, Dep. Sheriff Weitzman, originally signed an affidavit that it was a 7.65 Mauser and then "changed" his thoughts at the witness table, the Commission did not give him the rifle in the Commission's hearing room to examine. Every witness on the 6th floor testified that Capt. Fritz stated it was a German Mauser when he handled it. Now, into the picture strode the best police lieutenant of Dallas, Lt. Day. According to the Commission, a witness who was always at the Commission's side to support what they desired to be supported. He was a police officer who always kept "losing" or "finding" just that type of evidence needed by the Commission. He "found" fingerprints; he "lost" palm prints; he "found" a 3-foot paper bag; he "lost" memos and he "found" memos. You name it, and Lt. Day either "found" it or "lost" it. He was worse than the girl in the song "who lost it at the Astor"; at least she knew where she had "lost it" and also what she had lost.[28]

In the 4th volume of the "Hearings" is the testimony of Lt. Day, the mysterious police officer who "found" essential evidence at the necessary time. The police officer admitted that he had written a memo describing the rifle in detail; however, that memo is mysteriously missing from the files of the National Archives! (287.) In the National Archives is a statement that another memo had been written by a policeman who evidently worked with Lt. Day in describing the weapon taken by Lt. Day from the 6th floor. That memo is also missing! (288.) Yet, all was not lost, it seemed, because in the same testimony given by Lt. Day

---

[28] Marks refers here to a tongue-in-cheek popular classic, "She Had to Go and Lose It at the Astor," written by Don Raye and Hughie Prince in 1939 and later recorded by Pearl Bailey.

is his statement that while he was being driven back to the police station by FBI Agent Odum, he agent radioed the description of the "rifle" to the Dallas FBI office. (289.) Thus, the proper legal procedure for the Commission would be for them to either call Agent Odum to the witness stand or subpoena the radio tapes of the FBI Dallas Office. The Commission did neither!

Was there a conspiracy to conceal the identity of the rifle? Was there a conspiracy by the Commission itself that they had no desire to have Weitzman's testimony substantiated by those missing memos and the FBI radio tape? The answer can only be "yes"! One memo, relating to the most vital piece of evidence regarding the lethal weapon, can be lost; but two? Never! The failure to obtain either the testimony of Agent Odum or the FBI radio tapes is indicative, not of negligence by the Commission, but an adherence to the preset Commission theory that Oswald was the man.

It is definitely known that a German Mauser was found on the 6th floor. It is also known that a deputy sheriff, with a German Mauser equipped with the latest telescopic sight, was stationed on the roof of the County Building and the "angle of fire" from that roof was in direct line with the president's body. (290.) A former deputy sheriff, Craig, stated that on the day of the murder, Sheriff Decker pulled his entire department "off-duty" with the exception of the deputy on the roof. There has been no denial, thus far, by the sheriff regarding this charge.

In addition to the multiplicity of both German Mausers and Italian Carcano rifles there is, in the possession of a private photographer, a photograph which showed a police detective at 1 p.m. walking out of the Depository Building with a [rifle with a] telescopic sight on it. (291.) As has been pointed out in a previous chapter, an Inspector Sawyer spoke to police hq. that he had discovered three cartridges on the 3rd floor at 12:45 p.m. Note that the cartridges were found on the 3rd floor at 12:45 p.m., and between 1 p.m. and 1:05 p.m. a rifle without a telescopic sight. (292.)

No conspiracy, Mr. Dulles?

The testimony in the "Hearings" is overloaded with the proof that Oswald was "wanted" by the Dallas police prior to the murder of Officer Tippit. On a police radio tape timed at 12:45 p.m.

is the police announcement that Lee Harvey Oswald was wanted for the murder of President Kennedy! No conspiracy, Mr. Dulles? Then why does all testimony and affidavits by the Dallas policemen taking part in the arrest of Oswald at the Texas Theater reveal the fact that every one of those policemen swear that the "tip" said Oswald was in the balcony, not on the first floor? How did McDonald, the last patrolman to arrive, know that Oswald, who was not wearing the clothes broadcasted by the police, was on the first floor and knew Oswald to be the suspect? (293.) Why did one of the Commission's three witnesses testify that one of the cops hit Oswald and said: "Kill the president, will you, you son of a bitch!" How did these cops know Oswald was the killer?

No conspiracy, Mr. Dulles?

Another fraudulent statement by the Commission is one that Oswald was unknown to the Dallas police. That is a lie, for the testimony in the "Hearings" revealed that not only did the Dallas police know Oswald's address on Berkley St. but they also knew his secret address on Elsbeth Street, which Oswald kept from the Paine's and his wife, Marina. The Dallas police had Oswald's secret address on Elspeth Street, and the Dallas police sent a party of policemen to arrest him there. This testimony is suppressed from the "Report," but, in the "Hearings," Detectives Carroll and Taylor made that statement, and it was substantiated by Detectives Westphal and Parks. (294.)

It is abundantly clear from the testimony in the "Hearings" or in the National Archive's files that some of the Dallas police were involved in the Tippit murder. In an effort to solve this "mystery," the Commission had the police submit their radio tapes to the FBI because of the deliberate lies made by the police in their transcription of those radio logs. (295.). The logs revealed that only 2 squad cars in the entire city of Dallas were instructed to move into the Oak Cliff area. One of the squad cars, however, went to the Book Depository; the other was driven by Officer Tippit, who immediately violated the instructions. At the time he was murdered, the radio logs and the FBI revealed that Tippit was not in District 91 where he was ordered to patrol but in District No. 109. Why? That Tippit was scheduled to die was revealed in the tape recordings; for when Mr. Bowley saw Tippit's body at 1:10 p.m. on the street and he called in the report over Tippit's squad car radio, the police dispatcher immediately called Tippit's squad car number, not the code number of the officer who was supposed to be on regular duty in that Oak Cliff area. How did the despatcher know to call Tippit's code number in an area where Tippit was never instructed to patrol? The radio tapes revealed that when Mr. Bowley spoke to the police despatcher Mr. Bowley never gave the despatcher Tippit's badge number or his squad car number–No. 10.

The same Dallas police also testified that although Tippit's clipboard was attached to his dashboard they never looked at it or read it! Do you believe that, Mr. Dulles? Would any police department fail to read a fellow officer's clipboard which would reveal where he had been, and who he had seen, in their efforts to locate and capture the murderer of a fellow officer unless some of the police, themselves, were involved in his death? Of course, the police would have had to come up with the answers to such questions as "Why did Tippit leave his district and go home two hours before he was murdered? What was so important that while on duty he had to visit his family? Why was a police squad car missing from 12:45 p.m. in front of the Book Depository until 3:45 p.m., when it was mysteriously returned? Could the answer to the last question be that it was that car that went to Oswald's Berkley Street Address and, at 1:02 p.m., "tooted twice" and Oswald then rushed out of his rooming house? (296.)

No conspiracy, Mr. Dulles? The willful and deliberate acts of the Dallas police, their deliberate commission of perjury, and their deliberate refusal to investigate the murder of Officer Tippit can only lead to the conclusion that some of those Dallas police were deeply involved not only in his murder but also as participants of the conspiracy that murdered President John F. Kennedy.

Other evidence of the "conspiracy" is seen in the illustrated section of this book, where one can read the "arrest report." Oswald was arrested, according to that report, at 1:40 p.m. by four police officers, none of them who signed the charge! He was arrested but never charged. However, at the time he was "booked," not arraigned, the invisible officer wrote in the section: "Other details of the arrest": "This man shot and killed President John J. Kennedy and Police Officer J. D. Tippit. He also wounded Governor John Connally." The reader is advised to note (1) the time of the arrest; (2) no policeman signed the "charge filed" section; (3) Oswald was not resisting arrest; (4) Oswald had no revolver!

According to the police, Oswald arrived at the police station at approximately 2:20 p.m. He was immediately booked by an officer who completed the "arrest report." That would be approximately 2:30 p.m. Oswald was not notified of any charges against him until after 6 p.m. The Commission and the police admitted no charge was filed against him relating to the President Kennedy murder until 1:30 a.m. on November 23, 1963. That, as will be shown, is another Commission falsehood.

The Commission stated that at the time of Oswald's arrest none of the police knew he was wanted or suspected in the murder of President Kennedy, although one witness testified that, during the struggle (?) to capture Oswald, a policeman did say he was the killer of President Kennedy. Thus, the vital question never answered by the Warren Commission is that, at the time the charge sheet was completed at 2:30 p.m., how did the policeman writing up the "arrest report" know that Oswald had "killed" the president and "wounded" governor Connelly?

No conspiracy, Mr. Dulles? Then why did the officer use the word "killed" instead of "arrested for suspicion of murder"? How did the Dallas police know that Oswald had killed President Kennedy at 2:30 p.m.? There was no fingerprint or palm print evidence, for Lt. Day discovered no "prints" on that rifle until 8:00 p. m. The FBI never traced that Italian rifle from Klein's of Chicago to "Hidell" until late in the day of November 23rd. The police chief of Dallas went on a national television and radio broadcast and admitted, at 4:30 p.m., that they had no eyewitness to the rifleman. Mr. Brennan admitted he could not identify the rifleman he saw. Then, Mr. Dulles, can you answer the question: 'How did the Dallas police know at 2:30 p.m. that Oswald had "killed" President Kennedy and "wounded" Governor Connelly?

Conclusive proof that Oswald was never legally arraigned for the murder of President Kennedy prior to his own murder by another conspirator can also be seen in the "Illustrated" section of this book. This "Alexander" affidavit was published in the "Report" as a true copy for the "arraignment" of Lee Harvey Oswald in the murder of President Kennedy. The background relating to this photograph was revealed in the testimony that on the night of November 22, 1963, Alexander showed this affidavit at the press conference as proof to the news media that Oswald had been legally arraigned for both murders. Minutes prior to this showing, Oswald cried out that he was not charged with the murder of President Kennedy, only with that of Officer Tippit, and then exclaimed that he was being used as a "patsy." He also stated that he was innocent of both charges and he desired a lawyer.

Photographers and reporters are not lawyers, so they accepted, as true, Alexander's statement that Oswald had been arraigned. What those members of the press media did not understand was that, in criminal law, the Alexander "affidavit" was a fake, since no person, either as the "affiant" or as a justice of the peace, had signed that "affidavit." Oswald was thus, according to the Alexander "affidavit," being accused by an unknown person; for no Dallas policeman, justice of the peace, or member of the D.A.'s office had signed that affidavit. That "affidavit" was a worthless piece of paper in any court of criminal law in any state of the United States. The Commission and its 26 lawyers knew that "affidavit" was absolutely worthless, but they published it under "the basic principles of American justice."

In an attempt to corroborate this fake Alexander "affidavit," the Commission then proceeded to pour additional oil on the flames by publishing another photograph in the "Report" titled: "Johnston Exhibit No. 4." This can be seen in the "Illustrated" section of this book. This photograph is another fraudulent example of manufactured evidence. As the reader can see, this "affidavit" is torn in half, and the two torn portions do not match! The Warren Commission gave the Alexander "affidavit" a full page; the Johnston Exhibit an eighth of a page. Since when, Mr. Dulles, is a torn affidavit admissible in any court of law especially in view of the evidence that the two torn parts do not match each other? It can be noticed that the printing on both the Alexander "affidavit" and the Johnson "Exhibit" are one and the same, yet no one knows whose handwriting it represents. The reader should also compare the "Alexander" affidavit to the "Johnston exhibit," for both reveal a blank space under the word "affiant." This could mean that both are one and the same, and that Mr. Wade's and Capt. Fritz's signature were simply added to the photograph of the "Johnson Exhibit." That may be why the "Johnston Exhibit" is torn! What is another problem is that on the side of that Johnston "'affidavit" is the strange writing that appears. A word "June" or "Jan." 26, 1964 appears, with "2 of 4" also written. What the meaning of those written words is was not explained by the Commission. It could mean that Oswald was "arraigned" after his death to pacify the citizenry.

Thus, from a reading of the testimony in the "Hearings," the legal fact is that Lee Harvey Oswald, while alive, was never legally arraigned for the murder of President Kennedy. The next question that must be answered is whether or not that statement can be supported by testimony.

Oswald, according to the Commission, was charged with the murder of President Kennedy at 1:30 a.m., on November 23, 1963 by Capt. Fritz of the Dallas Police Department before Texas Justice of the Peace Johnston. (297.) The Commission said that, but the testimony in the "Hearings" informed the reader the Commission lied. Based on the testimony of Officer Hider, the Commission lied. This police officer testified that he was the duty officer in charge of the identification bureau where arraignments are made of accused persons. Officer Hider testified that he was on duty until 2:15 a.m. on November 23, 1963. He further testified that at 1:30 a.m. of the same day he never saw Capt. Fritz or J. P. Johnson make any arraignment of Oswald for the murder of President Kennedy. (298.)

On the basis of the testimony in the "'Hearings," Lee Harvey Oswald was never charged by any legal body in the State of Texas with the murder of President Kennedy or the wounding of Governor Connelly. In a legal sense, Oswald died innocent of any charge of being involved in the murder of President Kennedy.

After the arrest of Oswald, he kept shouting "I'm not resisting arrest, I'm not resisting arrest." According to the various affidavits in the "Hearing," namely Comm. Exh. No. 2003, Oswald's "gun" was in the possession of several policemen and "marked" by several other policemen with six live bullets, but, when given to Capt. Fritz by Sgt. Hill, the Captain announced that the revolver now had 4 live bullets and 2 spent ones. (299.) Since the Captain received the revolver directly from the hands of Sgt. Hill and he signed for it, how did 6 live bullets become reduced to 4 live bullets and 2 spent ones? Was the "Oswald" gun the weapon taken from him or was it planted? (300.)

With Oswald's refusal to run and be gunned down near the theater with several dozen witnesses looking on, the Dallas police now had a live "patsy" on their hands. It would take all of the 23rd to make the preparations that would lead to Oswald's murder, on the 24th of November. The "Report" has admitted that the Dallas police were warned several times that Oswald would be murdered. (301.) Hoover tried several times to contact Police Chief Curry and personally warn the chief that Oswald was going to be murdered. However, the police chief testified that on the night of the 23rd he went to bed with the telephone receiver "off the hook." As one can see, that is a new method to run a police department.

Jack Ruby, the alleged murderer of Oswald, who was a fringe member of the conspiracy that murdered President John F. Kennedy, now became the lead character actor in the conspiracy. Jack Ruby was well-known by the Dallas police and the district attorney's office In fact, there is a suppressed document in the National Archives, Com. Exh. No. 1467, which proved Ruby knew, by sight or personally, more than 70% of the Dallas Police Department. Jack Ruby was also well known by members of the staff of the Dallas district attorney. Ruby was even well known among the legal profession; for, at the Texas State Bar Association Meeting in 1963, Ruby was a nonparticipating member and introduced to many members of the Texas Bar. (302.)

Jack Ruby, on the day prior to the murder of Oswald, visited several high police executives and their offices on the 3rd floor of the Police station. When Chief Curry announced on the 23rd that Oswald would be transferred the next day at 10:00 a.m., Ruby continued his exploration of the police building. (303.) In spite of the fact that the Commission said that Jack Ruby acted emotionally in his "murder" of Oswald, the testimony revealed that it was, beyond doubt, premeditated. For, in the presence of his own attorney, Ruby, prior to taking a "lie" test, and in the presence of Asst. D.A. Alexander, admitted that he had informed his roommate, George Senator, that he was going to murder Oswald on the morning of November 24 in the police station. (304.) Ruby's smuggled confession, which was reprinted in full in "Ramparts," revealed the fact that he was ordered to murder Oswald. Dorothy Kilgallen's death was due to the statements Ruby gave to her, privately, in Judge Brown's chambers. Her murder was to come later! Why she kept Ruby's statement in her apartment and made no carbon statement to be "opened upon her death" remains a mystery. Of course, the main conspirators, with their influence in the federal government, could have located those notes and destroyed them.

With Oswald alive in the Dallas police station, it became absolutely essential that he be kept incommunicado from any legal advice. No attorney was permitted to see him privately, and the Dallas Civil Liberties Union was given false information by the Dallas police that Oswald wanted no legal advice. The last statement the reporters heard Oswald make was his plea that he desired to be represented by an attorney. But the Commission was to say none of Oswald's legal rights were denied. Who was lying? The Commission or Oswald?

The Commission in its attempt to prove that no one assisted Ruby in his plan to murder Oswald conveniently overlooked positive testimony that proved Ruby was given assistance by some members of the Dallas police. The Commission contended that Ruby entered the Dallas police station's basement via the ramp on Main St. about 10 minutes prior to the murder. However, Patrolman Vaughn, the guardian of the entrance, testified he never saw Ruby at any time prior to the shooting of Oswald. To substantiate Patrolman Vaughn was Lt. Pierce and Police Sgts. Maxey and Putman. (305.) However, since some of the police are involved, the investigator must seek impartial testimony to solve this entry problem.

Buried in the National Archives is an affidavit given to the FBI by a UPI reporter, Mr. T. McGarry, who testified that, ten minutes prior to the shooting of Oswald by Ruby, the reporter was standing in the middle of the basement looking at the Main

St. ramp entrance. He did not see Jack Ruby enter from the ramp entrance at the time stipulated by Warren Commission. (306.) The reporter's sworn testimony was, in turn, upheld by Mr. Tasker, a taxicab driver who was stationed at the Main St. ramp entrance across the street. He testified that while he was at the entrance during a time period, which was about fifteen minutes prior to the shooting, he did not see Jack Ruby enter the building through that ramp entrance. (307.)

Of course no policeman or civilian saw Jack Ruby enter the police building for the reason he was already in the building! By a strange coincidence he stationed himself in the exact spot where Oswald had to walk to the truck which was to take him out of that building. With an inaudible sign of resignation, the Commission 'accepted" the "testimony" of the police that by "accident" the police ordered a truck that could not fit the space within the platform from which Oswald was to step off and into that truck. It was also a "coincidence" that the police walked Oswald with no police in front of him, just to the side, so that Ruby had a perfect shot at Oswald. It was an "accident" that the police walked Oswald directly in front of Ruby. It was "coincidence" that the police failed to check all the credentials of the civilians in the basement. It was a "coincidence" that Chief Curry did not talk to the FBI and Secret Service bureaus who desired to inform him that they suspected Oswald would be murdered at the time he was to be transferred.

If any person with common sense can accept those "accidents" and "coincidences" they can accept the infallibility of the Commission's "Report."

In an attempt to discredit the testimony of the four police officers, three of whom knew Jack Ruby personally, and the two civilian witnesses who upheld the testimony of those four policemen, the Commission summoned three other police officers whose testimony revealed flagrant perjury. When Ruby was interrogated after the shooting of Oswald, FBI Agent Hall testified that Ruby made no mention of entering the police building at the ramp entrance. The official report of those three officers revealed that none of them made any statement that Ruby informed them he had entered through the ramp entrance. They "remembered" it after days or months had passed, but not in their official report.

In two of the most remarkable documents ever written and given under oath is the positive proof that a conspiracy murdered President Kennedy and Lee Harvey Oswald. Both documents are suppressed from the "Report" and buried in the 19th and 21st volumes of the "Hearings." To prevent an investigator from exposing the conspiracy, the Commission deliberately buried the evidence that Oswald was to be murdered by scattering that evidence in the National Archives or in the 26 volumes of the "Hearings." (308.)

Volume 21 contains the famous "Price" exhibit[29] which refers to the activities of the various members of Parkland Hospital from November 22 to and including November 24, 1963–the Oswald murder. This Exhibit contains testimony so inflammable that the Commission buried it deep in the "Hearings." What is contained in the "Price" Exhibit?

Approximately one-half hour prior to the shooting of Lee Harvey Oswald the staff of the hospital was instructed to prepare the operating room to receive the body of Lee Harvey Oswald! (309.)

A few of the staff members were to say that they suspected Oswald would be murdered or injured when they heard that Oswald was to be transferred on the morning of November 24th. But the Dallas police suspected nothing; the Dallas Sheriff's Office suspected nothing; those two police agencies suspected nothing. Just the staff at the hospital, but who warned them that Oswald was to be shot thirty minutes prior to the shooting? Is this not another example of the invisible "tipster," as in the one who "tipped" off Officer McDonald that Oswald was not in the balcony but on the first floor?

No conspiracy, Mr. Dulles?

---

[29] Marks is referring to an affidavit featured in Price Exhibit Number 7 (*Warren Commission Hearings and Exhibits*, volume 21), dated November 24, 1963. Charles Jack Price was administrator, Dallas County hospital district, which included Parkland Memorial Hospital and Woodlawn Hospital.

Did Ruby shoot or murder Oswald? The autopsy report relating to Lee Harvey Oswald revealed that Oswald was struck down by a bullet that entered his stomach area. In view of modern medical practice that wound is not a fatal wound if treatment is made promptly. The autopsy report also stated that Oswald's death was hastened by the loss of blood. Where certain acts occur which promote the original nonfatal wound into a fatal wound, the law presumes that the person who caused the nonfatal wound is not guilty of murder where he did nothing to convert that wound from the nonfatal to the fatal. For example, if a doctor operates on a patient for the removal of the appendix, and his assistant deliberately leaves in the wound an instrument which infects the wound after the operation, the second doctor could be found guilty of murder, since he did his act deliberately, not negligently. This example is applicable to the shooting, thus in the murder of Lee Harvey Oswald.

In Volume 19, pages 410-413, is a statement by a Dallas policeman, Davenport, who gave a sworn affidavit to the events that occurred after the shooting of Oswald. This policeman testified that he saw a man assist television technicians move their equipment into the basement on the morning of the shooting. This "assistant" was dressed in a physician's standard white uniform with a stethoscope hung around his neck. How he could be an "assistant" and a "physician" at the same time was not explained. Nor did the Commission explain their statement that "all" persons who entered the basement had their credentials "checked." The policeman neither checked the credentials of the television crew or the "physician." This "doctor" looked to be about 22 to 23 years old, which made this "doctor" the youngest "doctor" in the United States! Just as Oswald was the world's fastest human, strongest man, and greatest rifle expert, Dallas now had the world's "youngest doctor."

When Oswald fell to the basement floor after receiving the Ruby bullet in his gut, this "doctor" rushed to Oswald's side and pressed down, not once but several times, while the blood rushed out of Oswald's wound. After a short time, this "doctor" did not wait for any ambulance, but simply got up from Oswald's body and vanished into the crowd. But, while this "doctor" was assisting Oswald to Death's Door, an unknown Dallas police officer was also pumping out Oswald's blood by giving him artificial respiration! In other words, the "doctor" and the "plainclothes policeman" were pumping out Oswald's blood on the basement floor! (310.) There is no policeman in any police force in the United States that is ever instructed to handle the body of a living person who has just been shot. The Dallas police regulations so instruct their policemen. Why was that disregarded?

The only evidence in the Oswald-Ruby affair is that Ruby shot Oswald; he did not murder him. The actual cause of death was "lack of blood," which was pumped out of Oswald by two unknown persons.

No conspiracy, Mr. Dulles?

Thus ends the official record of Lee Harvey Oswald. A young man of 24 involved in matters far over his head. A man selected to enact the role of a "patsy," but when he was engaged to play that role the producer failed to inform him that the final scene was to be enacted on a dirty, damp, oil-stained floor in a police station basement with the spotlight slowly being dimmed on his own red blood gushing out of a wound given to him by a fellow conspirator.

This small book was not written to name the conspirators, for they are known only to the CIA, the FBI, the Secret Service, the Dallas Police Department, the Miami, Fla., Police Department and probably to the former president of the United States, Mr. Johnson. The author does not know, for he is only one of the "general public" and, "in the interests of national security," the Commission decided that those names should not be given to the "general public." The tape recording taken by the Miami, Fla., Police Department, by which they warned the FBI and Secret Service of the possibility of President Kennedy being assassinated in Dallas, Texas, on November 22nd, is the key to the conspiracy. Since both agencies had that recording in their possession a minimum of 13 days prior to the murder, both of them must be deemed grossly negligent in their protection of President Kennedy. For the FBI to interview the man who gave that recording to the Miami, Fla., Police Department five days after the murder simply revealed the feeling the Bureau expressed toward President Kennedy. That can also be said of the PRS division of the United States Secret Service.

That the FBI was disturbed by the recording can be seen in the "telefax"[30] message sent by the FBI Washington Hq. to their southern bureaus, but there is no evidence that the FBI even slightly warned the actual security guards around the president or even the Dallas Division of the Secret Service. Why? Did the FBI believe that, when all this came out, they would be like knights in shining armor? At no time did the FBI ever inform their superior, Attorney General Robert F. Kennedy, that the president of the United States would be under an assassin's rifle if the president visited Dallas, Texas in November, 1963. Why? Did the operating heads of the FBI let their personal hatred of the two brothers interfere with their sworn duty? Is the shield of the FBI now to be used as the personal shield of the present and future head of the FBI?

The strange activity of the FBI was brought to the public's attention in an article in the "Saturday Evening Post" of February 27, 1967, by an article written by Jules Witcover, who was writing about Richard Nixon's presidential opportunity in the following year, 1968.

Mr. Nixon related the following to Mr. Witcover:

> "I was in a taxicab when I got the news," Nixon says. "I had been in Dallas attending a meeting. I flew back to New York the next morning [Nov. 22nd]. It must have happened just as my plane was landing. [12:30 Dallas; 1:30 p.m. N.Y. time.] My cab was stopped for a light in Queens, and a guy ran over and said: 'Have you got a radio? The president's been wounded!' I thought, 'Oh, my God, it must have been one of those nuts.' A half hour later I got to my apartment, and the doorman told me he was dead. [1:00 Dallas; 2:00 p.m. N. Y. time.] I called J. Edgar Hoover and asked him, 'What happened? Was it one of the nuts?' Hoover said, 'No, it was a Communist.'"

---

[30] A forerunner of the Fax machine.

When Mr. Nixon arrived at his home apartment in Manhattan, the doorman told him the president was dead. Upon reaching his apartment, he immediately telephoned Mr. Hoover and Mr. Hoover informed him it was not a "nut" but a "Communist." How did Mr. Hoover know the arrested man was the murderer?

Strange? What was the distinction between Hoover's "nut" and a "Communist"? Stranger still is how did Mr. Hoover know that "it was a Communist" for, at the time Mr. Nixon spoke to Mr. Hoover, Oswald was not yet booked in the police station!

The official announcement of the death of the president was made at 1:00 p.m. The time in New York City was 2:00 p.m. Oswald was not in the Dallas police station until 2:15 p.m. or 3:15 p.m. The card in Oswald's billfold was listed, according to the FBI, to an "Alex James Hidell." The first fingerprinting of Oswald occurred at 6 p.m. (Dallas time), or 7 p.m. New York time. The FBI did not trace the "Hidell" rifle to Oswald until the next day. The first interrogation session did not commence until 5:20 p.m. Washington, D.C. time. Yet, Mr. Hoover said the "killer" was also a "Communist." What amazing foresight within the FBI Chief!

Mr. Dulles: How did J. Edgar Hoover, at 2:15 p.m. know that a "Communist" killed President Kennedy? Did he know it in the same manner that a Dallas cop, at 2 p.m. telephoned the Dallas Police Hq. and said: "I think we have got a man on both counts!" (311) or the cop who hit Oswald and kept saying: "Kill the president, will you!" (312.) How did the FBI and the Dallas police "know" Oswald killed President Kennedy before he was booked for the murder or his prints taken?

The FBI gave to the Commission more than sufficient evidence to prove beyond a reasonable doubt that Lee Harvey Oswald was not "the sole and exclusive assassin of the president." That the Commission disregarded that evidence is not the fault of the FBI or its operating heads. That responsibility rested solely upon the character of each commissioner. That the character was weak is to their disgrace.

The tremendous implication of the Commission's finding that conspirators may assassinate future presidents with impunity can be seen in the various political murders since the assassination of President Kennedy. For if the right-wing forces can murder with impunity then that practice may have to be taken by the left-wing forces. A Martin Luther King threatened no one with violence; neither did Senator Robert F. Kennedy; nor does a George McGovern or a Gene McCarthy, or a Ted Kennedy; but as long as the Commission's philosophy remains in our history books the political assassinations will continue. As long as the CIA, the FBI, and the Secret Service refuse to permit the American people to know the words on the original tape recording made by the Miami police, the greater the danger to our democratic form of government. For if those conspirators can murder two Kennedys, they can, with impunity, murder another Kennedy, a Humphrey, a Javits, a Ribicoff, a Fulbright, a Warren, a Lindsey, a Muskie; yea, even a Nixon, a Rockefeller, a Dirksen, a Smith; all those who disagree with the Minutemen, the KKK, the Birchers, Wallacites, and Nazis.

History has proven that once assassination has become the weapon to change the government, that style and form of government preceding the assassination falls beneath the hard-nailed boots of the assassins. Both Right and Left favor no democratic spirit in the people. The cold of Siberia and the gas ovens of the concentration camps have proved it.

The tragedy of the Warren Commission is that they helped set those boots on the road to the destruction of American democracy.

It would not be fair to Mr. Dulles not to accept his challenge flung to the American people to prove a conspiracy and name the assassins. To "name the assassins" cannot be done, either by the author or the "general public." A conspiracy has been proven beyond a reasonable doubt. But what was the purpose of the conspiracy?

History has shown that an invisible coup d'état occurred when President Kennedy was murdered. It is the belief of the author that more than the murder of a head of state was involved. This belief is based on two events that occurred during the three years President Kennedy occupied the White House; (1) The Bay of Pigs; and (2) the Cuban Missile Crisis.

The citizens of the United States, living in a dream world concocted by the mass communication systems, have been constantly told that a conspiracy to murder any president would be impossible since that kind of secret could not be kept. Overlooked, or rather not brought to their attention, is that all political assassinations involve a conspiracy. Some are exposed, some are successful. President De Gaulle of France was the target of 5 conspiracies, each a failure. More than 500 to 750 persons were involved in the conspiracies, with the leaders of those attacks being in the highest places of the French Government. Yet, outside of those persons involved, the French general public never learned of the conspiracies until the arrest, capture, and imprisonment of the conspirators. So, as History has shown, conspirators do keep their mouths shut.

The involvement of various executives and police officers of the Dallas Police Department has been proven beyond a reasonable doubt. With the police department riddled by members of the Birch Society and the KKK (a Lieutenant of the Dallas Police Department was a "Grand Dragon" in 1963), it was an easy task for the Texas oil and steel industry to organize the "task force" that murdered President Kennedy. After the murder of Senator Robert Kennedy, a newspaper of national renown investigated various police departments throughout the country, and they found the number of policemen who were active members of various fascist organizations to be incredibly high. ("Wall Street Journal," Sept. 1968.) These men operated on the philosophy of supplying the money but left the details with others.

The Warren Commission not only revealed a strange reluctance to question members and leaders of the KKK but a downright fear of questioning the leaders of the John Birch Society in Texas, although their names were brought into the testimony. The Commission, for example, showed a blind eye to the fact that the FBI could not locate any member of the H. L. Hunt family who put up some of the immoral advertisement money calling for the death of a "red"–President Kennedy. Nor did the Commission have the moral guts to ask another member of that same family why he was so highly regarded by the FBI that they secretly rushed him, in an FBI private automobile, to the American Airlines, purchased a ticket for him under a false name, and hid him away for approximately three weeks.

The solicitude of the FBI for this, and other fascist groups, is not applicable to those persons who disagree with Mr. Hoover.

There is no question that many agents of both the FBI and Secret Service are fervent believers of the Birch and Wallace philosophy. Many news reporters covering the 1968 Wallace campaign wrote news reports which exposed the feelings of the various police agencies, local, state, and federal, that revealed the anti-American philosophy of those staunch upholders of "law and order." (L.A. "Times" Oct. 11, 1968.) The FBI thought so little of President Kennedy that the Bureau, although notified 13 days prior to the assassination, waited until five days had elapsed after President's murder to interview the person who had given the Miami, Fla., the "tip" about the president's murder to be made in the next Southern city he visited. But this same Bureau gave physical protection to the man who furnished the funds for the "Kennedy is a traitor" advertisement.

Mr. Hoover expressed his concept of democracy and his basic attitude toward the philosophy upon which is constructed the American Society: "Law and order must take precedence over justice." (J. Edgar Hoover–November, 1968.) He believed that "justice" is a mere incident in the life of man. One must follow Hoover's life philosophy to its bitter logical conclusion: if the "law" orders blacks into a gas oven, it is the moral responsibility of the black to enter! If the "law" states that no person can wear a red tie or face imprisonment for a period of not less than 10 years, then any person violating that law should be imprisoned for that period. After World War I such a law was actually enacted! If the "law" says that a black man can only live in a rat infested, plague-ridden building, the black man should be happy to comply. If the "law" states that all persons of the Catholic or Jewish faith cannot attend their own parochial schools and a violation of that "law" be imprisonment of the parents for a period of not less than ten years, so be the law. Mr. Hoover's belief in "law and order" is on the exact same level as Hitler's "law and order"; Stalin's "law and order"; Mussolini's "law and order"; Tojo's "law and order"; "Batista's "law and order"; the Greek Colonel's "law and order, 1968 version"; and so forth. Mr. Hoover's basic philosophy is identical with the philosophy of any other "police state" objective.

Is it more than a mere coincidence that the private secretary to the president of the Lone Star Steel Company was appointed to be the right hand confidential secretary to the president of the United States, Lyndon B. Johnson, and then promoted to be the Postmaster General of the United States when the Lone Star Steel Company's president is on the executive board of the John Birch Society of Texas?[31] Who derided the author's statement that the murder of President Kennedy changed the course of history?

The life of President Kennedy was only an incident to bring into operation the main purpose of the conspiracy. The conspiracy was a four-pronged affair: (1) the murder of President Kennedy; (2) the invasion and overthrow of the Castro regime in Cuba, with the installation of a right-wing dictatorship under the direct control of the CIA, which is, in turn, controlled by the fascist forces in the United States; (3) involvement with a war with the Soviet Union, but, if that not be possible, a complete diplomatic break with the Soviet Union, isolating that nation by the new government in the United States by exerting economic pressure upon NATO and nations receiving our foreign aid; and (4) a "coup d'état."

The testimony in the 'Hearings" has given some glimmering that the three-prong conspiracy is not speculation. The background of Lee Harvey Oswald supports the thesis, for he did everything that would cast suspicion on the Soviet Union that they were involved. The willingness of all agencies of the federal government–State, Navy, Army, Marine, Secret Service, Bureau of Immigration and Naturalization, Office of Naval Intelligence, the CIA and the FBI–to assist Oswald in maintaining his fiction that he was a loyal and willing servant of Communism. Oswald's ease in obtaining passports was not due to his good looks; nor would an intelligence agent acting on behalf of the Soviet Union openly appear on the steps of the Mexican Cuban or Soviet Consulate so that "hidden" FBI and CIA agents could

---

[31] W. Marvin Watson, Jr., was executive assistant to the president of the Lone Star Steel Company in Dallas. President Johnson tapped him to serve as "appointments secretary" in January 1965. According to Watson's *Washington Post* obit, he was LBJ's "chief of staff in all but name." He also served as postmaster general.

snap his picture. Hitler, to convince his people that the Polish soldiers had invaded Germany, in Sept. 1939, simply had prisoners shot who were dressed in Polish Army uniforms, placed their bodies near the German-Polish border, and took their pictures. Millions of Germans were absolutely convinced that Poland had invaded Germany! Oswald was to be the "Communist" that was guided by Castro to kill President Kennedy. That was script.

The research done by Popkin in his "The Two Oswalds," by Mark Lane's two excellent books, by Weisberg's four volumes of "Whitewash" and Meagher's "Accessories After the Fact" prove beyond a reasonable doubt that Lee Harvey Oswald had more than one double traveling around the southern part of the United States. Why?

In Popkin's book he uncovered the evidence that three days prior to the murder two men and a woman appeared at the Red Bird Airfield outside of Dallas and attempted to hire an airplane that had a long-range capacity. The plane was to be hired for a flight on the day of November 22, 1963, for an unknown destination. The owner of the airport refused the request and stated one of the men "looked" like Oswald. He was never shown a picture of Mr. Ferrie, the man charged by Mr. Garrison, the D.A. of New Orleans, as being one of the conspirators. Nor did the Warren Commission deem it fit and proper to investigate Professor Popkin's facts. Strangely, Oswald and Ferrie were both members of the Civil Air Patrol, which is limited to loyal American citizens whose references and background must be approved by the Federal Bureau of Investigation. The big question is "How did and why did the FBI approve Lee Harvey Oswald's membership in the Civil Air Patrol"? Is that also the reason why the FBI informed the Dallas Police Intelligence Division that Oswald was "all right," according to that Division's memo dated February 14, 1964? Oswald was known by the FBI to be on the payroll of the CIA, and, in turn, Oswald was a paid informer for the FBI.

After the murder of President Kennedy, members of the conspiracy were to take off from the Dallas independent airport and fly direct to Cuba. Upon landing they were to proclaim the fact that they had murdered the president of the United States and were seeking political asylum. With Oswald's background secure in the smokescreen that he was an outstanding "Communist," the reader can well imagine what would have happened to the United States. Bismarck, by changing a word in a telegram prior to the French-German War in the 1870's, brought about the defeat of France. The mass communication media, backed by the right-wing forces in Congress and among the public, would have whipped the public into a frenzy to invade Cuba. And that would have happened. In '98 it was "Remember the Maine!" In '63: "Kennedy!"

But, the reader will ask, "Where did the Soviet Union come into the picture?"

In Manchester's book "The Death of a President" is a single paragraph which far too many people who have read the book overlooked. That author claims that on the afternoon after the death of President Kennedy, Assistant District Attorney Alexander, that mysterious man who has been kept on Wade's staff even though he threatened to pistol whip another attorney in the courtroom where Alexander was losing a criminal case, sought to present to the press and television media an affidavit charging the Soviet Union as being the principal agent in the murder! This method of insanity would have brought on a war, for no nation could accept such a charge that it had directed the murder of the head of another nation. That is a charge of war under international law. There is no doubt that the mass communication media would have accepted Alexander's charges, for they accepted everything that was "dished" out by the Dallas authorities. They have even accepted, as of today, the blatant lies "dished" out by the Commission, so what was a "little atomic war" to that media? They accepted, *in toto*, the "faked" indictment held by Alexander in pictures; why would they not accept another faked piece of paper held by Alexander for a few more pictures? Manchester stated that when the State Department heard of his proposed insane act, they rushed an assistant secretary of state to plead with Alexander not to do this rash act. What other pleading was made by the State Department is not known. But it is significant that the Warren Commission made no comment upon Alexander's proposed act.

But the Warren Commission never questioned Mr. Alexander,

either to his "faked" affidavit charging Oswald with the murder of President Kennedy or to his proposed legal indictment charging the Soviet Union with the murder. Why? It stands to reason that if Mr. Manchester, from his study of the murder, was able to uncover this proposed act of insanity, then why did the Commission fail to uncover it? Or did the Commission know of the act and hide it from the light of day? Manchester's story was confirmed by the "Herald-Tribune," May 16, 1964.

Of course, when Alexander's political background and public utterances are investigated, it is seen that he is a fervent right-winger, a right-winger that has repeatedly demanded war with the Soviet Union. He acts openly and is repeatedly quoted by various Dallasites as "a man to be reckoned with." His attitude and interpretation of "law and order" is the same as Gov. Reagan's: "If a person is arrested by any cop, throw the arrested one in prison." Reagan refuses to understand that his philosophy runs parallel to all dictators. The Soviet citizens obeyed the "law" and marched all the way to Siberia. The German Christian and Jew who dissented from Hitler marched all the way to the gas ovens. If it be morally correct for the Czech students to defy Stalinism, should not it be morally correct to defy Reaganism? The word of the police is superior to that of the citizen, therefore, save public money by eliminating trials. The Bill of Rights should be used or applied to only "good, decent people." What is "good" and "decent" seems to be interpreted that as long as the civilian obeys the law, like the one sending Germans to the gas ovens of Buchenwald, they remain "good, decent citizens."

The deterioration of the American Dream in the minds of the present Establishment can be seen in comparing three "leading" Americans to that of a "leading" German: Governor Reagan, as has been seen, desired "law and order." FBI Chief, Mr. Hoover, in 1968, after the murder of Senator R. Kennedy, proclaimed that "Justice is incidental to law and order." The former "gang-buster" from the State of New York, and twice the Republican presidential nominee, [Thomas Dewey], approved this doctrine when, in the fall of 1968, [he] issued his concept of justice by advocating the elimination of the 5th Amendment to both the Constitution of the United States and all state constitutions. In view of the fact that the U.S. historical record has revealed that, as a class, it was the well-to-do and the wealthy that have used the 5th Amendment far more than the poor, that was an astonishing statement from a would-be president of the United States. However, Mr. Dewey did carefully explain that the right to use the 5th Amendment should be withheld from the criminal class–whatever that means.[32]

"The streets of our country are in turmoil. The universities are full of students rebelling and rioting. Communists are seeking to destroy our country. Russia is threatening us with her might and the republic is in danger."

Yes, danger from within and from without. We need law and order. Without law and order our nation cannot survive.

"Elect us and we shall restore law and order. We will be respected by the nations of the world for law and order. Without law and order, our republic will fail."

Governor Reagan did not say those words. Nor Mr. Hoover. Nor Thomas E. Dewey. Nor Spiro Agnew. Nor President Nixon. Not even Senator Barry Goldwater, or Senator Mundt. None of them used those words. But a man became mad as he directed his nation toward his solution to those words. Adolph Hitler spoke those words during his campaign in 1932, and in less than a generation his nation lay in ruins.

Words may be spoken in German, English, Greek, Russian, Vietnamese, Mexican, Spanish, French, Chinese, Hebrew, or Arabic, but it is the thought that counts. The Constitution of the United States and the Pledge of Allegiance to the Flag does not contain any reference to "law and order," only to "justice." To eliminate the meaning of "justice" from "law and order" will only lead to the concentration camps of the 1940s.

The reader should not have forgotten that at 2 p.m. on Nov.

---

[32] Compare the author's comments on the post-Kennedy "deterioration of the American Dream" to these remarks made by former French President Valéry Giscard d'Estaing: "In the assassination of Kennedy, there is, in a sense, the idea of the assassination of a dream. When one murders a dream, it is not just the person who is murdered, the dream is killed together with him." As quoted by the French radio network, RTL (online), fall 2020.

22nd, the new president of the United States ordered an immediate "red alert." This was applicable, as he explained, to all our military forces in all parts of the world, including our Polaris submarines and our bases on the fringes of the USSR. The plot was a hair's breathe from success. An itchy trigger finger on one of those bases, in one of those subs, in one of those airplanes flying toward Soviet territory, and war would occur.

In this crisis, President Johnson turned not to the CIA but to the former ambassador to the Soviet Union. It was the ambassador who convinced the new president that the Soviets do not engage in the policy of murdering heads of state and never have. A canvass of foreign embassies revealed that there was no "out of the ordinary" movement by either the Russian military or the citizenry, which convinced the president that the Soviets were not involved in any adventure. A phone call to our Cuban naval base also revealed that that sector was quiet. It was close, very close.

It may seem like a screen scenario, but, if one looks back into history, the United States was nearly led into war by the CIA on two other occasions. The first one was the U-2 affair which destroyed, for the time, any detente between the U.S. and USSR. That affair was strictly a CIA affair designed for the long-sought war between the two countries. It must be recalled that a mysterious "red alert" was flashed to the armed services while President Eisenhower was in Paris with the premier of the Soviet Union sitting right beside the president. Why the Soviets would seek a war with their premier and the Soviet defense minister in Paris is unknown. But, at the same time that "red alert" was flashed, the CIA, in violation of the president's order, again sent a U-2 over the borders of the Soviet Union near the Turkish border. The CIA, as reported in recent memoirs of President Kennedy's associates and in histories of the CIA, has revealed that the CIA attempted to inject our wheat shipments to the Soviet Union with poison. The Canadian government also discovered that ground glass had been mixed with several shiploads of Canadian wheat sent to Red China and the Soviet Union. The CIA was then, as it is now, more powerful than the president of the United States.

The other example of CIA interference with the commander-in-chief of the Armed Forces, the president, occurred during the

Cuban Missile Crisis. Again, in direct violation of President Kennedy's orders, the CIA, during the negotiations on the third and fourth day of the crisis, sent a U-2 plane in Soviet Siberia. The excuse was that "the plane had strayed off its course." What was it doing there in the first place?

That was the four-pronged conspiracy; the conspiracy obtained only two if its objectives: the murder of President Kennedy and the coup d'état.

CHAPTER X

A SHORT REPRISE OF THE EVIDENCE

The responsibility for the "success" of the Warren Commission and its "Report" must rest solely upon the mass communication media, which went out of its way to protect the duplicity, deceit, and deception practiced by the Commission upon the American people. Why the "lords" of the press decided upon that course of action can only be answered by those people. Whatever the reason, both the "lords" and the "peasants" will pay a high price–the gradual erosion of the "freedom of the press."

The investigators of the "Report" have presented the result of their investigations to the public; but the silence of the press lords to further an investigation of the Commission's allegations has led to a further decline of the general public's faith in all forms of mass communication. It has been stated in a previous chapter that "freedom of the press" is a two-way street. If one-way is closed, the other is sure to follow.

The critics' primary failure was their repeated implication that the murder of President Kennedy could not be solved unless, at the same time, they proved a conspiracy. The critics have constantly proclaimed that unless the Zapruder film, the X-Rays, and other photographic evidence was released from the National Archives, no solution could be obtained. Their demands obscure the main issue: "Was Lee Harvey Oswald the 'sole and exclusive assassin of President Kennedy' as charged by the Warren Commission?"

The film, X-rays, and other photographic evidence is not the prime evidence in securing an affirmative or negative answer. That evidence is secondary.

The prosecution, in this case the Warren Commission, must affirmatively prove three elements: (1) Lee Harvey Oswald was at the 6th-floor S.E. corner window at the time the shots were fired; (2) those bullets which caused the death of President Kennedy came from a weapon he used at that time; and (3) the rifle allegedly used was a functional operating lethal weapon from which those bullets were discharged.

In a court of law those three elements must be proved beyond a reasonable doubt by the evidence in the possession of the Warren Commission. Each of the three must be proved; not just one, or two, but all three.

Thus, if Oswald was not at the S.E. corner window at the exact time those three bullets were fired, he could not be found" guilty" even though the remaining two elements be proved in the affirmative. If element (2) be proved in the affirmative but element (1) in the negative, then a trial judge would rule Oswald "not guilty." If element (3) was proved affirmatively, the trial judge would still rule Oswald "not guilty" if (1) or (2) not be proven by the evidence given in court. Further, if (2) be proved but (3) proves that the rifle could not discharge those bullets because it was defective and incapable of firing bullets through its barrel, then Oswald would be found "not guilty." A consensus does not operate in a criminal courtroom.

As can be seen, the failure of the critics to stress those three elements have confused and bewildered the public. Any attorney worth his law degree and license to practice would have obtained a "not guilty" verdict by simply using the power of subpoena and applying the rules of cross-examination to the witnesses for the prosecution (the Warren Commission). That is, of course, provided the judge and the prosecution practiced the "basic principles of American justice," which the Warren Commission did not.

An intelligent attorney would not have permitted Oswald go on the witness stand. Oswald's attorney would not have been disturbed by a failure to obtain an answer to the question of what article did he carry into the Book Depository at 8 a.m. on November 22, 1963. Whether the object was a disassembled rifle or curtain rods would have no bearing on the case. The prosecution would still have the three elements to answer. Nor is the tracing of Oswald's movements involved, for the critical issue remains the answers to those three elements.

Thus, those three elements must each be answered affirmatively to prove Oswald guilty.

In reference to the Tippit murder, the identical three elements are involved, and those answers must also be in the affirmative. Simply substitute the time of the murder, was Oswald there at the time, and did the bullets come from the weapon that murdered Tippit? However, in the Tippit murder, the Warren Commission failed to "prove" that Tippit died as the result of bullets. There is no autopsy report concerning his death.

The lack of X-rays neither affirms nor denies Oswald's guilt for, under American law, secondary evidence can be used to disprove or prove "innocence" or "guilt." The autopsy chart, No. 397, and the testimony of the physicians from both hospitals were sufficient to prove that Oswald was not "the sole and exclusive assassin of President Kennedy." With every physician from Parkland Hospital testifying that there was a bullet hole caused by a bullet entering the front of the president's throat; and Commander Humes, supported by assisting physicians and the president's suit jacket, testifying that there was a bullet hole 6 inches below the back of the neck and in the president's right shoulder, that evidence was sufficient to give Oswald a verdict of "not guilty" to the Commission's accusation.

Since the Zapruder film and the X-rays were available to the Commission, then under the rules of subpoena the failure to exercise that rule was not the responsibility of dead Oswald. The "basic principles of American justice" applies to both the accuser and the accused. The deliberate failure by the prosecution (Warren Commission) to use the subpoena when evidence is in the possession of another federal or state agency does not obviate the implication, in a law court, that such evidence would be favorable to the accused.

Far too many critics have attempted to prove that not only was Oswald innocent but that a conspiracy murdered the president. The author agrees but the primary function of a defense attorney is to bring forth the evidence that proves his client not guilty. The critics overlooked the essential fact that proving Oswald innocent axiomatically proved the existence of a conspiracy. The names of the conspirators were not, and are not, necessary. It is not his function to prove the identity of the actual killer. That may occur in the "Perry Mason" series but not in an American courtroom. Since the Commission constantly repeated the statement that no conspiracy existed then the only question that was involved was the validity of the Commission's accusation against Oswald.

The author contends that the evidence has proven beyond a reasonable doubt that a conspiracy murdered President Kennedy. Of course, the author relies upon his interpretation of the evidence in the same manner as if he were a member of the jury listening in judgment upon Lee Harvey Oswald. The seven commissioners may have believed that they were Gods but the author contends, like the little boy seeing a naked king who said he was clothed, that the question of whether or not the commissioners were God must be left to the judgment of the person who heard their statement.

The author, therefore, presents to the reader, the members of the Warren Commission, the Federal Bureau of Investigation, the Secret Service, the CIA, the Dallas Police Department, the Dallas Sheriff Department, the ABC, CBS, and NBC television and radio system, and to the Press Lords which, in the opinion of the author, proved that the 7 God Commissioners were mere mortals with feet of clay.

On the following pages are the volumes which have been used by the author to substantiate his accusation against the Warren Commission that those seven commissioners knowingly, willfully, and deceitfully accused Lee Harvey Oswald of being the "sole and exclusive assassin of President Kennedy."

* * *

FBI testimony and affidavits proving Oswald innocent

FBI Reports: Vols. 1-5 incl. National Archives. Suppressed by Commission. (Nov. 26, Dec. 9, 1963; Jan. 13, 1964.)

Report on Code Number on All Italian Rifles. Com. Dec. 2562. Rifle Sling Differences. Com. Exh. 1403 cf. Com. Exh. 139 cf. 3H25, 397; 4H289.

FBI statement: Oswald "owned" rifle; never "used" rifle. FBI Reports, 1-5 inc.

Rifle Barrel Changed. FBI Reports. Vol. 1-5 incl.

No ammunition clip with Rifle. Com. Exh. 2003, 26H449.

No fingerprints on ammunition clip. id.; 4H23.

No Oswald finger or palm prints on rifle. 4H24, 29.

FBI testimony that "found" palm print that was flat, not curved. 4H20-29.

Oswald's "flat" palm print taken in police station. 4H218; 71-1284.

Lt. Day's admission: "no identifiable Oswald palm or fingerprints on rifle." 4H260-3.

FBI calling Lt. Day "mistaken." 4H20-29 cf. 26H832 cf. R123 cf. 4H260.

Rifle repaired by FBI prior to testing. 3H443.

Rifle repaired so it could shoot accurately. 26H104.

Trigger on rifle worthless. 3H447; R193.

Telescopic sight mounted for left-handed person. Com. Exh. 2560.

Oswald was always right-handed. Com. Exh. 1401; IH293-4.

Telescopic sight "structurally defective." 3H405. 26H104.

White smoke emitted from rifle when discharged. 26H811.

Rust on firing pin; pin worn down. Com. Exh. 26H104. CE2974.

Shims necessary to hold telescopic sight. None found or used. 3H405; 15H779; 3H444.

Rifle inaccurate when discharged. 26H104.

FBI examination of cartridges from 6th floor. CD 1245; FBI No. DL 100-1046; C.E. 2968; Com. Exh. 543.

Fake rifle cartridges given to FBI by police. 4H205, 253-55; 26H449.

Commission's deceit in discussing rifle "coupon." "American Rifleman," Feb. 1963. cf. "Field and Stream," Nov. 1962. Holmes Exh. 2; RI 19; 7H294; 20H174.

Deformed cartridge given to FBI by police; no bullet fired from Italian rifle, 26H449.

"Life" and "AP" photographs faked. 4H281,21H453,456-8. Illus. section.

Phony Commission rifle tests. Height and time changed. 3H403-07; 441-47.

Rifle received in "well-oiled condition" FBI Reports. V. 1-5; CE 2974.

No oil stains or impressions in or on "brown paper bag."

No "brown paper bag" found on 6th floor. 3H288; 6H268; 7H65, 298.

FBI "manufactured" brown paper bag in Dallas office. 4H93; 16H513. Dallas police switching invisible brown paper bag. 7H103-04; cf. 4H266-68; 3H4, 8; cf. 7H143-44.

Police perjury re: brown paper bag. 4H57, 97 cf. 7H103-04. FBI finding brown paper bag in Irving, Tex., Post Office. FBI File Dec. 205, p. 148.

Official Dallas police list showing no brown paper bag on 6th floor. 7H289.

No oil stains or telescopic sight indentations on blanket. 9H424-5, 461; FBI Reports, 1-5.

Based on the testimony and affidavits of the FBI, Lee Harvey Oswald was proved, by that Bureau, to be innocent of being the "sole and exclusive assassin of President Kennedy." Under the "basic principles of American justice," no person accused of murder can be found "guilty" when the alleged weapon allegedly used to commit the murder was proved to be a nonlethal weapon.

FBI testimony and affidavits proving Oswald was not at 6th-floor window when shots were fired at President Kennedy

Edw. Piper saw Oswald near lunch room at 12:10 p.m. FBI File CD-5. Mrs. Arnold saw Oswald between 12:15 and 12:25 p.m. Id., p .41.

Oswald saw Jr. Jarman at lunchroom between 12 noon and 12:15 p.m. 3H276.

Oswald saw and talked to Mr. Allman. Suppressed. Nat'l Archives. Doc. 354.

Mr. Hoover's letter to Commission. Jan. 20, 1964. Re: Hughes photo. FBI Exh. 29.

Lovelady's affidavit: "Wore red & white striped shirt, buttoned up," Com. Exh. 457.

Shelley's affidavit: "Lovelady seated on steps, not standing.' Com. Exh. 1831.

Brennan's affidavit: "Could not identify man in window." Com. Exh. 5323; FBI File CD-5; DL 89-43; 3H147-48; cf.

R145, 146, 250.

Brennan saw no smoke; FBI disputing his statement. 3H144 cf. 26H811.

Brennan saw no telescopic sight. 3H144.

Brennan saw rifleman standing up and firing last shot. 3H144 cf. Com. Exh. 1311-12; cf. R80,138.

Cross-examination of Bonnie Ray Williams: Oswald not on 6th floor. 3H169-73.

Mrs. Adams proving Lovelady committed perjury. 6H392.

U.S. Secret Service Inspector Sorrels proving Oswald innocent. 7H732.

Police Capt. Fritz impugning Brennan's testimony. 4H237.

Medical testimony proving Oswald innocent

Autopsy Chart No. 397; RI 11; 2Hg1, 123, 143, cf. 2H82.

Cause of death of President Kennedy. 6H30-35; Ce. 392.

FBI Report: Back wound, not wound in back of neck, Nat'l Archives. File 89, , R97; CE886-A; CF 5H175.

FBI Report: Location of Back wound. National Archives: File No. 59,60; CD7. Sibert-O'Neill Report-suppressed; cf. CE 385-6.

Comdr. Humes' Agreement with FBI: 2H365, cf. ZH30.

No proof of Commission's Bullet 399; tracing: 3H428,497; 6H125-34; 11H468; 18H799; 24H412. Legally, this bullet was a plant.

Ballistic expert Nicols' testimony that No. 399 was a fake. 3H443, 497.

Physicians "bullet in lung" statement. N.Y. 'Times" 11/23/63; substantiated in 3H9,361; 5H78; 6H42,51; 7H4; 17H848.

U.S. Secret Service Report & Survey proving Oswald innocent. Suppressed. Nat'l Archives. Files 87, 88, 2H127.

As can be seen, if Lee Harvey Oswald was on trial for the murder of President John F. Kennedy as being the "sole and exclusive assassin," an impartial judge would direct the jury to bring in a verdict of not guilty. The FBI submitted to the Warren Commission the evidence and affidavits that proved Oswald did not "use" the Italian Mannlicher-Carcano rifle; that the cartridges "found" on the 6th floor and given to them by the police were not discharged from that rifle; that the rifle was not a lethal weapon. The FBI furnished the Commission with evidence that proved that Oswald was not at the 6th-floor window when those shots were fired; and the U.S. Secret Service proved that bullets fired from a rifle located at the 6th-floor window could not strike President Kennedy or Governor Connelly. To substantiate both the Secret Service and the FBI testimony, affidavits, charts, and photographs supported the testimony of all the Parkland and Bethesda Hospital physicians.

The Tippit murder case

Evidence proving Oswald innocent. Mrs. Markham admits she did not recognize Oswald. 3H310-11,391.

Mr. Benavides admits he did not recognize Oswald. 3H327, 4H452.

Tippit shot by a left-handed person. 17H416.

Time of death of Tippit. 3H304-11; 24H202; 215.

Mr. Bowley supporting time of Tippit's death. 1:06-1:08 p.m. Com. Exh. 2003, p. 11.

Oswald's location at 1:04 p.m. 6H440; 7H439.

Police radio description of Tippit's killer. Com. Exh. 1974.

Oswald not a suspect by police. Com. Exh. 1974, pp. 59, 74.

Oswald had no revolver when arrested. 3H300; 7H20-23; illus. sec. .38 automatic shell found at Tippit murder site. Oswald owned a revolver. 17H417-20; Com. Exh. 1974, p. 74, 78.

Two guns used to murder Tippit. Com. Exh. 1974, p. 78; 17H417-20.

Oswald never had holster in rooming house. 6H420-22.

Capt. Westbrook never found jacket. 7H30-33, 115-117.

Jacket, manufactured evidence by police. 7H30-33; Batchelor & Lawrence Exh. R175 cf. 74 115, CE 1974, pp. 62-77.

McDonald receiving "tip" that Oswald was on first floor, not balcony. 3H298-302.

Police perjury relating to Tippit's whereabouts prior to his murder. 4H443; 26H195; Com. Exh. 705; 1947; 2985.

U.S. Secret Service Memorandum; suppressed by Commission. Relates to number of bullet holes and number of bodies involved as "Tippit." File No. 87, 88. code No. M63-352, November 22, 1963. Signed by Agent Moore.

Police perjury relating to number of bullets. 20H465, 24H253, cf. 3H447-48, Ex.1974, King Exh. No. 5; 20H465.

Dallas police testifying Tippit shot only 3 times. 20H465; 24H253.

FBI Testifying 4 bullets given to them by police. Unidentifiable. 3H473; 24H263.

Dallas policeman failure to find his mark "JMP" on cartridges and shells given to him at murder site. 7H66.

Dallas Police Sgt. Barnes failing to identify Tippit shells. 7H69. 275-6, 24H415.

FBI evidence that one bullet carried button into body. 3H473. McDonald's perjury. R304 cf. 3H298, 301-2; 7H20-23; R560.

Det. Carroll "jerking" a revolver from "unknown" person. 3H300.

McDonald placed his "mark" on gun in police station. 3H298-302.

FBI statement: "one bullet from two shells," 3H473.

Commission statement that 5 bullets were fired at Tippit. 3H347-8, 3H477-8.

Oswald, without taking the witness stand, and relying simply upon the above testimony, would walk out of any court practicing the "Basic principles of American justice," innocent of the accusation placed upon him by the Commission. He was not at the scene of the crime, his revolver was not the murder weapon, and the bullets "taken" from Tippit's body did not come from that weapon.

The evidence that proved a conspiracy

In response to the former head of the CIA, Mr. Dulles, who challenged the Commission critics to "let them produce their evidence" that a conspiracy murdered President Kennedy, the author believes that the following testimony would substantiate that belief: The Commission admits a conspiracy! [See] pp. 116,

127, 134!

The only published map of the president's motorcade route. Dallas "Morning News," November 22, 1963.

The published and selected route had no "double detour." R30-41.

Who planned "double detour"? Ask Police Chief Curry. Dallas "News." 11/23/63.

Miami, Fla., police tape recordings of plot to murder president, Miami "News." 2/2/67.

"Telefax" Message by FBI to southern offices Nov. 17, 1963.

"Playboy"–Garrison interview.

Deputy Sheriff Craig's testimony and Capt. Fritz's crack-up. 6H226 cf. 23H817.

Craig's testimony corroborated by Mr. Robinson. CD-5; 19H524.

Commission's refusal to purchase TV tapes. Com. Ex. 962.

The bombshell–The FBI's W. S. Walter affidavit in Dist. Att. Garrison's possession accusing the FBI of being a silent accomplice in Pres. Kennedy's murder! ("Kennedy Conspiracy" by P. Flammonde 1969.)

Commission's refusal to purchase TV tapes. Com. Exh. 962.

Time of Murder: 12:20 & 12:25 p.m. Dallas "Times Herald," "News." 11/23/63.

Decker's announcement of time of murder, 12:25 p.m. Dallas police tapes.

Rifleman arrested in Dal-Tex Bldg. Disappears in police station. 19H526-27; 20H499.

Shots also came from Dal-Tex Bldg. Suppressed. Com. Doc. CD-5; 24H385; "Herald" 11/23/63.

Marine Corps cleared Oswald of "treason," Com. Exh. 2718.

FBI approves Oswald as "alright." Dallas police memo. Feb. 14, 1964; Suppressed.

Hudkin's statements, Secret Service: Informed by Dallas Chief Sweatt, Oswald an FBI informer, paid $200.00 per month. Code 30-030, 767, cf. "Latitudes" [magazine]–Feb. 1967.

Man arrested, and identified as rifleman on grassy knoll. "Times Herald." 11/23/63.

Oswald known to Dallas police prior to murder. Com. Exh. 709; 2003; 4H207.

Three (3) spent cartridges found on 3rd floor at 12:45 p.m. Com. Exh. 705, p. 492.

Rifle, with no telescopic sight, carried from Depository. "Playboy," Oct. 1967.

Phone call to Secret Service: "Oswald not the man." 4H356.

Dallas police knowledge of Tippit murder prior to its happening. Com. Exh. 2003, 79-83; Curry's Testimony, Vol. 4.

Men impersonating Secret Service agents during Tippit murder.

No brown bag found on 6th floor. 3H288, 6H268, 7H65, 289.

Fingerprints "lost" and "found" on brown paper bag. 3H3-8. 4H266-68; 7H97-98, 104, 143, 288.

Curtain rods found in Paine garage by FBI and aide. 9H425.

"FBI" and "CIA" agents disturbance in Parkland Hospital. 181-1795.

FBI Agent Hosty statement, at 3 p.m., Oswald, a "Communist" murderer. 5H34-37.

Police Chief Curry, prior to Tippit murder and prior to arrest of Oswald, that suspect had been captured for both Tippit and President Kennedy murder. 4H.

Police charging Oswald with President Kennedy murder at 2:20 p.m. Illus. sec.

Phony affidavit charging Oswald with Tippit and President Kennedy murder. Id.

Oswald never arraigned for murder of President Kennedy. 4H200; 7H289.

Switching of cartridge shells found at Tippit murder site.

Secret Service Report: No gun or person in 6th-floor window. Suppressed. National Archives: File CD-5, p.44.

Mysterious FBI statements referring to TWO types of reports to the Commission. 5H112.

FBI testimony proving a conspiracy. File No.89-30, Nov.26, 1963; Files 59, 60.

Secret Service testimony proving a conspiracy. 2H93; 127, 143, 368.

Comdr. Humes upholding FBI testimony proving a conspiracy. 2H365.

Governor Connally struck by 2 or more bullets. 4H109, 121.

Physicians' testimony proving a conspiracy. 3H9; 5H78;

6H42,51; 7H4; 17H848, 2H30, 6H5, 14, 22, 23, 36, 42, 55, 65, 67, 71, 143.

Physician's testimony proving aide Spector wrong. 2H347, 375.

Autopsy Chart 397 proving a conspiracy. WR95, 105, 111.

Specter's admission proving a conspiracy. "U.S. News," Oct. 1966; "Phil, Mag," Aug. 1966.

Milton Jones affidavit: police seeking killer on a bus at 12:25-12:30. Com. Exh. 2641.

Lt. Day's memo referring to description of rifle. Lost! 4H260; Com. Exh. 2003.

Commission referring to Lt. Day's "lost" memo. 4H260. Impersonation of Secret Service agents. 18H722; Com. Exh. 2003, No. 79. Policeman informing unknown person at 2 p.m. by telephone that Oswald captured for both murders. 7H12. Brown paper bag found in Irving, Texas, Post Office by FBI. Suppressed. FBI File 205.

Mr. J. Edgar Hoover's strange statement to Mr. Richard Nixon that by 2:30 p.m. Dallas time the FBI knew a "Communist" killed President Kennedy. Sat. Eve. Post. 2/25/67.

Finally: The HUGHES photograph which proved NO person was at the 6th-floor window of the Depository when the shots rang out.

This photograph can be seen in the FBI file, Exh. No. 29, and is reprinted in this book. Mr. J. Edgar Hoover's letter to the Warren Commission confirming this statement is dated January 20, 1964. Mr. Hoover, in analyzing this Hughes photograph said: "Presidential motorcade proceeding east on Main Street, north on Houston Street and left on Elm Street, directly in front of Texas School Book Depository building." Notice the phrase: "directly in front of TSBDB." This is the KEY frame of the Hughes 8-millimeter film.

Conclusion: Oswald was innocent, as proven by testimony and photographs, of "being the sole and exclusive assassin of President Kennedy." QED: A CONSPIRACY MURDERED PRESIDENT JOHN F. KENNEDY.

Oswald's death as the result of a conspiracy

Ruby's premeditation. 15H491, lie test. National Archives.
Ruby in basement. Perjury by Dallas policemen. 15H682-83; 5H255-56; 12H340; Com. Exh. 2050, 2002.
Conspirator impersonating physician pumping out Oswald's blood. 19H410-13.
Hospital prepares autopsy room for Oswald 30 minutes prior to shooting.
Ruby in police station; never entered through ramp. Com. Exh. 2050; 15H682-83.
Oswald shot 10 minutes after requesting lawyer via Secret Service. 4H223.

Odds and ends

FBI surveillance of Oswald prior to murder. Com. Doc. 2718. Suppressed.
Mrs. Marina Oswald statements to Secret Service. Com. Doc. 344.
Weitzman affidavit: rifle was a German Mauser. 24H228; upheld in 7H105-9.
Kantor sees and talks to Jack Ruby. Kantor Exh., Nat'l Archives.
Kantor's testimony upheld by Mrs. Tice. 15H388; 25H216, 317.
Warren Commission suppressed all statements made by all physicians to FBI and Secret Service agents. Suppressed until the year 2036. see 6H7-139.
Oswald as a CIA agent. 2H84-85, 192, 203; 5H104; 8H260, 297-98; 19H680; CD320; CD931; Com. Exh. 2718.
Strange U.S. Dept. of Justice statement alleging Shaw and "Clay Bertrand" were "same guy"–Washington "Star" 3/2/67 and "Post" 3/3/67, AP-3/4/67.
Pres. Johnson's press statement on Shaw. AP 3/2/67.
Lt. Col. Finck's admission as Shaw's defense witness that the Bethesda autopsy was false! Only a partial autopsy was performed! N. Y. "Times" –March, 1969.

Dr. Perry's press statement–NBC "70 Hours"–Random House–1966.

The author has produced the evidence; it was the duty of Mr. Dulles and his commissioners to name the names of the assassins and the conspirators.

That failure is theirs, not the responsibility of the American citizen.

Picture Notes

No. 1. The official map published in the Dallas "Morning News," November 22, 1963. As the Warren Commission admitted, there was no "double detour." (R31-40.)

No. 2. The front page of the Dallas "Times-Herald, Evening Edition. November 22, 1963. The Commission again overlooked the vital evidence contained in the article: (1) The shots came from (a) the Dal-Tex Building; (b) the deputy police chief also stated shots came from the triple overpass. (2) Six or seven shots were distinctly heard by witnesses. (3) The police went to the railroad tracks behind the fence on the grassy knoll. (4) The police broadcast for the arrest of a man that never matched Oswald's description. (5) The "time" of the shooting was announced by Sheriff Decker at 12:25 p.m.!

No. 3. The official FBI reenactment photographs showing the exact location of the bullet hole in the president's back!

No. 4. The only legal autopsy chart of President Kennedy which reveals the bullet hole in the front of the throat. If the bullet had entered the throat from the rear, then the notations written on the front of the chart would have been placed on the chart showing the rear portion of the body. The bullet hole shown on the chart's rear portion is in the exact location of the bullet hole in the jacket. This legal autopsy chart also supports the Parkland physician's statement that a bullet "coursed downward after entering the front of the throat and lodged in the lungs."

No. 5. The "phony" and manufactured photographs used by the Commission to "convict" Oswald. No. 1 and 2 were used by "Life" and "Associated Press." No. 3 is the one taken by the UPI of Capt. Fritz holding the rifle. Notice the "white sling" on the first three; the dark 2-piece sling on No. 4. A magnifier placed upon all three rifles shows definite discrepancies which proved someone in the Dallas Police Department switched rifles. The trigger guards are different, the sights are different, and the stock in No. 3 is clearly different!

No. 6. Lee Harvey Oswald photographed at the entrance of the Book Depository. The FBI submitted Lovelady's affidavit that at the time of the shooting he was wearing a "red and white short-sleeved shirt, buttoned up to the neck.". (J. E. Hoover–letter to Commission–March 9, 1964. Suppressed–National Archives!)

No. 7. Billie Lovelady posing for the FBI in the "red and white vertical striped, short sleeve" shirt he wore at 12:30 p.m. on November 22, 1963. This photograph was suppressed by the Warren Commission.

No. 8. The mysterious "arrest report" filed by an unknown policeman. This report was filed at approximately 2:20 p.m. Notice the blank unfilled spaces, required completed by Texas criminal law codes. (1) The police had no witnesses to (a) the arrest; or (b) to the murderer of Tippit. (2) How did that unknown policeman know those facts when Oswald was never identified, his fingerprints and palm print never found on the Italian rifle; and no rifle or revolver ballistic tests have been made? (3) Oswald did not "resist" arrest; nor did he fight any policeman; nor did he attempt to murder McDonald by drawing a gun from his waist since (4) the "arrest report" showed no revolver taken from Oswald! Based upon this legal document, the police manufactured the evidence.

No. 9. The Johnson Exhibit No. 4. In law, another fake affidavit. Also notice that the two torn parts do not match each other! A torn affidavit is legally worthless. Since the two parts do not match, could it be that this affidavit was made on Jan. 26, 1964? Could it be that this is a fake, and, after the murder of Oswald, the signature of Capt. Fritz and D.A. Wade were, unknown to them, torn from another affidavit, then photographed? The following five photographs, suppressed by the Warren Commission from its "Report" and "Hearings," can be found in the National Archives in Washington, D.C. The reason for the suppression is self-evident, for these five proved, beyond a reasonable doubt, that Lee Harvey Oswald was innocent of the Commission's accusation of being the "sole assassin."

No. 10a. The official location of the President Kennedy's automobile at the (10b) exact moment he was struck by bullets. This is the official U.S. Secret Service reenactment and was not published by the Commission. The reenactment proved that those bullets came from three ambush sites: (1) the Dal-Tex Bldg., (2) the County Bldg., and (3) grassy knoll's fence. (19H626-27; 20H499)

No. 11. The official legal survey, conducted by R. West, for the U.S. Secret Service and suppressed by the Warren Commission. It supported the reenactment location of the president's car and proved no bullets were fired from the 6th floor.

No. 12. Conclusive, damning proof that the Commission willfully, knowingly, and deceitfully "convicted" a man who was absolutely innocent of being the "sole assassin of President Kennedy." Hoover's letter, Jan. 20, 1964, to J. Lee Rankin, that at the exact moment the president was being shot the president's automobile was in such a location that no rifleman stationed at the 6th-floor window could discharge three bullets which could hit him.

No. 13. The suppressed Hughes photograph. The photograph shows no person at any window, the 5th or 6th floor! The FBI testified that the president's auto was "directly in front of the Texas School Book Depository." This photograph, the U.S. Secret Service Survey, the "angle of fire" into the president's body, conclusively upheld Inspector Sorrel's sworn testimony that at the time the shots rang out he "saw no body, saw no activity, saw no object" at the 6th-floor window.

No. 14. The picture of a man, pointed out by witnesses as one of the "grassy knoll" riflemen who shot President Kennedy. This man disappeared in the police station. See 19H626-27; 20H499.

No. 15. The FBI's official sketch of the man who was wanted for questioning in the murder of Dr. Martin Luther King. This sketch was developed by artists who received information from witnesses who stated the sketched man was the man they saw shoot Dr. King. It is not James Earl Ray but the man in No. 14! Strangely, this man is not now on the FBI's "Ten Most Wanted" list. Why?

THE DALLAS TIMES HERALD

PRESIDENT DEAD

Connally Also Hit By Sniper

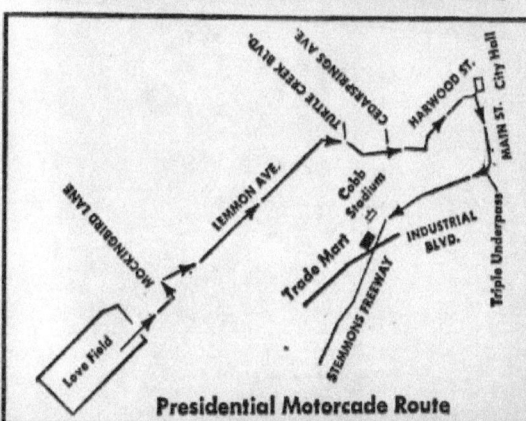

Presidential Motorcade Route

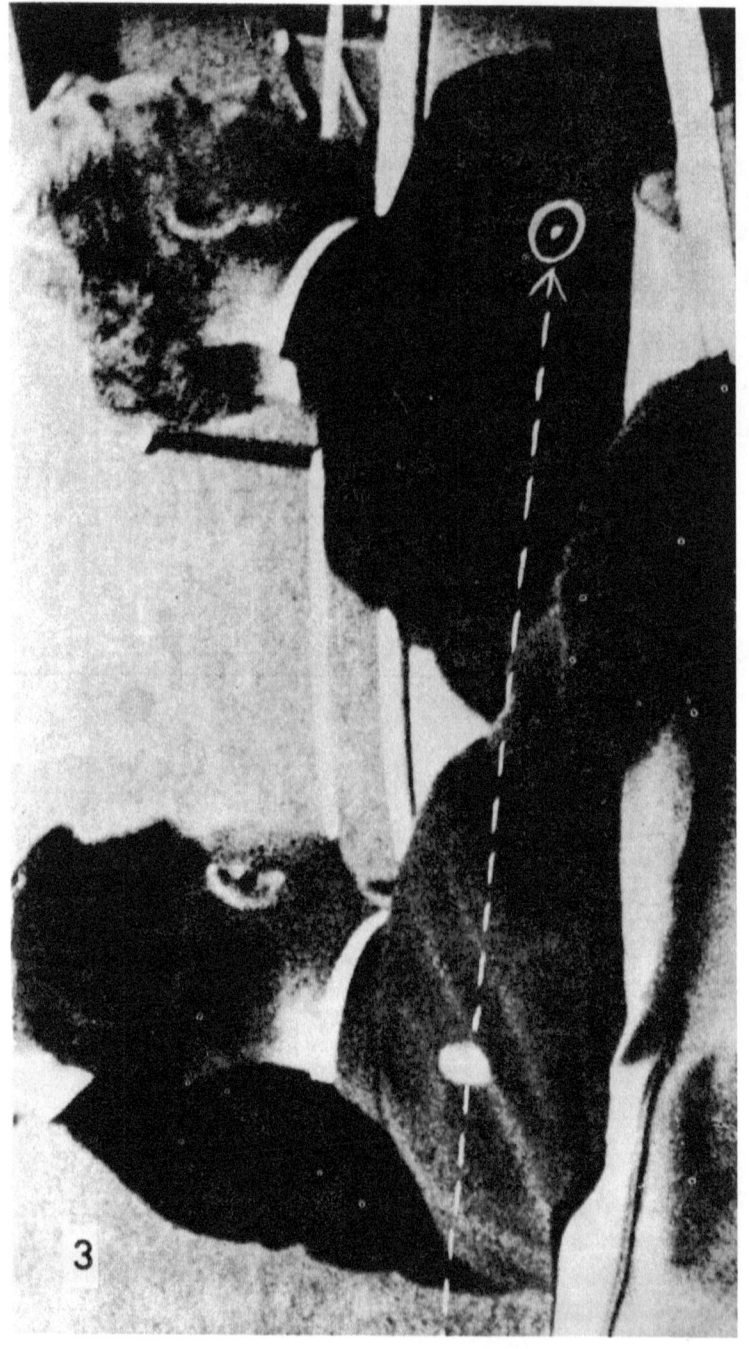

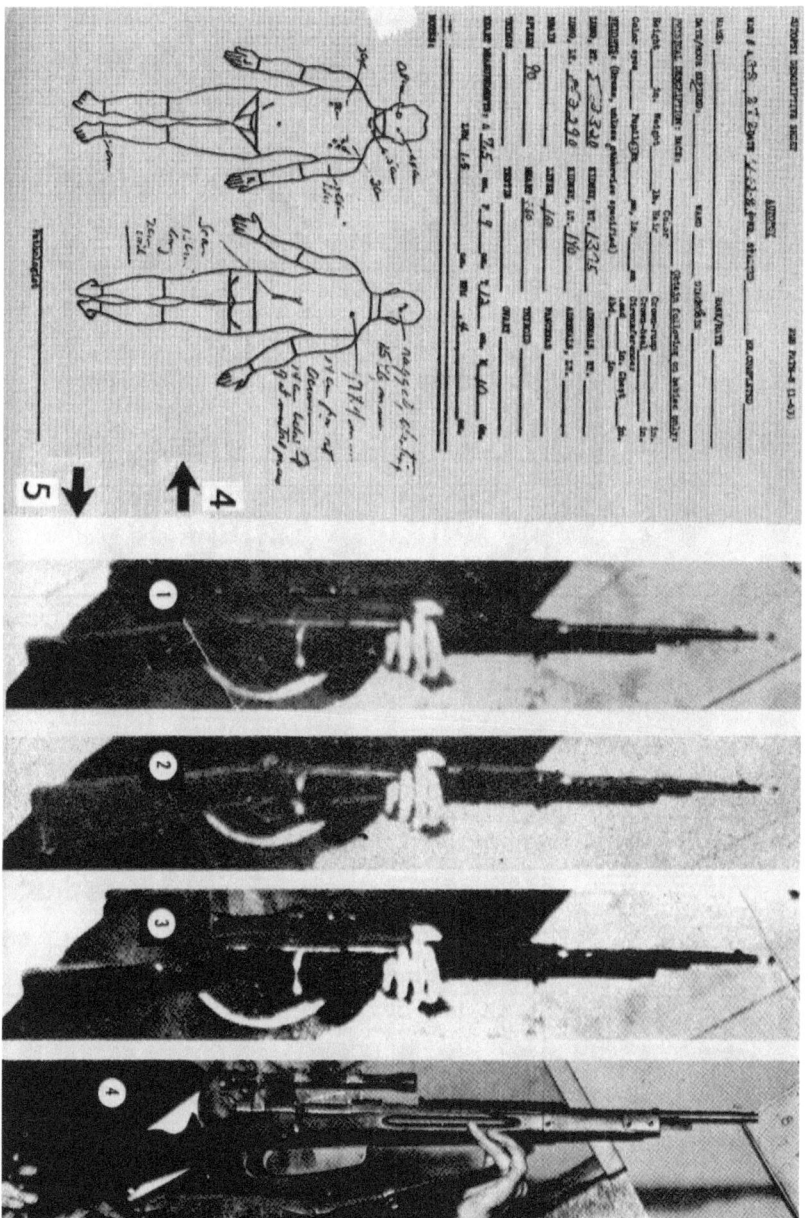

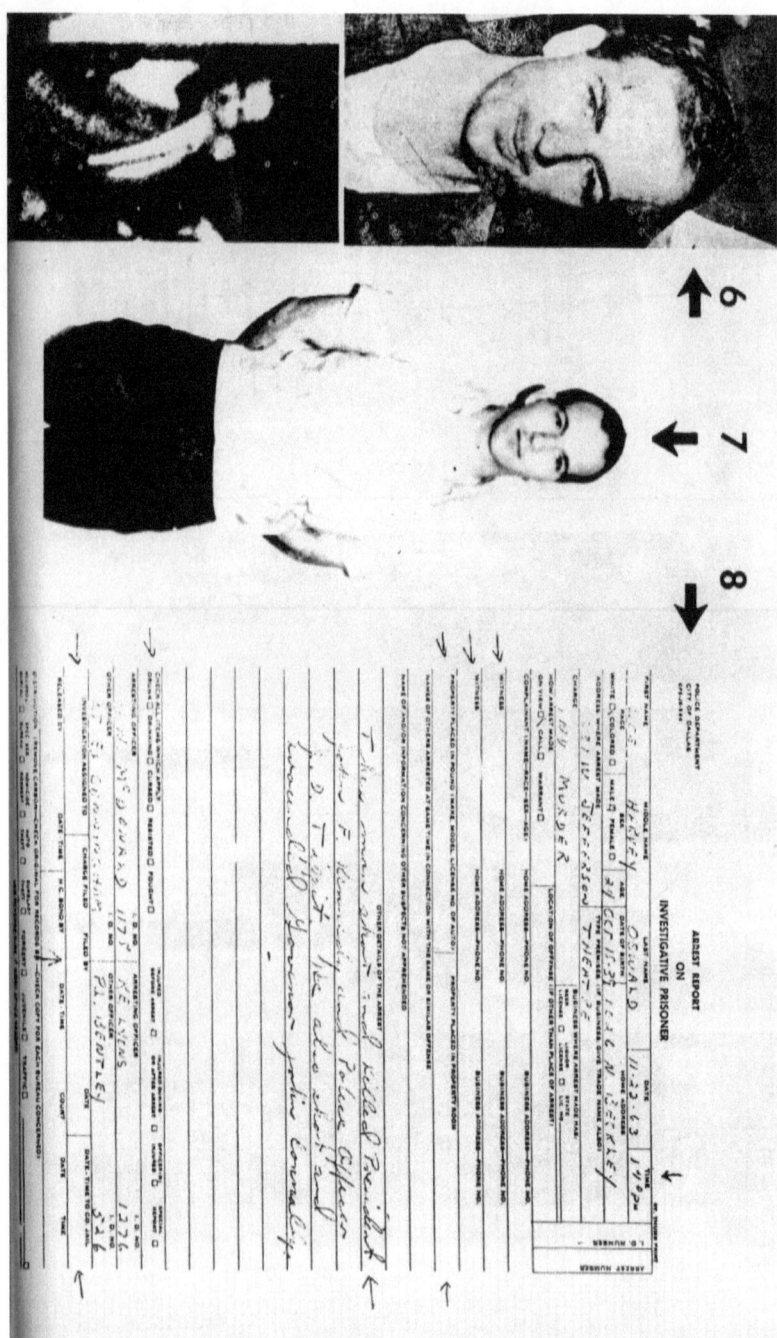

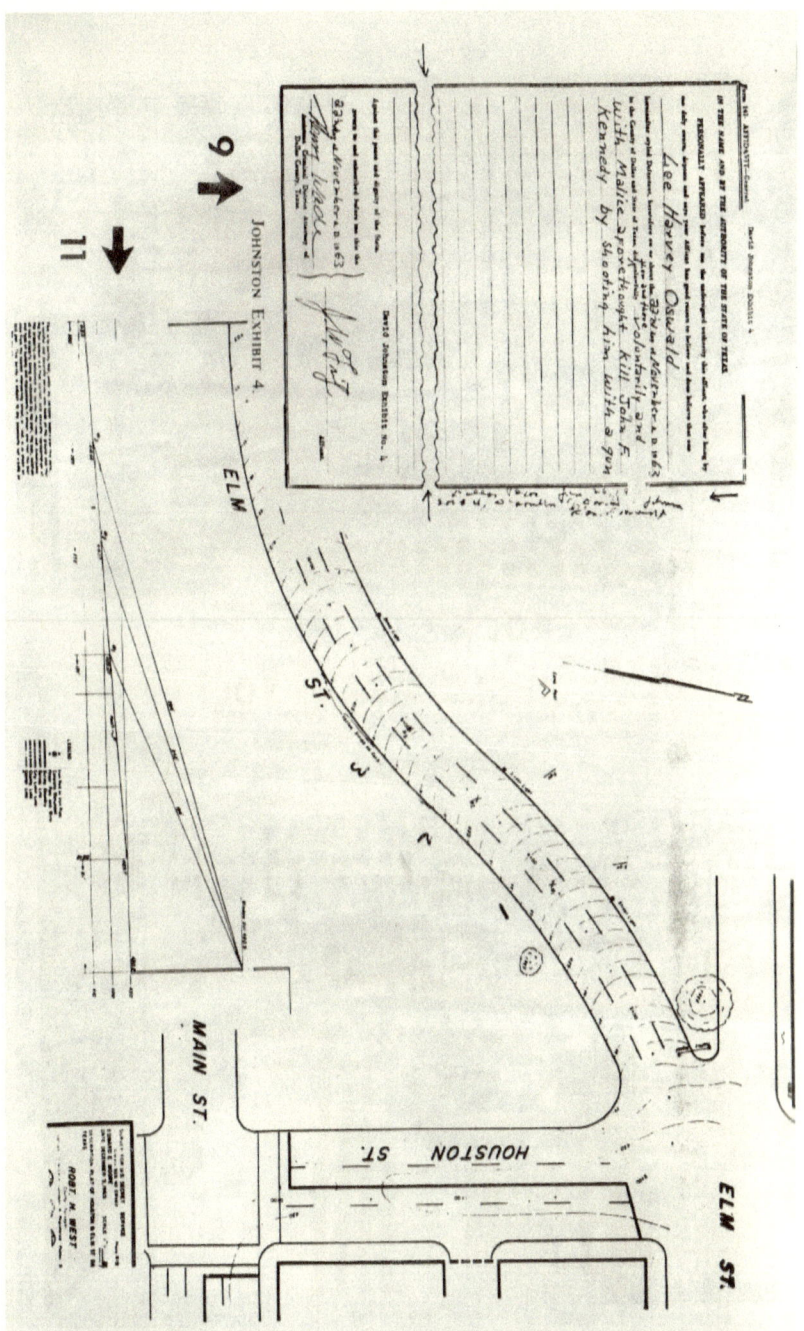

10 A

10 B

UNITED STATES DEPARTMENT OF JUSTICE
FEDERAL BUREAU OF INVESTIGATION

WASHINGTON 25, D.C.

January 20, 1964

Honorable J. Lee Rankin
General Counsel
The President's Commission
200 Maryland Avenue, N. E.
Washington, D. C.

Dear Mr. Rankin:

        With reference to the discussion had by you with J. R. Malley of this Bureau on January 17, 1964, concerning various films which are available of the assassination of President John F. Kennedy, set forth hereinafter is a list of the films that can be shown at any time at the office of the President's Commission:

Type	Subject	Submitted by
8 millimeter color	Presidential motorcade proceeding east on Main Street, north on Houston Street and left on Elm Street, directly in front of Texas School Book Depository Building	Robert J. E. Hughes Dallas, Texas
8 and 16 millimeter color	Assassination of President (taken from President's side of vehicle)	Abraham Zapruder Dallas, Texas
8 millimeter color	Assassination of President (taken from Mrs. Kennedy's side of vehicle)	Orville O. Nix Dallas, Texas
Video Tape black and white	Oswald shooting as shown on television (can be shown only with TV Station equipment)	TV station KRLD-TV Dallas, Texas
16 millimeter black and white	Oswald shooting as shown on television (this is copy of above video tape)	TV station KRLD-TV Dallas, Texas
16 millimeter black and white	Oswald shooting	Cameraman George Phenix TV station KRLD-TV Dallas, Texas
16 millimeter black and white	Oswald shooting	J. Jamison - station WBAP-TV, Ft. Worth, Texas

        Concerning the above, it is noted the film taken by Abraham Zapruder, Dallas, Texas, was sold by Zapruder to "Life" magazine and a number of the photographs which have appeared in "Life" magazine were apparently taken from this film. Information is not available as to what use has been made of the other films listed above.

Sincerely yours,

J. Edgar Hoover

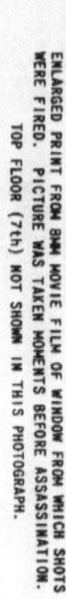

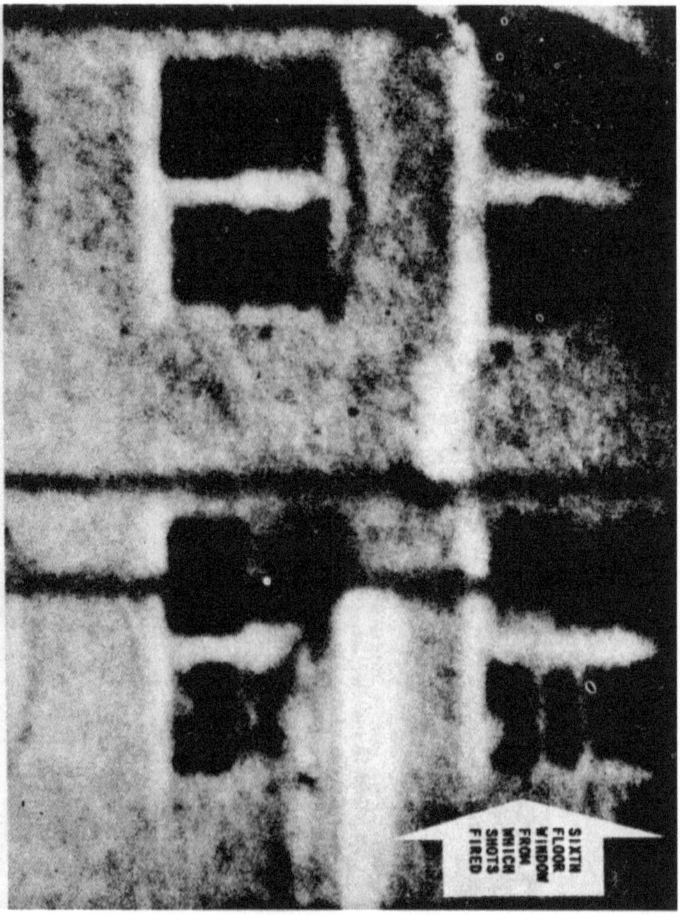

ENLARGED PRINT FROM 8MM MOVIE FILM OF WINDOW FROM WHICH SHOTS WERE FIRED. PICTURE WAS TAKEN MOMENTS BEFORE ASSASSINATION. TOP FLOOR (7th) NOT SHOWN IN THIS PHOTOGRAPH.

SIXTH FLOOR WINDOW FROM WHICH SHOTS FIRED

Author's Notes

CHAPTER II

1. 24H228
2. 7H108
3. 24H228
4. R81, 235; 3H294-99
5. R79, 553-54, 654; 4H202-09; 7H401-04; 15H145-54
6. 26H829-31
7. 3H204
8. 1H78-79; 7H325; 18H541-47
9. 1H12-21
10. R118
11. 17H636, 677-8
12. R119
13. Holmes Exh. N.A.
14. 24H228
15. 4H289
16. C.E.1403; 3H25
17. 4H289
18. 3H397
19. 26H104
20. 1H293; C.E. 2560
21. 3H443
22. 3H403-07, 441-47
23. C.E. 2003, p. 135
24. 3H398
25. Dallas "News" 12-12-63
26. LA "Free Press" 3-1-68[, p. 25.]
27. 17H467, 492
28. 26H449
29. 4h205, 253-55, 23
30. 3H296; 4H205, 253-55; 26H449
31. 26H62, 600
32. 7H404

33. 17H467, 492
34. U.S. Secret Service Files 87, 88, N.A.
35. 2H137-38; 2H370
36. N.Y. "Times" 11-23-63
37. N.Y. "Times" 11-23-63; 3H9, 361; 5H78; 6H42, 51; 7H4; 17H848
38. C.E. 397
39. 6H30-33, 48; 17H12
39a. Phil. "Bulletin" 12-24-63
40. C.E.585; 6H292-3; 17H262
41. 2H30
41a. 2H365
42. FBI Exh. 59, 60
43. 2H93
44. 2H127
45. 2H143; 18H780-83
46. 2H368
47. Mr. McCloy, NBC-TV 7-15-67
48. 2H371
49. 2H365
50. 4H109
51. 6H111
52. 2H374-82; 3H340; 4H113; 17H418
53. 18H799-800
54. 24H412
55. 24H412
56. 3H428
57. 3H497
58. 11H468; 24H412
59. 6H 130-34
60. 6H125
61. 6H126-27
62. 3H497
63. 3H443, 497
64. 18H795
65. 18H795
66. ABC-Bishop 6-8-68
67. 20H443
68. 15H388-89; 25H216-17, 317

69. LA "Free Press," 4-4-68

CHAPTER III

70. 23H402
71. C.E. 2003, No. 78
71a. R574
72. 7H197, 438, 441; 20H276
73. 23H402
74. C.E. 2160
75. Vol. 4H
75a. R118-19
76. C.E. 3119, p. 5, 11
77. C.E. 2718
78. 26H831
79. 4H20-21
79a. 26H832
80. 4H20-29
81. C.E. 139
82. R123
83. 4H24
84. 26H832
85. 26H832-33
86. 4H261-63
87. 4H261; 26H831
88. 26H273
88a. 26H831
89. 26H832
90. 4H260
91. 4H260-63
92. 4H218; 7H284
93. 4H81, 97
94. R125-28
95. N.A. Com. Doc. 344
96. R125-28; 21H443-48
97. 21H450-53
98. 4H281
99. R129, 628-29; 24H423, 269

100. 7H209, C.f. 7H194, 213, 231; C.E. 2557
101. 21H456-58
102. 21H453
102a. 1H49
102b. C.E. 1155; C.E. 1404
103. R128
104. FBI Reports V. 1-5
105. 2H462-63; 414; 3H19, 25; 9H442-43

CHAPTER IV

106. 2H246-48
107. 2H210
108. R131-34
109. 2H288
110. 2H210, 248-50; 19H408
111. 2H226-29, 239-44
112. 2H21; 7H190; 14H602; 24H293
113. 2H226
113a. 9H4, 425-25, 461
114. 4H93; 16H513
115. C.D. 205
116. 2H356; 4H91
117. FBI Reports V. 1-5; 4H57, 97
118. 4H97
119. 4H266
120. 2H226
121. 4H266
122. C.E. 628
123. 3H288; 6H268; 7H65, 289
124. 7H97-98
125. 7H103-04
126. 7H143
127. 7H143
128. 7H103-04
129. 4H57, 97
130. 4H266-68
131. 3H3-8

132. 3H3-8
133. 7H289
134. C.E. FBI File 205, 12-4-63
135. 9H425
136. 16H513

CHAPTER V

137. 3H169-70
138. 3H288; 6H268; 7H65, 289
139. 3H276
140. FBI File No. 89-43, 11-26-63, Agent Harrison, N.A. "CDs"
141. DL100-10461, 3-18-64
142. Dallas police tapes, Dallas "Herald," 11-22-63
143. 7H732
144. R149
145. 22H749; C.E. 457
146. C.E. 1381
147. 6H392
148. R145
149. 14H762, 780-81
150. 26H811
151. 3H144-45
152. C.E. 5323; 3H144
153. C.E. 1311, 1312; 22H484
154. 3H144
155. R80, 138
155a. R6
156. 7H342
157. 4H237
158. 6H321-22; 21H392
159. 3H148
160. 6H322; 21H392; 23H843-44
161. 7H349
162. 19H524; C.E. 2641
163. 19H524

164. N.A. File "CD-5"
165. 6H266
166. 6H266, 70; 23H317
167. C.E. 2003, 2H270, 279; 19H347
168. 4H412; 6H409-13
169. C.D. 2641
170. R604-05, 622
171. 2H254-59

CHAPTER VI

172. 6H438-40
173. 6H434
174. 3H303; 24H215
175. 24H202
176. 23H857-58; 24H202
177. 24H253
178. 3H473
179. R235; 6H321; 17H10; 21H393
180. R156; 3H187; 6H382-86; 3H294; 22H655-56; 23H843
181. C.E. 705, p. 492
181a. 3H319
182. R167
183. 4H212; 7H262
184. 3H310-11
185. 6H452; 17H416
186. 3H327; 335-37
187. 3H333-37
188. 3H327
189. FBI Reports V. 1-5
190. R175; 7H30-33
191. C.E. 162; 2H311-12
192. C.E. 163
193. 3H328
194. 3H347
195. 3H356
196. 6H439
197. 2H238

198. 7H30-33
199. Lawrence–Batchelor [Exh.]
200. C.E. 1843; C.D. 1066, pp. 993,1245; C.D. FBI 868, C.D. 7, p. 205
201. R175
202. C.E. 1843; C.D. 1066, pp. 993,1245; C.D. FBI 868, C.D. 7, p. 205.
203. C.E. 1974, p. 74
204. C.E. 1974, p. 78
205. 3H29B
206. 3H302
207. 3H300; 7H20
208. 7H720
208a. R304
209. 7H20-22
210. R304 c.f. 301; 7H20-3
211. 6H440
212. R560
213. 24H253; 20H465
214. 3H473
215. 3H347-8
216. C.E. 1974,p. 74; 17H417-20
217. 3H473
218. 3H473
219. 7H66,415
220. 7H69;275-6
220a. C.E. 2003,Exh. 85-
220b. 1d
221. U.S.V. Wolfson, 6-27-68
222. 5H33-37

CHAPTER VII

223. Dallas police memo, 2-14-64
223a. 2H174,178,183
224. 19H16-18
225. 19H18
226. C.E. 434, N.A.

227. R128, 184, 145
228. 3H447
229. 1H293
230. 3H405; 26H104; 2H104
231. C.E. 2974
232. 3H405
233. 15H779; 26H104
234. 26H104
235. 26H449
236. 26H449
237. 3H404; 3H441-47

CHAPTER VIII

238. N. Y. "Times," 10-23-66
239. U.S. "Week" 10-10-66
240. WBAI Radio, 10-30-66
241. 5H112, 242
242. Dallas "Herald," 12-9-63
243. 5H34-37
244. R29-30
245. 2H109-110
246. 4H556
247. 18H735
248. 8H298
249. Vols. 19, 20
250. C.D. 917, 918, C.E. 1915
251. R711; C.D. 2718-N.A.
252. "Greater Phil." 8-66

CHAPTER IX

253. U.S. "Week," 8-66
254. "Playboy," 10-67
255. 2H109-11; 4H356
256. Dallas "News," "Herald," 11-22-63, 11-23-63; police tapes

257. R30-41
258. R31
259. 7H538-39
260. C.E. 875
261. 2H43-5; 3H226; 6H223; 7H440, 487
262. 4H161
263. 19H616
264. 19514
265. 19H530
266. 3H238
267. 7H345
268. C.E. 0283-84
269. 19H530
270. C.E. 2003
271. C.E. 2099
272. C.E. 2091
273. C.E. 2084
274. C.E. 2003
275. Id.
276. 7H571
277. 3H288
278. 6H230
279. 6H243
280. C.D. 3, PT 1; 6H312
281. 7H107, 18 H722-799
282. C.D. 5-N.A.; 24H385
283. N.A. C.D.-5
284. 19H1526-7
285. 20H499
286. Dallas "Herald," 11-22-63
287. 4H260
288. C.D. 2000, p. 195
289. 4H264
290. L.A. "Free Press," 4-68, 5-68; "Playboy," 10-68
291. "Playboy," 10-68
292. C.E. 705, p. 492
293. C.E. 2003
294. 4H207-10; 5H34, 41-42; C.E. 709; C.E. 2008, p. 127
295. C.E. 705; C.E. 1947

296. 4H443; 26H195, C.E. 2985
297. R198
298. 4H200; 7H289
299. CBS and NBC, 11-26-63
300. C.E. 2003
301. 4H223; 19H770
302. Midlothian Press, 5-68
303. C.D. 407, 2449; 15H401, 603, 617; Eberhardt Ex. 5026
304. 15H491
305. C.E. 2002, p. 130
306. C.E. 2050
307. 15H682-83
308. Vols. 4, 5, 12, 15, 19, 21
309. 21H170-1182, 215, 227
310. 19H410-13
311. 7H12
312. 7H6

POSTSCRIPT

After five years of research, the answer to the question "Where did the bullet that entered the president's throat go?" was finally located!

The author was able to locate the November 28, 1963 interview published in the now defunct "Herald-Tribune." An interview between Dr. R. R. Shaw of the Parkland Hospital staff, who was part of the group of physicians striving to save President Kennedy's life on November 22, 1963, and Mr. Martin J. Steadman of that newspaper, revealed the answer. Dr. Shaw informed the columnist that the bullet which entered the front of the president's throat and "coursed downward into his lung was removed in the Bethesda Naval Hospital, where the autopsy was performed"!

This statement now explains why Lt. Col. Finck admitted at the [Clay] Shaw trial that the Bethesda Naval Hospital team conducted an incomplete autopsy. It explains why Lt. Col. Finck was a nervous witness on Shaw's behalf; for, if that information was known to District Attorney Garrison the Army physician would have had to admit that a complete bullet had been recovered from the president's body. The illegal autopsy report, not the chart which revealed the existence of a bullet in the president's body, was nothing more than a "cover-up" ordered by the high military officers. This is not hearsay, for Lt. Col. Finck swore under oath at the Shaw trial that military brass were in that room. This also explains why the autopsy report is undated and the reason why Lt. Col. Humes destroyed his original notes. He admitted to the Warren Commission that he made several autopsy drafts! In other words, the military physicians were under orders from the highest level of the new power running the government to make the "facts" conform to the theory that no conspiracy existed. The bullet extracted from the president's body was thrown away, but in the locked files is a statement that it was not a 7.65-mm bullet!

One last postscript regarding the Tippit murder. There is an

"AP" story of November 23, 1963 signed by Patrolman McDonald, the "capturer" of Oswald. In it he states that the revolver he "took" from Oswald did not discharge, because of a "dented firing pin." The FBI ballistics expert upheld this "dented firing pin" when the expert testified that there were no firing pin marks on any of the cartridges given to them by the Dallas police. Thus, the statement and the testimony can only be interpreted one way: Since Tippit was shot at 1:08 p.m. and Oswald captured at 1:50 p.m. with the "identical" weapon, how could that weapon have been used to murder Tippit when the revolver was so defective that its firing pin could not strike any of the cartridges?" The two Dallas policemen who obtained the cartridges testified that those given to them by the Commission aide were not the cartridges they initialed at the Tippit murder scene. The Dallas police planted the revolver, the bullets which were extracted from five dead bodies in the police morgue, and the cartridges. QED Oswald was framed by the police.

SELECTED BOOKS AND ARTICLES
CITED IN *TWO DAYS OF INFAMY*

Epstein, Edward Jay. *Inquest: the Warren Commission and the Establishment of Truth.* New York: The Viking Press, 1966.

Flammonde, Paris. *The Kennedy Conspiracy.* New York: Meredith Press, 1969.

Fonzi, Gaeton. "The Warren Commission, the Truth, and Arlen Specter." *Greater Philadelphia Magazine*, August 1, 1966, pp. 38-45, 79-88, 91.

Garrison, Jim. Interview in *Playboy*, 1967.

Joesten, Joachim. *Oswald: Assassin or Fall Guy?* New York: Marzani & Munsell, 1964.

Jones, Penn. *Forgive My Grief.* Midlothian, TX: The Midlothian Mirror, 1966.

Manchester, William. *The Death of a President.* New York: Harper & Row, 1967.

Lane, Mark. *A Citizen's Dissent. Mark Lane Replies.* New York: Holt, Rinehart & Winston, 1966.
– *Rush to Judgment.* New York: Holt, Rinehart & Winston, 1966.

Meagher, Sylvia. *Accessories After the Fact.* Indianapolis: Bobbs-Merrill, 1967.

Popkin, Richard. *The Second Oswald.* New York: Avon, 1966.

Weisberg, Harold. *Whitewash.* Vols. I-III. Hyattstown, MD: Harold Weisberg, 1965, 1966, 1967.

ABOUT STANLEY J. MARKS

When Stanley Marks was four years old, his parents died from the 1918 influenza pandemic and he was placed in the care of foster parents in Chicago. During the Great Depression he wrote publicity for the DNC; worked as a billboard salesman; and conducted research for *The Bear that Walks Like a Man: A Diplomatic and Military Analysis of Soviet Russia*. While working on the book, Marks received assistance from FDR's Secretary of State, who gave him access to State Department files. In 1943 *The Bear* was published by a vanity press yet it became a bestseller, receiving positive reviews in over thirty mainstream papers. The *Chicago Tribune* featured a major review by John Cudahy, FDR's former ambassador to Poland. Marks then pursued a teaching career at the Abraham Lincoln School, an innovative institution founded by a Black civil rights activist. He also published book reviews in the *Chicago Defender*, an African American newspaper that played a key role in the Civil Rights Movement by encouraging blacks to leave the South and join "The Great Migration" to the North. Both the Abraham Lincoln School and the *Chicago Defender* were placed under FBI surveillance, and in 1944 Marks was blacklisted by HUAC. Despite the blacklist, he was commissioned by the Army to write a history of military science, and from 1945-46 he served in the Pacific Theatre under General MacArthur. In 1967 Marks published *Murder Most Foul!*, a book about the Kennedy assassination. When the House of Representatives Select Subcommittee on Assassinations issued its report, it cited five of Marks' titles, including *Murder Most Foul!* and *Two Days of Infamy*. Marks was also one of the first American researchers to draw a direct connection between the assassinations of JFK, MLK, and RFK. As a result of speculation that Bob Dylan's ballad "Murder Most Foul" may have been influenced by Marks' text, interest in the author has been reawakened.

About Roberta Marks

Roberta (Bobbie) Marks was born and raised in Chicago. Upon graduating college with a degree in art, she moved to Los Angeles to work in the California fashion industry as a clothing designer. During this period she started a clothing-manufacturing company and owned two retail women's clothing stores.

In the 1980's she switched from clothing to interior design and opened the Los Angeles franchise of Designer Previews, the highly successful New York company run by Karen Fisher, which matched clients with interior designers. The LA office represented over sixty design professionals whose works were often showcased in top-shelf publications.

Now retired, Roberta continues to create, utilizing paper as her main medium. She makes figures that are clothed in all forms of paper, from heavy butcher paper to fine tissue, then paints and embellishes the paper and forms it into clothing. Papier-mâché and clay are also used to make heads that are adorned with elaborate headpieces. Roberta says that she's now come full circle: using her pattern-making training to make paper clothing.

About Rob Couteau

Rob Couteau's work as a literary critic, interviewer, and social commentator has been featured in books such as *Gabriel Garcia Marquez's 'Love in the Time of Cholera'* by Thomas Fahy, *Conversations with Ray Bradbury* edited by Steven Aggelis, *Ghetto Images in Twentieth-Century American Literature* by Tyrone Simpson, and David Cohen's *Forgotten Millions*, a book about the homeless mentally ill.

His published interviews include conversations with Ray Bradbury, Pulitzer Prize-winning author Justin Kaplan, *Last Exit to Brooklyn* novelist Hubert Selby, Simon & Schuster editor Michael Korda, LSD discoverer Dr. Albert Hofmann, Picasso's model and muse Sylvette David, Nabokov biographer Robert Roper, music producer Danny Goldberg, poet and publisher Ed Foster, and historian Philip Willan, author *Puppetmasters: The Political Use of Terrorism in Italy*.

In his early years as a writer, Couteau won the North American Essay Award, a competition sponsored by the American Humanist Association. His books, including the novel *Doctor Pluss*, the anthology *More Collected Couteau*, and the poetry collection *The Sleeping Mermaid*, have been praised in the *Midwest Book Review*, *Publishers Weekly*, and *Evergreen Review*.

His essays and interviews on the Sixties assassinations have been featured at the Kennedys and King website, and he has appeared several times as a guest on Len Osanic's Black Op Radio.

Visit his website at robcouteau.com

INDEX

A

Adams, Victoria Elizabeth, 96, 206
Alexander, William F., 77, 152, 179, 180, 182, 194, 195
Allman, Pierce, 96, 138, 159, 205
Altgens, James William, 94, 95, 96
American Rifleman, 26, 204
Army, xxii, 192, 238
Arnold, Carolyn, 90, 91, 96, 205
Associated Press, 29, 30, 69, 204, 212, 214, 239
Aynesworth, Hugh Grant, 152

B

Ball, Joseph A., 147
Barker, W. E., 173
Barnes, W. E., 130, 208
Batchelor, Charles, 207
Batista, Fulgencio, xx, 51, 191
Bay of Pigs, 143, 189
Belin, David W., 147
Benavides, Domingo, 118, 119, 130, 207
Bethesda Naval Hospital, xxxix, xl, 10, 40, 42, 44, 74, 207, 212, 238
Bill of Rights, 18, 195
Bledsoe, Mary E., 77, 105, 106
Boggs, Thomas Hale, 90, 127, 142, 144
Boone, Eugene Lawrence, 23, 80
Bowley, Temple Ford, 113, 114, 132, 176, 177, 207
Brennan, Howard Leslie, 4, 77, 92, 97, 98, 99, 100, 103, 112, 149, 178, 205, 206
Brewer, Edwin D., 80, 81, 82, 89, 123
Brown, Earle V., 170
Brown, Joe B., 182
Bullet No. 399, xvi, 45, 46, 47, 48, 49, 54, 77, 125, 143, 147, 148, 163, 171
Bureau of Immigration and Naturalization, 192

C

Carroll, Bob K., 123, 124, 125, 131, 144, 176, 208
Castro, Fidel, 51, 153, 192, 193
Chaney, James, 170

Chism, John Arthur, 172
Civil Liberties Union, 182
Clark, Ramsey R., 166
Clark, William Kemp, 40
Communism, 50, 101, 137, 152, 156, 157, 187, 188, 192, 193, 194, 196, 210, 211
Communist Party, 137
Connally, John Bowden, 12, 13, 17, 45, 178, 210
Cooper, John Sherman, 90, 124, 142, 143, 144, 163
coup d'état, 9, xi, xxii, xxv, xli, 165, 189, 192, 198
Craig, Roger Dean, 33, 34, 80, 89, 101, 102, 103, 104, 136, 175, 209
Cuban Missile Crisis, 189, 198
Cunningham, Cortlandt, 24, 127, 129, 131

D

Dallas Morning News, 69, 122, 153, 170, 171, 173, 209, 214
Dallas Police Department, 5, 10, 31, 32, 33, 57, 61, 63, 64, 67, 78, 82, 83, 93, 110, 120, 122, 123, 129, 132, 135, 137, 138, 140, 153, 167, 170, 180, 181, 186, 190, 203, 215
Dallas Times Herald, 52, 93, 167, 209, 214, 232, 235, 236
Dal-Tex Building, xvi, 44, 146, 159, 169, 170, 173, 214
Davenport, R. A., 115, 185
Day, John Carl, 23, 31, 32, 33, 58, 63, 64, 65, 66, 67, 77, 79, 80, 81, 82, 83, 85, 160, 174, 178, 204, 211
de Gaulle, Charles, 190
Dean, Patrick, 77
Decker, James Eric, xxxix, 77, 93, 98, 160, 167, 171, 172, 174, 175, 209, 214
Detroit Free Press, 69
Dorman, Elsie, 173
double detour, 8, 29, 159, 168, 169, 170, 171, 209, 214
Drain, Vincent, 37, 50, 51
Dreyfus, Alfred, 70
Dulles, Allen, 9, xvii, xviii, xix, xxviii, 45, 88, 90, 142, 143, 144, 147, 155, 162, 163, 164, 169, 170, 172, 173, 174, 175, 176, 177, 178, 179, 184, 186, 188, 189, 208, 213

E

Eberhardt, A. M., 237
Eisenberg, Melvin Aron, 47, 48, 49
Epstein, Edward, 42, 148

F

Federal Bureau of Investigation (FBI), xix, xx, xxi, xxix, xliii, 8, 9, 24, 27, 31, 33, 34, 37, 46, 49, 51, 74, 78, 79, 85, 126, 128, 129, 134, 136, 137, 146, 149, 150, 151, 152, 153, 155, 157, 158, 159, 163, 164, 165, 166, 167, 168, 175, 176, 178, 182, 183, 186, 187, 188, 189, 190, 191, 192, 193, 195, 203, 204, 205, 206, 207, 208, 209, 210, 211, 212, 214, 215, 216, 217, 239

Field and Stream, 204
Finck, Pierre Antoine, xl, xliii, 43, 212, 238
Flammonde, Paris, xxviii, xxxix, xl, xli, 209
Ford, Gerald, 90, 142
Frazier, Buell Wesley, 14, 75, 76, 77, 78, 79, 84, 119
Frazier, Robert A., 28, 31, 46, 47
Fritz, Will, xxxix, 23, 37, 64, 65, 67, 77, 89, 96, 99, 101, 102, 103, 104, 106, 125, 126, 132, 135, 136, 174, 180, 181, 206, 209, 214, 215

G

Gallagher, John, 47, 48
Garrison, Jim, xi, xxv, xxviii, xxxvii, xxxix, xl, xli, xliii, 35, 193, 209, 238
Giesecke, Adolf H., 42
Givens, Charles, 137
Goldberg, Alfred, 147, 148
Greer, William Robert, 43
Griffin, J. T., 77, 119

H

Hall, C. Ray, 183
Haygood, Clyde A., 89
Herald-Tribune, 195, 238
Hester, Charles, 172
Hester, Mrs. Charles, 172
Hicks, J. B., 33, 80, 83
Hidell alias, 26, 27, 28, 32, 56, 57, 58, 61, 62, 178, 188
Hill, Gerald, 80, 89, 121, 125, 181
Holland, S. M., 172
Holmes, Harry D., 25, 27, 62, 204
Hoover, J. Edgar, 9, xix, xx, xxi, xxiv, 24, 27, 31, 33, 36, 42, 95, 98, 129, 146, 151, 153, 169, 181, 187, 188, 191, 195, 196, 205, 211, 215, 216
Hop-along Cassidy, 122
Hosty, James Patrick, 77, 136, 137, 151, 152, 210
Houston Post, 152
Huber, Oscar L., 42
Hudkins, Lonnie, 152, 153
Hughes, Robert J., 146, 151, 159, 205, 211, 216
Humes, James J., 40, 41, 43, 44, 45, 77, 163, 171, 202, 206, 210, 238
Hunt, H. L., 190
Hutson, Thomas Alexander, 77, 119

I

Inquest, 42, 43, 148
International Trade Mart, 130, 131, 132, 168

J

Jarman, James (Junior), 89, 90, 91, 96, 138, 205
Jenkins. Marion Thomas, 42
Jimison, R. J., 48
Joesten, Joachim, xi, xl
John Birch Society, 110, 190, 192
Johnsen, Richard E., 46, 47, 51
Johnson, James, 81, 82, 89, 179, 180, 215
Johnson, Lyndon Baines, xvii, xxiv, 6, 38, 59, 61, 142, 146, 172, 186, 192, 197, 212
Johnston, David, 180
Jones, Penn, xxiv
Jones, Roy Milton, 60, 101, 104, 105, 106, 211

K

Kantor, Seth, 52, 53, 212
Kellerman, Roy H., 43, 154, 165
Kelley, Thomas J., 115, 150
Kennedy, John F., xi, xiii, xiv, xv, xvi, xxi, xxiv, xxv, xxvi, xxxvii, xxxviii, xxxix, xl, xli, xliv, ii, 4, 5, 8, 10, 11, 12, 13, 15, 16, 17, 20, 21, 22, 27, 28, 29, 30, 35, 38, 39, 40, 42, 43, 44, 47, 48, 50, 51, 52, 55, 56, 59, 60, 63, 66, 69, 73, 74, 77, 78, 84, 90, 93, 101, 103, 106, 110, 114, 122, 125, 132, 136, 137, 138, 140, 141, 142, 143, 144, 146, 149, 151, 152, 153, 155, 159, 160, 162, 163, 164, 165, 166, 167, 169, 170, 172, 174, 176, 177, 178, 179, 180, 181, 184, 186, 188, 189, 190, 191, 192, 193, 194, 195, 197, 198, 200, 202, 203, 205, 206, 207, 208, 209, 211, 214, 216, 238
Kennedy, Robert F., xi, xix, xxiii, xxiv, xxv, xxvi, xxxvii, xxxviii, xli, xlii, xliii, xliv, 44, 51, 145, 146, 187, 189, 190, 195
Kilgallen, Dorothy, 54, 182
King, Glen, 127, 208
King, Martin Luther, xi, xxxvii, xxxviii, xli, xliii, xliv, 132, 189, 217
Klein's Sporting Goods, 25, 26, 27, 28, 32, 54, 57, 62, 63, 71, 72, 178
Ku Klux Klan, 189

L

Landis, Paul, 172
Lane, Mark, xl, 193
Latitudes, 209
Leavelle, James R., 127
Liebeler, Wesley J., 147, 148
Life, 28, 29, 30, 62, 68, 69, 70, 73, 144, 145, 151, 159, 204, 214
Lone Star Steel Company, 191, 192
Look magazine, xviii, 162, 164
Los Angeles Times, 191
Lovelady, Billy Nolan, 77, 94, 95, 96, 97, 150, 205, 206, 215

M

Manchester, William, 194
Mannlicher-Carcano rifle, 4, 9, 21, 23, 24, 25, 26, 27, 28, 30, 37, 49, 56, 62, 64, 100, 134, 207
Marine Corps, 34, 37, 139, 156, 157, 158, 192, 209
Markham, Helen L., 4, 5, 77, 112, 113, 114, 117, 118, 119, 128, 207
Marks, Roberta, xxxi, 242
Marks, Stanley J., xxix, 184
Mauser rifle, 9, 22, 23, 24, 29, 32, 37, 54, 64, 80, 100, 101, 103, 138, 174, 175, 212
Maxey, Billy Joe, 182
McClelland, Robert N., 41
McCloy, John Jay, 43, 44, 90, 142, 143
McDonald, Maurice N., 77, 122, 123, 124, 125, 126, 133, 138, 143, 144, 163, 176, 184, 207, 208, 215, 239
McGarry, Terrance, 182
McWatters, Cecil J., 104, 105, 106
Meagher, Sylvia, xxviii, xl, 193
Miami News, 165, 166, 209
Miami Police Department, xxxix, xliv, 8, 165, 166, 186
Midlothian Press, 29
Miller, Austin, 172
Milteer, Joseph S., 8
Minutemen, 189
Montgomery, Leslie Dell, 80, 81, 82, 89
Mooney, Luke, 80, 89, 172
Moore, Elmer W., 115, 208
Mudd, F. Lee, 173
Murder Most Foul!, 9, x, xii, xvii, xxiv, xxv, xxvi, xxviii, xl, 146
Mussolini, Benito, xix, 191

N

National Archives, x, xv, xviii, 4, 6, 9, 11, 12, 15, 23, 25, 26, 30, 33, 35, 38, 39, 44, 55, 63, 69, 74, 84, 89, 90, 95, 96, 102, 113, 115, 132, 137, 139, 141, 145, 146, 148, 150, 152, 154, 158, 162, 164, 169, 173, 174, 181, 182, 184, 200, 203, 206, 210, 212, 215
national security, xiii, 8, 10, 17, 62, 113, 171, 186
NATO, 192
Navy, 43, 158, 192
Nazis, 101, 189
New York Times, 171, 212
Newman, William E., 172
Newsweek, 69
Nicol, Joseph D., 48, 49, 206

O

O'Neill, Francis, 43, 206

Odum, Bardwell D. (Hart), 47, 48, 117, 175
Office of Naval Intelligence (ONI), 157, 158, 192
Oswald, Lee Harvey, x, xiii, xv, xvi, xx, xxi, xxxviii, xl, ii, 3, 4, 5, 6, 7, 9, 10, 11, 12, 13, 14, 15, 16, 17, 18, 20, 21, 22, 24, 25, 26, 27, 28, 30, 31, 32, 33, 34, 36, 37, 38, 39, 41, 44, 47, 53, 54, 55, 56, 57, 58, 59, 60, 61, 62, 63, 64, 65, 66, 67, 68, 69, 70, 71, 72, 73, 74, 75, 76, 77, 78, 79, 81, 83, 84, 85, 86, 87, 88, 89, 90, 91, 92, 93, 94, 95, 96, 97, 98, 99, 101, 102, 103, 104, 105, 106, 107, 108, 110, 111, 112, 113, 114, 116, 117, 118, 119, 120, 121, 122, 123, 124, 125, 126, 128, 129, 130, 131, 132, 133, 134, 135, 136, 137, 138, 139, 140, 141, 143, 144, 145, 147, 148, 149, 150, 151, 152, 153, 154, 155, 156, 157, 158, 159, 160, 162, 163, 164, 165, 168, 170, 173, 175, 176, 177, 178, 179, 180, 181, 182, 183, 184, 185, 186, 188, 192, 193, 194, 195, 200, 201, 202, 203, 204, 205, 206, 207, 208, 209, 210, 211, 212, 214, 215, 216, 239
Oswald, Marina, 24, 25, 38, 56, 63, 69, 71, 72, 75, 77, 120, 121, 159, 176, 212
Oxford, J. L., 171

P

Paine, Ruth, 10, 14, 24, 28, 38, 63, 69, 72, 76, 77, 79, 84, 102, 103, 104, 151, 176, 210
Parkland Memorial Hospital, xvii, xxxix, 10, 40, 41, 42, 46, 47, 50, 51, 52, 53, 54, 55, 58, 74, 93, 94, 103, 132, 145, 155, 167, 171, 172, 184, 202, 207, 210, 214, 238
Parks, P. M., 176
Pierce, Sam Rio, 182
Piper, Edward, 90, 91, 96, 205
Poe, J. M. (Joe), 130
Popkin, Richard, 193
Price Exhibit, 184
Price, Charles Jack, 184
Price, Jessie C., 172

R

Ramparts, 182
Randle, Linnie Mae, 75, 76, 77, 78, 79
Rankin, James Lee, 6, 58, 59, 147, 148, 216
Ray, James Earl, 5, xli, xliii, xliv, 217
Reagan, Ronald, 9, 35, 51, 195, 196
Redlich, Norman, 148
Reilly, Frank E., 172
Revill, Jack, 137, 152
Roberts, Earlene, 101, 104, 107, 111, 112, 119, 125
Robinson, Marvin C., 102, 104, 209
Rose, Earl Forrest, 115
Rowley, James Jose, 46, 47, 49
Ruby, Jack, 7, 51, 52, 53, 114, 146, 170, 181, 182, 183, 185, 186, 212
Russell, Richard Brevard, 90, 143

S

Saturday Evening Post, 187
Sawyer, Herbert J., 100, 116, 175
Scoggins, William Henry, 121, 128
Secret Service, 5, xvii, xxvi, xxxix, xliv, 3, 8, 10, 20, 32, 37, 38, 43, 44, 45, 46, 47, 48, 49, 50, 51, 54, 56, 59, 61, 63, 68, 74, 77, 78, 84, 94, 96, 99, 100, 102, 103, 105, 115, 116, 117, 120, 127, 129, 131, 132, 136, 144, 145, 146, 149, 150, 151, 152, 153, 154, 155, 159, 160, 165, 166, 167, 168, 169, 170, 171, 172, 183, 186, 187, 189, 191, 192, 203, 206, 207, 208, 209, 210, 211, 212, 216, 229
   Protective Research Section (PRS) and, 154, 165, 186
Senator, George, 182
Shaneyfelt, Lyndal L., 28, 68
Shaw, Clay, xxxvii, xxxviii, xxxix, xl, xli, xliii, ii, 212, 238
Shaw, Robert R., 40, 42, 45, 238
Shelley, William Hoyt, 95, 205
Shires, George T., 45, 46
Sibert, James, 43, 206
Simmons, Ronald, 31
Sims, Richard, 80
Smith, L. C., 171
Sorrels, Forrest V., 94, 96, 97, 98, 99, 100, 159, 171, 172, 206
Soviet Union, 156, 192, 194, 195, 197
Specter, Arlen, xvii, 45, 143, 147, 148, 163, 171, 211
Stalin, Joseph, xix, 70, 107, 191
Steadman, Martin J., 238
Stevenson, Adlai E., 154, 155, 167
Studebaker, Robert Lee, 77, 80, 81, 83
Summers, H. W., 120, 121, 123
Sweatt, 153, 160, 172, 209

T

Tague, James, 39
Tasker, Harry, 183
Taylor, Warren, 176
Texas Rangers, 37, 136
Texas School Book Depository, xiii, xvi, 4, 10, 11, 13, 14, 15, 21, 32, 35, 37, 38, 41, 44, 45, 54, 75, 76, 78, 84, 89, 91, 92, 93, 94, 95, 96, 97, 100, 101, 102, 103, 104, 108, 116, 120, 122, 130, 131, 132, 137, 145, 146, 150, 159, 169, 170, 171, 173, 175, 176, 177, 201, 210, 211, 215, 216
Texas Theatre, 60, 101, 120, 121, 123, 131, 132, 133
The Bear That Walks Like a Man, xxiii
The Death of a President, 194
Tice, Wilma, 53
Tippit, J. D., 7, xviii, xxxix, 4, 5, 9, 10, 12, 13, 14, 15, 16, 25, 58, 59, 60, 61, 68, 77, 110, 111, 112, 113, 114, 115, 116, 117, 118, 119, 120, 121, 122, 123, 124, 125, 126, 127, 128, 129, 130, 131, 132, 133, 136, 137, 138, 143, 144, 145, 149, 151, 158, 160, 163, 175, 176, 177, 178, 179, 202, 207, 208, 210, 215, 238, 239

Todd, Elmer L., 46, 47
Tojo, Hideki, xix, 70, 191
Tomlinson, Darrell C., 46, 47, 48, 50, 51
triple underpass, 168, 172
Truly, Roy, 91, 170, 172

U

U-2 spy plane, 156, 197, 198

V

Vaughn, Roy E., 182

W

Wade, Henry Menasco, 5, 23, 52, 77, 113, 135, 180, 194, 215
Walker, Edwin Anderson, 9, 12, 13, 15, 16, 17, 134, 138
Wall Street Journal, 190
Wallace, George, 191
Walters, W. S., xxxix
Warren Commission, 5, 7, x, xi, xii, xiv, xv, xix, xx, xxii, xxiv, xxvi, xxxviii, xl, xli, xliii, xliv, ii, 3, 4, 5, 6, 8, 11, 12, 15, 17, 20, 22, 24, 29, 30, 34, 37, 44, 51, 55, 61, 63, 73, 77, 79, 82, 85, 89, 92, 96, 99, 103, 104, 108, 112, 114, 116, 117, 120, 131, 133, 141, 142, 152, 155, 160, 162, 164, 170, 178, 179, 183, 184, 189, 190, 193, 194, 200, 201, 202, 203, 206, 211, 212, 214, 215, 216, 238
  aides and, 6, 20, 78, 107, 111, 122, 124, 134, 147, 148, 154, 164
  commissioners and, x, xvii, xix, xxii, xxix, 15, 17, 46, 70, 87, 88, 97, 99, 122, 124, 127, 142, 143, 144, 146, 147, 151, 160, 162, 163, 164, 173, 188, 203, 213
Washington Post, 44, 192
Weisberg, Harold, xl, 51, 193, 240
Weitzman, Seymour, 9, 22, 23, 24, 28, 29, 32, 80, 174, 175, 212
West, Robert, 150, 216
West, Troy Eugene, 78
Westbrook, William R., 77, 118, 119, 207
Westphal, R. W., 176
Whaley, William, 77, 107
Williams, Bonnie Ray, 80, 86, 87, 88, 89, 91, 92, 143, 163, 206
Williams, J. Doyle, 51
Wisdom, Robert, 113
Witcover, Jules, 187
Wolfer, DeWayne, xlii
Woodward, Mary, 170, 172
Wright, O. P., 46, 47, 48

Y

Yarborough, Ralph, 170

Z

Zapruder film, xv, 42, 145, 172, 200, 202
Zapruder, Abraham, 145

www.ingramcontent.com/pod-product-compliance
Lightning Source LLC
Chambersburg PA
CBHW030903080526
44589CB00010B/118